T0367962

It was easy to persecute me without people feeling ashamed. It was easy to vilify me and project me as a woman who was not following the tradition of a 'good African woman' and as a 'highly educated [unlikeable, insolent] elitist woman' who was trying to show innocent African women ways of doing things that were not acceptable to African men.

—Wangari Mathai, Kenyan environmental political activist, Nobel Laureate

Gender is a Choice

INSPIRED, PROACTIVE, AND SELF-ACTUALISED

How anyone can become inspired and proactive to
disrupt disempowering gender myths, attitudes,
and behaviour and lead a nice, beautiful life

GRACE ALICE MUKASA

authorHOUSE®

AuthorHouse™ UK
1663 Liberty Drive
Bloomington, IN 47403 USA
www.authorhouse.co.uk
Phone: 0800.197.4150

Published by AuthorHouse 10/30/2018

ISBN: 978-1-5462-9149-7 (sc)
ISBN: 978-1-5462-9150-3 (hc)
ISBN: 978-1-5462-9148-0 (e)

Library of Congress Control Number: 2018912422

Print information available on the last page.

Any people depicted in stock imagery provided by Getty Images are models, and such images are being used for illustrative purposes only. Certain stock imagery © Getty Images.

This book is printed on acid-free paper.

Gender Book Series One
Gender Concepts and Meanings

DEDICATION

On 4 September 2016, I suffered a massive stroke which paralysed my left side. Since then, I have been literally climbing my personal Everest. I dedicate this book especially to my children, biological and otherwise, and a myriad of friends and pastors across the world, who have shown me unconditional love, care, and support.

To all my children, I commend you for showing me the mystery of unrequited love during my time of greatest need. May God grant all of you his exceedingly abundant grace and mercy.

- Mariam, whose childhood was stolen by my stroke. She amazingly transformed herself into my main feisty carer.
- Hussein, a young man who became my dedicated driver and surprisingly never felt stigmatised or tired while pushing his old, vulnerable mother in London's high streets and shopping malls.
- Jessica, my daughter inlaw, who gave me a timely gift of a precious grandson, King, from the mysteriously working God.
- Jo, my patient host and cook. If you could handle me so well in that delicate state and cope patiently with my unending demands, I am confident you can handle any woman.
- Ronnie, who could hardly miss a day without talking to your mum despite the distance. I have learned to anticipate and depend on your voice to uplift me from fear, pain, sadness, and loneliness.
- Joel, my young brother whom I brought up, you really showed me how love begets love.
- Yusuf, your calm respect uplifted my maternal instincts.

Thank you, all my children. I know that we socialised you well with humility, respect, love, and kindness. You have made me experience compassion and the elusive pride of motherhood through your great love. I believe I passed on to you very strong values. Whenever I think of you, imagining what you have become, my joy overflows.

Abdu, you nursed me with dedication and love at my weakest point soon after the stroke. You also taught me that a marriage can exist without domestic violence. Thank you. I will forever be grateful.

Irene Guijt, you first introduced me to the mystery of gender and the notion of intra-communal difference. The rest is now history. Can you see how far we have come? You are the greatest facilitator I have ever met. You are a dear friend who saw my potential and chose to harness it. Can you see how far we have come?

All my dear friends, relatives, and religious leaders, who gifted me with an incredible amount of spiritual guidance, support, and prayers: may God bless you all. All the pastors, prophets and apostles, in Uganda, Kenya, Zambia, the UK, and the US, you gave me spiritual guidance, freedom from fear, godly peace, prayer, and support to bring Jesus and the Holy Spirit into my life. That was the greatest gift I have ever received. I humbly say *thank you*.

PREFACE

This book may make some people uncomfortable. Many times they may feel like they are teetering on the edge of a slippery slope with nowhere to hold, seeing only the hard ground packed with truth below. They may feel relentlessly and mercilessly provoked to the core. They may wonder, 'How did they find me out? Who released my well-kept secrets?' However, this book is based on facts and real-life stories of people. Facts and lived realities don't lie.

Consequently this book cannot protect anyone's personal sensitivities or emotions. It will push for straight talk and the damnedest realities of gender discrimination that women everywhere silently suffer from. These injustices are often shrouded in our sociocultural and religious taboos. These realities are often kept in silence. These taboos are ones we have been trained well not to talk about publicly.

Before you go through emotional turmoil and become angry, self-loathing, defensive, guilty, or self-righteous—slow down, take a deep breath, and slow down some more. Don't throw away your precious book. Read to the end. If you do so, you will also conclude that this book is merely a mirror of our society today, a maze with only one invisible and elusive exit. You may feel trapped and forced to self-criticise, self-judge, or even despise yourself and those who are closest to you for what you have done or seen others do to women and girls.

Don't despair. Stay focused on the future, like a car with its widest window at the front. You will soon acquire a different value system and mindset from which to see the world. Ultimately you will surprise yourself by discovering the light at the end of the tunnel.

Since you were made in the image of God, this book will not leave you unchanged. It will help you claim back your humanity, compassion, love, and respect towards the people in your life. It will turn you into a precious human being who radiates truth, compassion, and love. You will proudly stand up for gender justice and women's rights because that is the only right thing to do. You will dream big, feel good, and be fulfilled. Above all, you will be proud of the new, real you that emerges.

Contents

Glossary of Key Terms Used in This Book

- *Advocacy*: Support for or recommendation of a particular cause or policy, e.g., advocacy of traditional family values, advocacy for more women in key government positions, etc.
- *Affirmative action*: Deliberate and usually short-term measures on only one side in order to create a balance, e.g., employment of only women in senior positions until equality in the workplace is achieved.
- *Agency*: In the social sciences, the capacity of individuals to act independently and to make their own free choices.
- *Authentic*: Original or true; not a copy.
- *Campaign*: An organised course of action to achieve a particular goal.
- *Complementary*: Two or more things that, when combined, add value to each other.
- *Conscientisation*: The process by which a person develops the ability to think critically about issues of power in relationships to privilege and oppressions in different spheres of influence (i.e., at local, national, or international levels).
- *Distinction*: Treating people differently on the basis of their diversity. For example, treating a woman differently from a man because they are of different sexes.
- *Emasculation*: (usually as adjective **emasculated**) Deprive (a man) of his male role or identity. *'he feels emasculated because he cannot control his sons' behaviour'* 1.1 (archaic) Castrate (a man or male animal); 2. Make (someone or something) weaker or less

effective. *'the refusal to allow them to testify effectively emasculated the committee'*

- *Empowerment*: Process and result of gaining new attitudes, beliefs, knowledge, and skills that position one to compete equally with others for available opportunities and resources.
- *Exclusion*: A preventive act. For example, women are excluded from positions of authority or are denied a chance to enjoy something on an equal basis. To keep somebody out.
- *Female genital cutting* or *mutilation*: Sometimes referred to as *female circumcision*. Procedures that intentionally alter or cause injury to the female genital organs for non-medical reasons.
- *Female infanticide*: The deliberate killing of newborn female children.
- *Femicide*: A sexual/gender hate crime term, broadly defined as the killing of women/girls (female homicide) or the murder of a person based on the fact that she is female. Definitions vary depending on the cultural context.
- *Feminist*: A person who advocates for gender justice and the rights of women and girls on the basis of the equality of the sexes.
- *Gender*: Unequal sociocultural expectations placed on men and women. Through these expectations, society assigns roles and status on men and women. The roles, status, and expectations are often unfair, especially for women. Gender is the way society sees us and trains us to behave as acceptable men and women in a particular society.
- *Gender discrimination*: Different treatment given to one gender relative to another gender. In most cases, the term describes how the treatment given to women and girls differs from that given to men and boys. Usually this is not a one-off situation but a systemic process of discrimination.
- *Homogenous*: Of the same kind; alike. This term is often used to highlight the fact that men or women are not of the same kind. They have differences and specific needs and interests due to age, economic status, geographical location, etc.
- *Lobby*: An organised attempt by members of the public to influence politicians or public officials to do something. Usually a lobby acts

in the interest of a specific group, e.g., a lobby for better salaries for teachers.

- *Patriarchal beliefs*: Through the socialisation process, every society develops a collection of religious, cultural, and ideological beliefs which it embeds in the psyche of its children and uses to legitimise practices of gender discrimination.

- *Patriarchal control*: Directly or indirect social promotion of a male monopoly or domination of decision making, especially over women with regard to division of labour, allocation of resources, women's bodies, benefits, opportunities, and rewards. For example, most societies overburden women and girls with domestic chores, place little value on their labour, and give boy children enhanced opportunity to complete their education.

- *Patriarchal interest*: The material interest which males have in perpetuating a particular discriminatory practice, because of the benefits which accrue to men from patriarchal control. An example is inheritance practices that only allow males to inherit, denying females the opportunity to exploit productive resources accumulated by the family.

- *Patriarchy*: Systemic discriminatory treatment through which men maintain their domination over women. It starts in the home and exists in the community and across the whole society.

- *Productive work*: Labour performed by women and men for pay in cash or kind. It includes both market production with an exchange value, and subsistence or home production with use value (and also potential exchange value).

- *Puberty*: The period during which adolescent human beings go through rapid changes and reach sexual maturity. Boys start to produce sperm, and girls to produce eggs that make them capable of reproduction.

- *Self-actualisation*: A term developed by Abraham Maslow to describe the growth potential, attendant needs, and motivations of the individual, progressing toward fulfilment of the highest needs—those for meaning in life, in particular. Maslow created a psychological hierarchy of needs, the fulfilment of which theoretically leads to realising 'being values', or the needs that are on the highest level of this hierarchy, representing meaning.

- *Socialisation agents*: Vehicles used by a society to make members behave in a certain acceptable way. Parents, peers, teachers, and governing bodies (through policies and legislation) are the main socialisers. They teach us how to behave, what is expected of us, what is considered good, and what is bad. For example, when you are a teenager, your biggest socialising agents are often your peers, who can pressure you into favoured ways of behaving, dressing, or talking.
- *Socialise*: The process through which someone (usually a child) is systematically trained and surrounded by the sociocultural norms that make her or him acquire the particular values, attitudes, and behaviours considered 'normal' for a woman or man in their society.
- *Stereotype*: A widely held but fixed and oversimplified image or idea of a type of person, e.g., the stereotype that a woman is a person who does all the housework.
- *Strategic gender needs*: Things necessary to change the balance of power between women and men in society, based on the premise that women in society are currently subordinate to men. Examples of strategic needs include the law, education, and income. Strategic needs are geared towards women's emancipation, equality, and empowerment.
- *Synopsis*: A brief summary of a written work.
- *Time poverty*: A social aspect of poverty. Women are time-poor because of the disproportional level of household tasks they are supposed to perform. As a consequence, they hardly have time for leisure or for self-development activities to improve the quality of their lives.
- *Women's empowerment*: Process of acquiring new knowledge, skills, experience, attitudes, and beliefs which women can use, leading to more equitable participation and agency in decision-making, enabling them to exercise control over their own lives.
- *Women's practical and/or reproductive work*: In most societies, women are primarily responsible for child-rearing plus the daily

tasks involved in the care and maintenance of the household and family. Despite the important role the women fill and how this type of work contributes to the economy, it is rarely considered as having the same value as the so-called 'productive' work that men do. Domestic work by women is also normally unpaid.

- *Women's special needs*: These are requirements that differ from men's requirements, due to biological differences. For example, because of their reproductive role and physiology, women require sanitary towels, antenatal clinics, maternity clinics, and postnatal clinics.
- *Women's triple burden*: Women are socially and culturally assigned reproductive, productive and communal roles. Significantly, they bear a lioness's share of routine, repetitive domestic responsibilities.

CHAPTER 1

The Painful Change

Here's to the crazy ones, the misfits, the rebels, the troublemakers, the round pegs in the square holes … the ones who see things differently—they're not fond of rules … You can quote them, disagree with them, glorify or vilify them, but the only thing you can't do is ignore them because they change things … they push the human race forward, and while some may see them as the crazy ones, we see genius, because the ones who are crazy enough to think they can change the world are the ones who do.

—Steve Jobs, American entrepreneur and business magnate, co-founder of Apple Inc.

Good change can be painful when only one group has all the fun and the other group suffers. In such a situation, the oppressed need strong leaders who are troublesome and optimistic to disrupt the status quo.

Former South African president and freedom fighter, the late Nelson Mandela, was tired of suffering. His African colleagues and contemporaries from other races were tired of being treated like slaves in their own country. They felt compassion for vulnerable black people and wanted to secure their freedom.

Some white people, also fed up with this inequitable treatment of black people, joined in this fight. Mandela was arrested for protesting against apartheid. In his speech against the apartheid regime during his trial at Rivonia, in the Pretoria Supreme Court, on 20 April 1964, he adamantly stated,

During my lifetime I have dedicated myself to this struggle of the African people. I have fought against white domination, and I have fought against black domination. I have cherished the ideal of a democratic and free society in which all persons live together in harmony and with equal opportunities. It is an ideal which I hope to live for and to achieve. But if needs be, it is an ideal for which I am prepared to die.

—Nelson Mandela Foundation

Since he was even ready to die, the apartheid government tossed him and his friends into the lonely Robben Island high-security prison, locked them up, and threw away the key. The government wanted to hear no more of that equal rights stuff. However, Mandela and his fellow prisoners continued to struggle for equality for all people in South Africa: black or white, women or men, girls or boys, young or old. Millions of people from around the world heard what happened to Mandela and took a keen interest in joining the struggle.

After twenty-seven gruesome years spent demanding change, it finally happened. South Africa became independent in 1990. That same year, Nelson Mandela was released from prison and became the first president of a free South Africa. Apartheid was banned not only in South Africa but also in neighbouring Namibia, which gained independence the same year. It took too long, and too many lives were lost, but they had trudged on. These men and women believed in the fundamental principle of success. Their motto might well have been, 'Failure is a Detour. Not a dead End Street.'

—Zig Ziglar, American author, salesman and motivational speaker

A small group of people demanded change, and they were willing to suffer, even die, to ensure all people enjoyed equal rights and opportunities in their nation. Today, South Africa continues that long journey toward equal rights and social justice for people of all races, ages, and sexes. They call themselves the Rainbow Nation.

Isn't that powerful? Isn't the goal of equal rights for everybody inspirational? Change is not easy. Nor does it happen as quickly as you want. The leaders of the apartheid regime learned the hard way that 'He who rejects change is the architect of decay. The only human institution which rejects progress is the cemetery.'

—Winston Churchill, British Prime minister.

Mandela realised he was not living his big dream of a free and equal South Africa. He took a risk and dared to dream. But not only did he dream. Mandela challenged all obstacles and took massive action. Mandela and other freedom fighters even risked the ultimate sacrifice of giving their lives to fight the good fight. Together with his contemporaries, Mandela went further and linked the country's future stability to the struggle for social justice. 'A dream is your creative vision for your life in the future. You must break out of your current comfort zone and become comfortable with the unfamiliar and the unknown.'

—Denis Waitley, American motivational speaker and writer

No wonder Chris Hani, one of the movement's firebrands, said, 'If you want peace then you must struggle for social justice.' The fight for social justice, similar to that against apartheid, is one in which we are all meant to become disrupters. We need to get angry—so angry that we see no other option but to challenge the status quo and fight for the rights of all people.

—Chris Hani, South African anti-apartheid freedom fighter

This is not a comfortable position. It places demands on you, demands that make intrinsic changes in you and create new values. 'If you put yourself in a position where you have to stretch outside your comfort zone, then you are forced to expand your consciousness.'

—Les Brown. American motivational speaker

I seek inspiration in people like Mandela and Hani, who faced extremely challenging experiences. Instead of looking on passively, they courageously and consciously decided to do something about the situation and bring about the change they desired. They made change that echoed. Their change echoed what Maya Angelou had described so beautifully, 'If you don't like something, change it. If you can't change it, change your attitude. Don't complain.'

—Maya Angelou. American writer and poet

CHANGE, CHANGE, CHANGE!

> Do you know how painful change can be?

As I mentioned earlier, change is painful when rights are provided selectively. Those who have experienced all the fun will not want to change. But those who are suffering will want the change. That is where the challenge comes in, and all kinds of tough things can happen. Those striving to be treated like those having all the fun must take a stand and fight for that change. There are lots of examples in history.

Until 1990, black South Africans suffered under the apartheid regime. This was a social system in which black people and people of other races, like Indians and mixed-race people, did not have the same political, social, and economic rights as white people. They had the worst jobs, the worst education, the worst places to live, and the worst health services. Worse still, they were not allowed to go anywhere they pleased, and they could not vote. The irony here is that this was all happening in a nation that belonged to black people in the first place!

There were jobs black South Africans were not allowed to apply for; hotels, offices, restaurants, malls, and parts of buses or trains they could not sit in; and clubs they were not allowed to enter unless they worked there as staff. Why? Because they were black Africans in South Africa! That was part of what the apartheid regime did. White people decided they were better than black people, so white people had the best homes, the best jobs, the best opportunities for health care, and the best access to all parts of the country. They had immense power.

The apartheid regime was so brutal and inhumane that it made both blacks and whites do unimaginable things to each other, things you would rarely expect from a fellow human being. They were outrageous and horrific. It is shocking what one human being can do to another without care, compassion, or conscience. History is replete with stories of such experiences.

Unfortunately, we usually see the affected people as mere victims or weaklings who need our pity. So we remember them for a short time and then forget them as mere statistics. But we must remember that behind those negative statistics, there are living people's stories—stories of women, men, boys, and girls who were demonised, dehumanised, humiliated, and treated in undignified ways. On the other hand, when one follows the stories of such people, we often find amazing human resilience, persistence, and survival— stories of the indomitable spirits of human beings.

I have decided to learn from the experiences of such legends. I want to stand on the very wide shoulders of these giants and take massive action to fight for social justice. That's why I decided to write this book. I know there is something in me that has changed significantly. I feel I can no longer wait for things to happen to me passively, as a spectator. I strongly believe I was born to be a passionate activist who can influence the direction of social justice.

I believe there is something I can do about change. I trust that I am blessed and greatly endowed. I trust that if I use my faith in God and combine it with a positive attitude and my international development expertise and leadership skills, I will make a difference. I can define my purpose. I will add value and inspire many women and men to fight for social justice, especially in Africa.

Deep inside me, I believe I am capable of making a personal contribution and leave a great and valuable legacy to the world. That's why I am always cheery and engaged. In this area I take an exaggerated view of myself. I know that it was not for nothing that my parents called me Grace!

CHAPTER 2

Be the Standard

The same analysis can be applied to another area of social injustice that must change. This area has to do with the way roles, resources, opportunities, and decision-making power are unfairly distributed among women and girls versus men and boys.

One group, the men and boys, seems to have all the fun, advantages, and privileges. The other group, women and girls, silently suffers with all the difficulties and gets ever-fewer opportunities in society. This is referred to as *gender discrimination*.

Similar to apartheid, gender discrimination is an unfair system for women and girls. It's a travesty every human being must stand up and fight until it is completely eliminated like apartheid.

Did you know that there are 145 million people in the East Africa Community (EAC)? Did you know that women and girls comprise 60 per cent (84 million people) of this population, yet 'women own only 1 per cent of all the businesses in East Africa' Is this not surprising to you?

—East African Community

Did you know that a report produced in 2015 by the Institute of Directors (IOD) indicated that among Kenya's banks, only 12 per cent have women on the boards where major decisions are made? Women comprise less than a third of the membership in professional associations for industries such as insurance (15 per cent), state-owned enterprises (26 per cent) and microfinance (26 per cent). Don't women also need to participate in making decisions that affect their lives?

—Institute of Directors

Did you know that, worldwide, while 55% of men report having an account at a formal financial institution, like a bank, only 47% women do worldwide. This gap is largest among lower and middle income economies like those of East Africa, as well as South Asia, and the Middle East and North Africa?

—World Bank FINEX, Financial Inclusion

Do you know that women farmers, who are 85 to 90 per cent responsible for household food production in Africa, control less land than men and also have limited access to inputs, seeds, credit and extension services? Gender differences in access to land and credit affect the relative ability of female and male farmers and entrepreneurs to invest, operate to scale, and benefit from new economic opportunities.

— Food and Agriculture Organisation (FAO)

Did you know that we are losing many African mothers to the human papillomavirus (HPV), transmitted through sex, that increases the risk of cervical cancer—yet it can be detected early through Pap smears and even vaccinated against?

—Hugo et al: The burden of HPV … in sub-Saharan Africa

Did you know that a Demographic and Health Survey (DHS) of Kenya in 2014 showed that '18 per cent of younger women aged 15–19 have given birth or are pregnant with their first child, and this has a great impact on women's education achievement overall? Don't you think education matters?

—Kenya DHS 2014

It's my assertion that these huge disparities in the way resources, opportunities, and decision-making powers are shared, are not a one-off incident, nor are they by accident. There are significant underlying causes of these differences and deliberate acts of omission and commission that discriminate women. Achieving gender equity and equality is another big struggle for social justice. Unlike apartheid, which was limited to South Africa, these inequities seem to be global and accepted across the world.

Addressing the issues related to gender always raises people's emotions. It is therefore a very difficult, culturally sensitive, and controversial area to deal with. This book has been written with lots of love, hope, and confidence that it will create greater awareness about gender discrimination and ultimately change millions of women and girls' lives and livelihoods. Hopefully it will touch the hearts of many other people who are vulnerable and suffering silently from gender injustice and other forms of discrimination.

Gender discrimination is experienced every day, everywhere, most of the time. You can observe and feel it daily. You are either a beneficiary or a victim of the unjust gender systems in our society. And you can take a stand, like Mandela and his colleagues did, to fight for change. You can fight for gender justice and women's rights, even if it does not affect you directly.

Alternatively, you can choose to be a hopeless and selfish bystander, who believes that you cannot do anything. Maybe your attitude is, as the popular saying goes, 'If it's not broken, do not fix it.' Remember that taking action is an important decision, and so is not taking action!

Certainly gender relations of power can change! In the past six thousand years that the world has been in existence, there have been only two things that are certain: death and change. I can assure you that if the world is still around for another six thousand years, the only things that will continue to be certain will be death and change. However, this time, part of that change will be in the gendered relations of power. 'Things don't happen overnight, but you can step in the water and have a good go.'

—Sir Elton John, British singer

9

RESPONSES TO CHANGE

When there is need for change, different people react differently. Generally you have four kinds of reactions:

1. critics who oppose the change
2. victims who panic about the change
3. bystanders who simply ignore the need for change
4. disrupters who are empowered by change

DISRUPTERS

Disrupters are the ones who seek deeper knowledge about what they are experiencing. They are the ones who navigate and rise to the occasion to assess their options and the risks involved. They arrive at solutions that can make a positive difference. They are the celebrated and disruptive forces of the world. As Steve Jobs incisively summarised, love or hate them, you cannot ignore them, for they make things happen in a positive way.

BYSTANDERS

Bystanders are the most dangerous group of people among these four categories. They ignore the need for change. As long as they are not affected, they consider it none of their business. As long as they are not the victims, they will not do anything about it. These people make the world sick.

One of the greatest inspirational speakers in the world, once observed that, 'The greatest sin of our time is not the few who have destroyed but the vast majority who sat idly by.' He went on to say, on another occasion, that 'In the end, we will remember not the words of our enemies but the silence of our friends.' I am certain you too, as you read this book, must remember many occasions when you expected some people to rise up and take a stand for what they knew was right, but they didn't. Unfortunately they are normally the majority!

—Martin Luther King Jr., American Baptist minister and civil rights leader

Many years before Dr King spoke these wise words, Napoleon Bonaparte, the greatest French general of all time, similarly observed, 'The world is a bad place, not because of the violence of bad people, but because of the inaction of good people.'

—Napoleon Bonaparte, French statesman and military leader

Personally reflect: when it comes to gender discrimination, on which side of history would you like to stand today? Would you like to be remembered as a critic, a victim, a bystander, or a disrupter? I challenge you to answer the call of your destiny as Nelson Mandela did and write a new page in the history of gender equality.

A great British politician who led his country during the Second World War, once said, 'History will be kind to me because I intend to write it.'

—Winston Churchill, British prime minister

When would you like to start writing your own story? What stops you from writing your history today? Thomas Carlyle was right when he said, 'The history of the world is but the biography of greatmen'—and women! Be one of them! *Work on gender discrimination.*

—Thomas Carlyle, Scottish philosopher

DON'T FOLLOW THE CROWD

Disrupters can stubbornly find a way where the rest see no way. Nelson Mandela and his colleagues took a stand and refused to follow the crowd into the abyss of apartheid misery. They followed the less trodden, risky, and lonely path of fighting for freedom. At the end of their struggle, they changed the destinies of millions of fellow black people. You can do the same if you chuck your fear.

A wise woman once said, 'Never doubt that a small group of thoughtful and committed citizens can change the world: Indeed it's the only thing that ever has.'

—Margaret Mead, American cultural anthropologist

A close friend of mine once challenged me too: 'Grace, never, ever allow yourself to be a spectator—'You were born an original, don't die a copy.' I listened and reflected on my purpose in life. I decided to take action, and one of the outcomes is this book.

—John Mason, best selling author, minister and speaker

Likewise, I challenge you. Don't be a spectator. Step up to the plate and take action against gender discrimination. Many history books tell us that change happens when people get sick and tired of being sick and tired! Change happens when people recognise that whatever affects one of us, affects all of us. Lets not stand as unaffected and selfish observers.

HAVE COMPASSION AND KINDNESS

A Ugandan singer, Philly Bongole Lutaaya, once rallied fellow Ugandans to become more compassionate towards people affected by HIV and AIDS.

Similarly gender inequality is not a women's issue only—it affects us all. It is about being human, in all our humanity in the image of God. Women and girls are not simply statistics. They are always in our lives. They are our mothers; they are our sisters; they are our wives; they are our aunties, grannies, and friends. We need them. We love and adore them. They are real humans with flesh and blood like us!

—Philly Bongole Lutaya, Ugandan singer

YOUR ARE ALSO IN PRISON!

Someone once said, 'As long as you keep a person down, some part of you has to be down there to hold the person down, so it means you cannot soar as you otherwise might.' The prison warders who kept Nelson Mandela jailed on Robben Island for twenty-seven years were in essence also prisoners on that island!

—Marian Anderson, singer

LEVERAGE BOOKS AND OTHER PEOPLE'S POWER

I once heard this from an African motivation speaker, 'Two things matter in life. The people you meet and the books you read.' So, start reading. To become great let us climb on the shoulders of great women and men. Definitely you cannot climb on your own shoulders. Otherwise, in Africa, you will be called a witch.

—Pepe Mirambo, motivational speaker and writer

Some schools of thought say that as long as women and girls do not participate fully in the development of the human race, half the world's innovation and progress will be stupidly sabotaged. During his his visit to Kenya in August 2015, President Obama echoed this when he talked about the status of women in Kenya

'Every person has inherent dignity- and the right to have that dignity respected and protected … There's no excuse for sexual assault or domestic violence. There's no reason that young girls should suffer genital mutilation … These traditions may date back centuries, they have no place in the 21st century. Treating women as second-class citizens is a bad tradition. It holds you back … Imagine if you have a team and you don't let half of the team to play. That's stupid. That makes no sense.'

—Barrack Obama, American president

Reflect on those nuggets of wisdom. The grace, beauty, confidence, growth, and strength that Michelle Obama his wife, exhibited as First Lady at the White House is a clear testimony of Obama's genuine ability to empower women and especially his wife at home.

Truly as men and women of the twenty-first century, we are the first generation in the history of mankind with the global technological opportunity to fundamentally make our great minds meet through media. Let us use the power of social media to defy negative gender myths and taboos and bring real change for the holistic and balanced progress of the entire human race. History will judge us harshly if we fail to seize this laudable opportunity. Decide today to be a voice of change on gender and women's rights.

GENDER ON THE DINNER TABLE

Another American president, once said, 'All great change in America begins at the dinner table.' There are dinner tables across the world where families sit daily and have opportunity to share food and interact with each other. Even though in many countries people sit down on mats and women are not expected or not allowed to sit at the table as equals to men. They eat from behind in the kitchen. Nevertheless, begin the discussion *now*. Let women to sit and eat together as one family. Open up and start to ask those uncomfortable questions *now*. Place gender on the agenda of the dinner table or mat *now*!

—Ronald Reagan, US President

Start a change conversation in your own family—or school, church, mosque, or workplace—in small ways. If every family or company takes the responsibility to discuss gender issues and transform the prevailing inequality of power in our society, I believe our children will grow up better enlightened than us. They will know that gender inequality exists and its bad for us all. They will work for gender equality and build a whole new world that is well balanced, where every member of the community is valued and has access to equal opportunities. Decide today to be a voice of change.

As an American president recently said, 'Change will not come if we wait for some other person or some other time. [REMEMBER], We are the ones we've been waiting for. We are the change that we seek.'

—Barrack Obama, American President

CALL TO ACTION

Today, make the decision to gain a deeper understanding of gender discrimination. Decide today on the strategies and tactics you will use to read this book to the end. One leadership guru once said that, leaders always 'start with the end in mind.'

—Steven Richards Covey, leadership authority, organisational consultant, teacher

- Peruse all the chapters of this book.
- Set your goal by deciding when you want to finish reading this book.
- Write down this goal on paper.
- Take a look at each chapter and set your daily targets.
- Allocate a specific time of the day when you will dedicate your time to reading this book.
- As you read each chapter, do these things:
  o Take at least ten minutes to focus and reflect on that chapter.
  o Summarise the lessons you have learned in your own words.
  o Jot down your action items for those lessons (What? When? How? With whom?).
  o Take massive action!

CHAPTER 3

Gender and Sex

The problem with gender is that it prescribes who we should be, rather than recognizing how we are.

—Chimamanda Ngozi Adichie, best seller Nigerian novelist and writer

There are two words that people use often. People mix these words up as if these words are the same. These words are *sex* and *gender*. Even when you are filling up applications, some will ask 'What is your gender?' and others will ask 'What is your sex?' However, these two words are different.

The word *sex* often appears when people want to identify whether you are biologically male or female.

Can you fill in the table below to show six physical differences between males and females?

Males	Females

Sex has to do with the physical and biological differences between males and females.

THE GENDER AND ENVIRONMENT ANALOGY

Years ago, some leaders of government in one country wanted to destroy a park and build a high-rise building in the city centre. This involved cutting down many indigenous trees, and turning that beautiful park into a huge construction zone. We have always witnessed such compromises when it comes to development.

Many people who valued nature held demonstrations and campaigns. They advertised in newspapers and on billboards about the importance of keeping the indigenous trees for the sake of protecting the environment. Trees provide habitat and shade, not forgetting their contribution to preserving climate and water sources.

The activists introduced a term to our vocabulary: *endangered species*. It referred to the indigenous tree species which, if destroyed today, would never be found again. Those species needed protection and propagation in order to continue existing in our environment.

Then there was another campaign about black rhinos, white rhinos, and elephants in Africa. Poachers were killing these animals for their valuable horns, which they used as expensive jewellery and medicine. The animals were being killed in large numbers and would soon disappear forever from the face of Africa.

Many things were done to help protect rhinos and elephants. These measures included banning the purchase of any products made from these animals, and making it illegal to hunt them. We wondered what was happening to the world.

After a while, there came another issue that troubled many people. As African society modernized, many young girls were not getting the same level of education as boys. Girls enrolled in large numbers at primary level but as they entered adolescence their numbers dwindled as their parents pulled them out of school to be married off or to help their mothers to look after their younger siblings.

This happened especially to girls with disabilities, because their parents placed very low value on them. Parents thought that educating them was a waste of money. Some schools refused to admit them. Can you imagine the isolation and stigma those children felt? There can be no genuine reason for their exclusion from school.

Further, there were jobs that women were not allowed to do. In offices, when women did the same job as men, they were paid less than their male counterparts. Do you see the discrimination here?

Nearly all companies had boards of directors and senior management teams comprised of men only. When women became pregnant, many organisations asked them to stop working because pregnancy was inconvenient.

Many women were dying during childbirth (and still dying today) because there were no trained midwives to attend births. Many left behind broken families and helpless orphans.

Every day, the media mentioned women and children (both boys and girls, but mostly girls) who had been maimed or even died as a result of domestic and sexual violence from their husbands, neighbours, teachers, and close relatives. Others were put at the mercy of traditional old women, who mutilated them with unsterilized, blunt, and crooked knives. Again, many were maimed for life or died in the process.

Similar things were happening in far-off countries like India and China. Girl children were aborted in large numbers or killed at birth because society placed very low value on them. That is what is commonly referred to as *femicide* or *infanticide*. Having a girl child meant that the parent had to pull together a high dowry to give to the boy's family at marriage. Many women whose parents could not raise high dowries were killed by their husbands and in-laws, or abused to the extent of committing suicide.

What a world it was for all these women! Is it surprising to you that in many African countries, where it's the men who pay the dowry, we do not kill men or force them to commit suicide because of failure to pay enough? So many opportunities were harder for women to achieve than for men because society thought women were less deserving.

It seemed like the pipeline for women's progress to the top was like a big sieve. Women kept falling through the holes like bad wheat. As a result, there were hardly any role models in high positions and professions for girls to emulate. Women were not promoted to decision-making bodies like senior leadership teams or governance boards.

This barrier to promotion into management and governance positions is often referred to as the *glass ceiling*. Women peep through it to observe the men making decisions that are going to affect their lives but they have no say in the process. However, they find it very hard to break through and sit at that decision-making table, to bring out their needs and interests, and ensure that leaders understand and take decisions in response to both the women and men's lived realities. The key questions were how and when this glass ceiling would be smashed, and by whom.

In many African traditional cultures, females could not inherit land from their parents. After all, thought the parents, they girls were about to leave the family and marry into another clan. They also could not inherit land where they married. They were seen as semi-permanent or quasi-foreigners who could at any time leave the husband, remarry, and take their husband's land to a new husband, or one day run back to their parents' home and take their land to their birth clan. As if women could shuffle the land in their suitcases or handbags and leave with it. Do those fears make sense? And if I may insolently ask a few more questions, Where do women belong? And if land is the main productive resource, in Africa, how will women ever accumulate wealth?

So where did women belong? What identity could they claim, given the fact that they would naturally always be deemed either transitory daughters or wives? When their marriages broke down, should they become destitute?

There were tasks girls were not allowed to perform once they started menstruating or gave birth. There were foodstuffs, often of the rich protein family, they could not eat. Those foods were reserved for their husbands (even if they were away) or served to boy children only. The foods included eggs, chicken, and goat meat. The prohibition continued even through pregnancy and lactation, when women had higher nutritional requirements to ensure their own health and that of their babies.

WOMEN'S TRIPLE BURDEN

Women and girls took on greater responsibilities at home, including reproductive care roles for the whole family. They also ensured the general well-being of the whole community.

At home, women collected water, firewood, and food. They cooked for the family. They cleaned the house, swept the compound, washed the dishes, washed and clothes ironed and folded up. This was part of women's role of ensuring total maintenance of the family and the country's productive workforce.

Women were the ones who nursed and nurtured children from infancy, ensuring they were well-fed and healthy. If any member of family fell sick, women and girls had to drop everything (including going to work or school) in order to care for the patient. This included taking the patient to hospital, often by carrying that person on their backs. In all these reproductive roles, women were neither recognised nor remunerated.

Even today, when you see a smart man wearing a nice, clean, ironed suit and shining shoes, remember some woman did the work to make him look smart and responsible—most likely without pay or appreciation! It's the same for smart children you see going to school. There is an incredibly hard-working woman doing the job.

In the *shambas* (gardens), the same women toil as smallholder farmers in the bristling sunshine with an exacting hoe. This is how they guarantee food security for their families. They populate the evening and weekend markets as farmers or traders, playing productive roles by selling their extra food and cash crops to cover daily home expenses.

In the evenings, women often ran kiosks or shops—part of their domination of Africa's formidable small and medium enterprise (SMEs) sector. These smallholder women farmers who also double as entrepreneurs constitute the backbone of the economy in Africa. Surprisingly, even in the productive sector, women are left behind. Lenders refuse to give them credit to expand their businesses because they lack collateral. Collateral is a tangible asset with monetary value, like a land title, car log book or building. Women are left out of inheritance, so they don't own land titles!

To be professionally employed, one needed high levels of education. Women were rarely professionally employed because the majority never got beyond primary education. Do you see how the cycle of poverty was propagated in our societies? Have you heard the term '*feminisation of poverty?*' That is one example.

At the community level, women played voluntary communal roles which entailed taking care of the sick as Community Health Workers (CHWs). They were the public entertainers at official functions, to please official government visitors on behalf of the community. They collected food, water, and firewood, then worked as cooks and servers at major community events like marriages and funerals. Unfortunately, for this work too, they were neither recognised nor remunerated. Do you see the unfairness?

This was what was referred to as the *triple burden*—women fulfilling reproductive, productive, and communal roles simultaneously. This was a big challenge, and it cut down women's dreams. They were extremely busy, hence suffered from *time poverty.*

The heavy workload at home, coupled with the low value parents placed on girls, hindered many girls from pursuing higher education beyond primary. They missed out on acquiring skills for harnessing their talents, and competing for employment. Girls did not have the resources to dream big and pursuing their passions to realise their full potential.

Then we began to hear the word *gender* being used everywhere as if it was a suffix. People talked about gender awareness, gender gap, gender balance, gender equity, gender equality, gender sensitivity, gender socialisation, gender integration, and gender mainstreaming. These unfamiliar terms were interspersed with other terms like *women's empowerment.* We also heard calls for gender quotas, affirmative action, and gender justice. What were the cause and meaning of all these words? Was it the same as the activism about the trees, the rhinos, and the elephants? Was gender another 'endangered species?'

All we knew was that there was a thing called gender, and everyone was talking about it. Gender was like a vitamin given to children—it had become part of our lives, but we didn't quite understand what it was about. We began to think that gender and sex were one and the same thing; that if someone talked about male or female private parts, that was the same as talking about gender. Yet in our culture, we were not allowed to discuss sex in public. In some cases, people got so confused that they presumed 'gender' meant females trying to change themselves into men! 'Over my dead body!' Some men exclaimed. The noise was too much, too loud, and too confusing.

Universities and international non-governmental organisations (NGOs) introduced courses whereby people could begin to study and understand gender issues in development. There was also a lot of media publicity about gender. Through education and media, we finally began to understand what gender is. People are slowly becoming sensitised to gender issues.

EXPLAINING SEX AND GENDER

Sex was easy to appreciate because it's biological and tangible. People could see and touch the differences. They could experience and observe the changes that boys and girls went through during adolescence. This meaning of the word *sex* was clear.

Gender was not so easy to understand. It was not an animal or a tree or an endangered species. It is not a part of the human body. It was intangible and intricately linked to our culture. It was shrouded in lots of complexity. Gender was an enigma because it involved very many terms and concepts that did not have concrete meanings in our local languages. What was certain is that the word *gender* tended to pit women and girls against men and boys.

The word *gender* seemed to challenge our deeply held and respected societal myths, beliefs, values, and attitudes. These are revered in every culture because they tell us how to be a 'normal man' or a 'normal woman' in that particular society. Gender activists analysed these myths from what they called a gender perspective and tried to change people's views about them. This was not pleasing at all

That is what this book is all about. My goal is to raise awareness about what is wrong with our culture's current values, myths, attitudes, and behaviours. Using stories, case studies, family portraits, and inspirational quotations, I carefully demystify the meanings of gender both conceptually and practically. I share famous quotes and anecdotes with you to emphasize some points, inspire the readers and to enable you to grasp certain gendered messages better. The book proposes another equilibrium based on holistic human well-being. It helps the reader to reflect and understand our culture and use that knowledge to audit our culture ourselves.

Complex change requires disrupters, like those mentioned in the Steve Jobs quotation in chapter 1: 'Disrupters have foresight. You can vilify them and demonise them. The only thing you cannot do is ignore them for they are crazy enough to imagine a new world. And that is why they are the ones who change the world.'

—Steve Jobs, American entrepreneur and business magnate, co-founder of Apple Inc.

Disruption may make people uncomfortable. Some may feel they are teetering on the edge of a slippery slope with nowhere to hang on. They may feel provoked to the core, wondering, 'How did they find me out? Who revealed my well-kept secrets?' However, this book is based on facts. People's real-life stories don't lie.

This book does not and cannot protect your sensitivities or emotions. It pushes for straight talk about the damnedest realities of gender injustice that are often shrouded in our sociocultural and religious taboos. These realities are often kept in silence, not talked about publicly.

Before you go through emotional turmoil, slow down and read to the end. If you do so, you will also conclude that this book is merely a mirror of our lives to date, a maze with only one invisible and elusive exit. You may feel trapped and forced to criticise, judge or even despise yourself and those who are closest to you for what you have done or seen them do to women.

Don't despair. Stay focused on the future, like the car with a wide windscreen at the front and a small one behind. You will soon acquire a different value system and mindset from which to see the world. Ultimately you may surprise yourself and discover the light at the end of the tunnel.

Since you were made in the image of God, this book will not leave you unchanged. You will be a human being who radiates truth, compassion, and love. You will proudly stand up for gender justice and women's rights because that is the only right way to go. You will dream big and feel fulfilled. Above all, you will be proud of the new, real you who emerges.

ACTION PLAN

1. Form two groups of peers. Ask each team to ask the following questions widely among friends, families, neighbours, and workmates, and to write down the answers they get.
    *   What words come to mind when you hear the word *gender*?
    *   What images come to mind when you hear the word *gender*? Give drawings if possible.
    *   What positive experiences do men and women experience in relation to their gender? What negative experiences do men and women experience in relation to their gender? Consider these aspects: division of labour, access to resources and services, inheritance, control and ownership of assets, and opportunities.
2. Convene the two groups to compile and discuss the answers received, especially the positive and negative aspects of gender experiences. Allow each team to define the word *gender* from their perspective.

CHAPTER 4

Gender Discrimination and Human Rights

All human beings ae born free and equal in dignity and rights. They are endowed with reason and conscience and should act towards one another in a spiri of brotherhood[sisterhood]

—Article 1, United Nations Declaration of Human Rights

Everyone is entitled to enjoy the human rights defined in the Declaration without distinction of any kind such as colour, race, sex, language, religion, political or other opinion, national or social origin, property, birth or other status.

If you want to become inspired, proactive, and self-actualised to the point that you can disrupt disempowering gender myths, attitudes, and beliefs, you need to know the legitimacy and credibility offered to all human beings through the Universal Declaration of Human Rights (UDHR). So it is imperative that, before embarking on the tedious journey of fighting for gender equality, you get a deep appreciation of the concept of human rights and mechanisms for enforcement of human rights. You also need a firm understanding of the links between gender, women, and human rights.

Before we start, remember:

- human rights have something to do with *being human*

- human rights are *free* and thus *grant freedoms*
- human rights are *entitlements*

Therefore human rights can be defined easily as 'rights, freedoms, and entitlements possessed by all persons by virtue of being human'.

SUMMARY OF HUMAN RIGHTS UNDER UDHR

1. Right to Equality	9. Freedom from Arbitrary Arrest and Exile	17. Right to Property	25. Right to Adequate Living Standard
2. Freedom from Discrimination	10. Right to Fair Public Hearing	18. Freedom of Belief and Religion	26. Right to Education
3. Right to Life, Liberty, and Personal Security	11. Right to be considered Innocent until Proved Guilty	19. Freedom of Opinion and Information	27. Right to our own way of life and to enjoy he good things that Science and Learning brings
4. Freedom from Slavery	12. Freedom from Interference with Privacy, Family, Home and Correspondence	20. Right to Peaceful Assembly and Association	28. Right to proper Order and Freedom
5. Freedom from Torture and Degrading Treatment	13. Right to Free Movement in and out of the Country	21. Right to participate in Government and in Free Elections	29. Duty to other People and protecting their Rights
6. Right of Recognition as a Person before the Law	14. Right to Nationality and the Freedom to Change it	22. Right to Social Security	30. Nobody can take away these Rights and Freedoms

7. Right to Equality before the Law	15. Right to Nationality and the Freedom to Change it	23. Right to Rest and Leisure	-
8. Right to Remedy by a Competent Court	16. Right to Marriage and Family	24. Right to Desirable Work and to join Trade Unions	-

Human rights are not static. They are dynamic and respond to social, economic, and political change; development issues; and the challenges of the day. Examples of major changes include industrialisation, the information age, climate change, terrorism, pollution, and technological advances. In other words, human rights cannot be tied up in a box and put away in a corner.

The way we enjoy individual human rights and respect others' human rights is conditioned by culture and the socialisation we experience, which are also dynamic and can be moderated by laws and regulations at different levels.

Characteristics of human rights
- human rights are founded on *respect* for the dignity and worth of each person in the society
- human rights are *universal*—applied equally without discrimination to all people
- human rights are *inalienable*— no one can have their rights taken away as a trade-off for another right
- Human rights are *indivisible*, *interrelated*, and *interdependent*

There are three sources of human rights and they exist at three levels: international, regional, and national.

1. International (UN) instruments
- treaties: formal agreements between nations that are legally binding

- conventions: same as above
- covenants: same as above
- declarations: expressions of principle
- resolutions: not contractual

2. Regional instruments

These are specific to a region and tackle issues pertinent to it. The best examples are those developed for Africa as a regional block, namely:
- The African Charter on Human and Peoples' Rights.
- The African Charter on the Rights and Welfare of the African Child
- The African Charter on the Rights of Women—additional protocol

3. National instruments
- national constitutions
- acts by national legislatures
- decentralisation and devolution statutes

I will highlight five key reference points for gender justice and women's rights in Africa, namely:

1. Universal Declaration of Human Rights (UDHR)—1948
2. UN Convention on the Elimination of all Forms of Discrimination Against Women (CEDAW)—1979
3. Maputo Protocol—2003
4. UN Convention on the Rights of Children (UNCRC)—1989
5. African Charter on the Rights and Welfare of the Child (The Africa Charter)—1999

Note that when developing the Africa Charter, the leaders of Africa wanted to emphasise the fact that in Africa, the child not only has *rights* but also has *responsibilities*—for example, to his parents and the elderly.

UNIVERSAL DECLARATION OF HUMAN RIGHTS (UDHR)

Current international human rights obligations are rooted in the charter of the United Nations, which was established on universally accepted principles of human dignity. After witnessing the atrocities and widespread abuses of individuals and groups, including genocide, mass killings, and other forms of violence against humanity, the governments of the time got inspired and saw an urgent call for action to demand and set standards for the treatment of people by their own national governments.

The first attempt to codify such standards was the Universal Declaration of Human Rights (UDHR) on 10 December 1948. The UDHR has since been the fundamental document on human rights, from which other rights instruments have been developed. In addition to framing a declaration, the UN established a covenant and mechanisms of implementation, including compliance monitoring, reporting and other procedures.

The UDHR was initially ratified by only a few states, then later by all emerging nations through a process of accession. It has become recognised the world over, and 10 December is celebrated annually as International Human Rights Day.

Below is a glossary of key terms you need to know in relation to UN conventions processes:

- *ratification*: a country's formal expression of consent to be bound by a treaty
- *reservation*: a country's commitment to only specific articles in a treaty
- *signing*: a county's formal indication of commitment
- *adoption*: a country's expression of acceptance of a treaty and willingness to put it into action
- *accession*: a country's consent to be bound by a statute when it has not previously signed the instrument

POLITICAL AND CIVIL RIGHTS

These address the states' traditional responsibilities for administering justice and maintaining the rule of law. Civil and political rights include the right to self-determination, the right to life, the right to liberty, the right to security, the right to religion, the right to peaceful assembly and association, the right to freedom from torture and arbitrary arrest, and the right to a fair and prompt trial.

ECONOMIC, CULTURAL, AND SOCIAL RIGHTS

These rights are designed to protect people based on the expectation that people can enjoy rights, freedoms, and social justice simultaneously. They include the right to work, the right to clothing, the right to food, the right to housing, the right to health, and the right to education, among others.

As you read and understand the relationships between gender, human rights, and discrimination, you will begin to realise how different rights are intertwined. You will appreciate that men and women lead holistic lives that encompass all these rights.

HUMAN RIGHTS ENFORCEMENT MECHANISMS

The sources of human rights exist at three levels: international, regional, and national. Similarly, enforcement mechanisms for those rights also exist at three levels.

International

- Charter-based bodies: these mechanisms are established by the UN Charter and are responsible for policy making, e.g., the UN General Assembly, UN Security Council, and UN Economic and Social Council.
- Treaty-based bodies: these mechanisms are established under a specific treaty and are responsible for monitoring that treaty's observance, e.g., the Committee on Elimination of all Forms of Discrimination Against Women, the Human Rights Committee, and the Committee on the Rights of the Child.
- Specialised agencies of the UN: these mechanisms focus on specific issues and address human rights at the practical level, e.g.,

UNICEF (children), UNIFEM (women), UNDP (development), ILO (labour), and WHO (health).

Regional

At the regional level, the UN uses different mechanisms to identify key issues and problems and to advise on policy and remedial action. These include:

- commissions, e.g., the African Commission on Human and Peoples' Rights
- the African Court on Human Rights
- committees
- working groups
- UN special rapporteurs and peacekeeping forces, like AMISON in Somalia

National

At the national level, the enforcement mechanisms of human rights include:

- human rights laws
- national courts
- police and prisons
- non-government organisations (NGOs)
- tribunals

UN CONVENTION ON THE ELIMINATION OF ALL FORMS OF DISCRIMINATION AGAINST WOMEN (CEDAW)

In this convention, the United Nations defines gender discrimination as 'treating men and women or boys and girls differently in a manner that disadvantages one group from enjoying entitlements, benefits, or opportunities.'

Special conventions are developed for vulnerable groups like women, girls, persons with disability, refugees and children to address their unique circumstances in life. The UN Convention on the Elimination of all Forms of Discrimination Against Women (CEDAW) is a treaty that seeks to address discrimination against women as a human rights issue.

CEDAW addresses the specific needs of women and girls, especially needs related to their reproductive roles in society and their low status, often conferred on them from childhood. Women and girls are universally discriminated against in all aspects of life. CEDAW is the central international convention that highlights the link between gender and human rights, as well as the links between women's rights and development.

CEDAW lays emphasis on the need to address discrimination as a major obstacle to women's advancement. More rights are addressed in the UNCRC. So if you wish to address gender and the rights of women and girls, you need to understand these two conventions.

CEDAW's main focus areas

- CEDAW emphasises discrimination as the fundamental barrier to women's rights and women's advancement.
- CEDAW highlights the link between gender and discrimination.
- CEDAW lays out strategies for achieving women's rights and development in the political, economic, and social spheres.

CEDAW was adopted by the UN General Assembly as a convention in 1979, but it only came into force as a UN treaty in 1981. Unfortunately, CEDAW has the highest number of reservations in the history of the UN! I believe that the reason for that is the low status most societies put on women under the guise of sociocultural norms, attitudes, and beliefs.

CEDAW'S SUMMARY OF DISCRIMINATIONS AGAINST WOMEN AND GIRLS

1. Through Socially Assigned Identities
2. Through the Buying and Selling of women and girls as well as the exploitation of Prostitution

3. In Political and Public life
4. In opportunities to represent their governments at the international level and to participate in the work of International Organizations
5. In matters of Nationality
6. In Education
7. In the field of Employment
8. In Health Care
9. In other areas of Economic and Social Life
10. Against women in Rural Areas
11. In equal treatment with men before the Law
12. Within Marriage and Family Life

THE MAPUTO PROTOCOL

The Maputo Declaration on Gender Mainstreaming and the effective participation (The Maputo Protocol)

The Protocol to the African Charter on Human and Peoples' Rights on the Rights of Women in Africa, better known as the Maputo Protocol, was a declaration made by African heads of government in 2003 as a commitment to ensure that African men and women are supported to meaningfully participate in all organs of the Africa Union (AU). For example, the protocol helps to ensure gender parity in the leadership of the AU, participation in the Pan-African Parliament, and membership in the Economic, Social, and Cultural Council. The Maputo Protocol also made commitments to other areas that are of special interest to African women, including:

- The New Partnership for Africa's Development (NEPAD) addressing specific issues faced by poor women in national Poverty Reduction Strategy Papers (PRSPs).
- adopting concrete legal, policy, and programmatic interventions to curb the high incidence of maternal mortality in Africa.
- supplying adequate financial resources to health and social care services.

- eradicating discriminatory and harmful practices against women, like female genital mutilation (FGM), that expose them to sicknesses, infection, and early death.
- ensuring that HIV and AIDS interventions take due cognisance of the gender implications of the epidemic and establish modalities to curb the disproportionate negative impacts on African women and girls.
- establishing an African food bank reserve to be used in cases of emergency, bearing in mind that in Africa, women are responsible for food security for their families.

NKOSAZANA DLAMINI-ZUMA: PIONEERING AFRICAN POLITICAL DISRUPTER

You can never force gender—it's elusive, resilient, and resistant to change. After the creation of the Maputo Protocol in 2003, it took another eleven years for African leaders to implement their resolutions!

Nkosazana Dlamini-Zuma, a South African politician and anti-apartheid activist, was elected in 2012 as the first woman chairperson of the African Union Commission—after more than fifty years of the organisation's existence!

In 2014, representatives of the Africa Union (AU) and the European Union (EU) gathered at the AU headquarters in Addis Ababa to exchange ideas on how to exploit the abundant renewable energy resource, which presents immense benefits for women in Africa. We were all shocked into sense the first time when we congregated around a wall that portrayed the former chairpersons of the AU. Amid gasps, the key question the delegates asked was 'Where are the women?' What an achievement, *Mother* Africa.

The challenge we now have is to ensure that Ms Zuma's formidable achievement is a huge one off opportunity for women. It is my sincere hope that Ms Zuma will mentor, coach, and inspire other African women to succeed her. I hope she will be proactively supported by African men to succeed in her role. I hope many other African women keenly understudy her and will dare to stand on her very wide shoulders, using them as a lever to defy gender discrimination at the AU and lead Africa into a prosperous future.

UN CONVENTION ON THE RIGHTS OF THE CHILD

I find it incomprehensible that in today's era of technology and advancement some three million children still die every year from under-nutrition.

—Andris Piebalgs, EU Commissioner for Development

In 1989, the UN developed the Convention on the Rights of the Child (UNCRC). This is the most comprehensive articulation of the rights of children in international law. It is meant to address their dependence on the actions and decisions of adults for survival, development, and protection from abuse and participation. Consequently childhood is a protected space According to the UNCRC, a child is any person below the age of 18 years.

Key things to remember about childhood

- Childhood is much more than just the space between birth and adulthood. It is recognised in the UDHR as a period when one is entitled to special care and assistance.
- Childhood is the time for children to be in school and at play. They should grow strong and become confident with the love and encouragement of their family and an extended community of caring adults.
- Children should live free from fear and protected from violence, abuse, and exploitation.

RIGHTS UNDER THE UNCRC: AN OVERVIEW

Children's rights are summarised under four main areas of survival, development, protection, and participation as follows:

Survival and development rights	• These are rights to resources, skills, and contributions necessary for the survival and full development of the child. • They include rights to food, shelter, clean water, formal education, primary health care, leisure and recreation, cultural activities, and information about their rights. • States' obligations are not only to put the necessary guarantees into place to realise these rights, but also to ensure universal access for all children and ensure compliance to attendant national rights laws. • Specific articles address children with special needs: refugees, unaccompanied children during conflict, child soldiers, children with disabilities, and children of minority or indigenous groups.
Protection rights	• These rights include protection from all forms of child abuse, neglect, exploitation, and cruelty, • Included are the rights to special protection in times of war and protection from abuse in the criminal justice system. • Categories included are children at risk of being exploited as child labourers, and children at risk of trafficking to become sex workers.
Participation rights	• Children are entitled to learn how to express their opinions and to have a say in matters affecting their social, economic, religious, cultural, and political lives. • Participation rights include the right to be heard, to access appropriate information, and to exercise freedom of association. • Engaging these rights as they mature helps children bring about the realisation of all their rights and prepares them for an active role as full citizens in their society

THE AFRICAN CHARTER ON THE RIGHTS AND WELFARE OF THE CHILD (AFRICAN CHARTER)

The African Charter on the Rights and Welfare of the Child (African Charter) was developed in recognition of the unique circumstances, cultural heritage, and vulnerabilities of the African child. The heads of government in Africa developed the charter specifically to complement the UNCRC. This charter came into force ten years after the UNCRC on 29 November 1999.

Similar to CEDAW, the Charter highlights the principles of non-discrimination, irrespective of the parents' or legal guardians' race, ethnic group, colour, sex, language, religion, political or other opinion, national or social origin, fortune, birth, or other status. Decisions affecting a child must always take into account the *best interests of the child*. The charter affirms the child's right to survival and development, and the child's right to various freedoms—of expression, association, thought, conscience, and religion.

The Africa Charter recognizes the right of African children to leisure and play, and the special needs of children with disabilities, adopted children, refugee children, children of imprisoned mothers, children caught up in conflict, and children who are sexually and economically exploited.

In summary, the Charter reinforces the fact that children in Africa don't only have *rights* but *responsibilities* as well. It defines a child as any person below the age of 18.

CALL TO ACTION

- From now on, try to identify the different forms of human rights abuse and acts of discrimination against women and girls.

---- ❧❀ CHAPTER 5 ❀❧ ----

Gender, Power, Participation, Domination, and Control

The concept of empowerment and participation lies at the heart of most social development strategies. The notion of power, its use, and its distribution are central to the understanding of social transformation, especially that of vulnerable women

Participation' has been assumed to be synonymous with 'equitable development' - yet it has largely tended to hide women and their views, by opting for public spaces in which to debate and decide. Simplistic assumptions about women, as a monolithic (homogeneous) block, have also hidden the often deep differences between older and younger women, or married women and unmarried young mothers.

'Participation' can, as is now increasingly accepted, under certain circumstances be manipulative of local (poor) women. It can be used for cosmetic, co-optation or empowerment objectives.'

—Robert Chambers, Emeritus fellow, IDS

For example, poor women and children can be used for fundraising objectives instead of empowering them in practice. Participation can be used for cosmetic, co-optation or empowerment objectives. Cosmetic and co-optation versions of participation sit within one of the two broad schools of participation in development: (a) the instrumental one, (b) the transformative school which focuses on participation for empowerment. The few transformatory processes differ from the many instrumental uses of participation by 'making' women important rather than making women feel important.

Men usually manipulate the socialisation processes and ideals of maternal altruism to exert overt and covert power over women. However, women are not totally powerless. Power is a not a commodity that outsiders or the more powerful men can hand over to the less powerful women. Women have strategic ways, within the limited choices available to them, to appropriate power and subvert subordination.

—Deniz Kandiyoti

Nevertheless, whenever we carefully observe gender facts and figures, especially those related to violence against women, we see that gender is about power and control, period! But to understand gendered power, you also need to understand the power dynamics that are played out by men and women in different ways, at different stages of their lives, and in different places. You need to understand the power every individual can potentially wield if given a chance, because 'deep within man [and woman], dwell those slumbering powers; powers that would astonish him [or her] that he [or she] never dreamed of possessing: forces that would revolutionalise his [or her] life if aroused and put into action.'

—Orison Swett Marden, American inspirational author

The socialisation process allocates particular rights, resources, decision-making power, and validation to men over women. Consequently, society fundamentally uplifts and amplifies men and boys voices. Meanwhile it locks women and girls in silence and restricts their exercise of power. Can you trace which type of discrimination this is in the areas identified in the CEDAW summary in Chapter four? (*through socially assigned identities*)

Gender analysis looks not only at roles and activities done by women and girls or men and boys, but also at the relationships between them. It asks not only who does what, but also who makes the decisions, and who derives the benefit from the activities, who uses productive resources such as land, or credit, and who controls these resources; and what other factors influence relationships, such as laws about property rights and inheritance.'

—Susanne, W., et al, OXFAM

VeneKlasen and Miller's (2002) book *'Power and Empowerment'* made great contributions to the definition of power in gender relationships. According to them, women's empowerment will not happen unless we address the way women and men experience power in the three realms or spaces: public space, private space, and intimate space.

- *Public space*: We can observe women and men's power in public space through their jobs, the public lives they lead, the legal rights they enjoy, and so on. Government plays a huge role here, through its legislative and public policy roles, to remove barriers to women's empowerment and enforce laws that protect women from discrimination.
- *Private space*: In private space, we glimpse women and men's power through the relationships they have and their roles in families, in friendships, in sexual partnerships, in marriage, and so on. Often the whole society works in tandem to enforce women's subordination and men's dominance.
- *Intimate space*: The power of women and men in intimate space can be observed through their self-esteem, their self-confidence, their 'can do' attitude, their agency, and their voice, which enables them to make the right decisions on issues affecting their lives. Power in intimate space enables their psychological and emotional stability and holistic development.

Intimate space is the most important realm of women's empowerment. It is this space that enables women to say no to abusive relationships. Empowered intimate space gives women courage to dream again after seeing all their dreams go up in flames. Intimate space is the space of possibilities, of future opportunities, and of expansion beyond limits, as

Pepe Minambo describes in his most transformative book, *Beyond Limits.* Intimate space, once women occupy it, enables them to become disrupters of their own reality and subordinate identity.

As Steve Jobs rightly said, when people become disrupters, they cannot be ignored. It's my hope that all women and girls will start to believe in themselves and devise ways to disrupt their subordination. Think about it. Imagine what would happen if all women overcame their discrimination. What nice and beautiful world it would be. What would be different for you?

Steven Covey, a theorist of leadership, wrote a famous book called *The 8th Habit.* In it, he discussed holistic development which can be related to gender and power. He said all human beings—as employees, irrespective of gender—have four intelligences and capacities they all deeply desire:

- *IQ*—creative and cognitive intelligence: This is the source of our thinking. We expect the people we relate to, especially our managers at work, to support us so we can develop and grow. Across the globe, girls are denied education. They miss the opportunity to grow and develop. We silence their voices and police their movements, killing their desire to explore and create.
- *EQ*—emotional and social intelligence: This is related to our feelings and matters of the heart and love. It's why we always seek to be loved, recognised, and treated with kindness and fairness. At the family level, this is crucial. At the workplace, it makes a big difference for staff to feel valued by employers and line managers. However, this is hardly done for women and girls, who toil every day for our well-being. We rarely recognise them. We never show them love and kindness. We don't even say thank you after eating their well-prepared meals. We take them for granted! Is that fair?
- *PQ*—physical and health intelligence: We use this to maintain ourselves in good shape through basic needs like food, water, and healthcare. If we are in employment, we desire to be paid well so that we can meet those needs. We want to live for a long time. At

home, we hardly pay women and girls for their labour. Instead, we overwork them, and it affects their health and well-being

- *SQ*—spiritual intelligence: This is exhibited in our need to serve, to contribute, with a conscience. We therefore always seek inspiration from the people around us. As we grow older, we desperately ask ourselves, 'What is my purpose in life? What will be my legacy? Will people remember me favourably? What will be in my obituary? What will be the inscription on my headstone? Will I be remembered for a great contribution to humanity or otherwise?' Women and girls are often too busy within the home. They miss out on leisure. They are easy to forget because most times they are invisible. Unfortunately because they don't earn a salary from their labour, women, an girls are often not valued for their labour. They are ignored and often have low self esteem.

One secondary school in Uganda creatively inspired Ugandans through a song. The song, full of deeply challenging lyrics, asked us to reflect on what legacy we would leave behind if, God forbid, we were to die tomorrow. Would we leave our families with the curse of large debt? Would we be remembered for over-drinking, over-eating, or being worthless vagabonds? One day, at a family function, the song was played for us. I jokingly asked the smartly dressed lady seated next to me about her legacy, she bluntly told me that, 'It's men who think about such issues. They are the ones with property, money, and time to spend on legacies. For us women, everything goes to food and our children, period!'

We have different types of power: visible, hidden, and invisible power. So it is important for both men and women to be empowered, to have a purpose in life, to live meaningful lives, and to leave a legacy. VeneKlasen and Miller describe how these three powers play out in our lives.

Visible power

Visible power is the process whereby some people have power and the ability to influence formal decision-making processes—for example, in a village meeting or as a member of Parliament.

When considering gender relations, power is often related to men and women's access, control and use of available resources, and thus a basis for wealth. Power is also related to knowledge, both as a source of power and a means for its acquisition. It is also related to the realisation of, to be able to and feeling more capable to use one's inherent abilities and propensity to improve one's wellbeing

—INTRAC1999

The people or particular interest groups which have mobilised and organised themselves can have power as *agency*, which they hold openly and use. Empowerment means having a voice and influence in formal processes. Empowered persons or groups can organise specific issue campaigns and hold demonstrations that influence public opinion.

Never underestimate the power of role models. We all have people who have inspired us, people we believe in and would like to emulate. They are incredibly influential. They fight for and are linked to a particular issue or cause. Take the example of the late Nobel laureate, Professor Wangari Maathai. You can't think of her without envisioning a forest or powerful and charismatic African women. Few people met her in real life, but her name evokes images of trees, environment, and nature in us all.

Hidden power

Hidden power exists when certain people or interest groups set the agenda and make decisions behind closed doors, excluding others. Have you ever heard of 'kitchen cabinets' like the one Tony Blair, former prime minister of the United Kingdom, had? He had a core team of reliable and incredibly powerful ministers who advised him on the best way to govern the country. Such people can quietly mobilise bias and influence interests to shape the agenda, decisions, and outcomes of governing processes.

Do you remember those days of the Poverty Reduction Strategy Papers (PRSPs)? A PRSP would set out a country's macroeconomic, structural, and social policies and programs to promote growth and reduce poverty, as well as associated external financing needs. People believed then that the real power to make key decisions in the PRSP was with the World Bank and the Ministry of Finance. They sat behind closed doors and decided on critical government policies which would later emerge in PRSP consultations. The core issues and related finances would be set and they hardly changed. In this case, empowerment would be the ability to influence what appears on the agenda of the World Bank and the Ministry of Finance, before they sat behind closed doors.

> Do you know that even in some international NGOs, staff can propose gender as an issue for discussion in senior leadership meetings—but unless the CEO is a champion for gender equality, that issue is usually put last on the agenda and discussed in a rash when people are already very tired, preparing to leave a weeklong meeting or eliminated from the agenda completely!

'Companies with three or more women on the Board are likely to have more women among senior executives, including the Chief Executive Officer (CEO) ... and other senior roles ... have higher female representation in other senior roles ... gender diversity among senior executives is correlated with better financial performance.'

—Noland et al., 2012

Invisible power

Invisible power is the one most related to gender and the way we were socialised. This power is exerted over the long term through deep social conditioning using culturally embedded norms. It affects one's knowledge, ideology, beliefs, world view, and what is considered within the realm of the possible.

In this realm, empowerment is related to self-esteem. A good example is the way some women in Africa are socialised to believe that a husband who beats you is in love with you; otherwise he would not bother to do so.

Another example is when women are socialised to believe that a good wife welcomes a co-wife into the family. She should silence all her fears about the future of her marital relationship and pretend to be happy, because a good wife accepts the new wife as her own younger sister. And she should continue to accept even when her husband is very disrespectful, or fragments the property (land) to give to the new family, or when her children's school fees are no longer being paid. 'A good wife is not jealous,' the saying goes. What does that really mean except that society is institutionalising and popularising deception? Otherwise why would so many stepchildren suffer abuse and violence from these very 'welcoming' stepmothers?

This type of power is very dangerous to women because it shapes their psychological and ideological boundaries of participation. As a result they learn to pretend, silence their real feelings and face major problems. Powerlessness is internalised in women's mindsets. Apart from not participating in the decisions affecting them, issues affecting women are also kept from the minds of those at the decision-making table.

Sarah Longwe, a celebrated gender and development consultant from Zambia, contributed a lot to our understanding of gender relations of power through what she called the women's empowerment framework. She identified five steps through which women can pass to become progressively empowered. A woman moves from welfare, to access, to conscientisation, to mobilisation, and finally to control.

In the development sector, many NGOs talk about empowerment of poor women in terms of access to and control of resources. Sarah Longwe saw the importance of women moving on from welfare, where they are passive recipients of development benefits, to a level where they have control over those resources. This challenges the usual approach of international NGOs to have a long term view of delivering sustainable development. NGOs should build the capacities of local people and their organisations, empowering local people to take control of their own development.

The process of empowerment enables women to recognise their gender needs. Empowered women can confidently play their socially assigned roles as mothers, wives, and community animators. They need to be near water. They need to have access to energy resources and infrastructure. They need to be near health centres. All of these facilities enable them fulfil their socially assigned, practical roles.

However, women need to go beyond access to owning and controlling these resources. Women need to participate in decision-making regarding issues affecting their lives They also need access to strategic services and resources that can transform their lives. For example, access to education means that women can have jobs in future and meet their economic needs and those of their families. A good education means a higher-level job, which can uplift a woman's position in society.

Good education also opens up doors for women to participate in politics and stand for political leadership positions, and to seek positions in corporate governance. They need access to financial products like loans to develop their entrepreneurial abilities. A woman whose strategic gender needs are addressed normally has choice and voice. She not only becomes independent but interdependent.

According to Sarah Longwe's model, access to resources, services, new knowledge, and networks will enable women to become conscientised. They will be able to understand issues of gender power, patriarchy, and oppression. They will be able to challenge their realities and use information about their rights, talents, and abilities to live transformed lives as full human beings.

This is when women will realise that they need to mobilise, organise, and acquire networking skills. With like-minded women, they will collectively demand their rights. Then they will feel and act as empowered women with access to *and* control over resources, services, and ultimately their lives.

Empowerment is a long process. It may not follow a logical=hierarchical process. It's messy, complex, and sometimes painful. But it's worth all the pain.

Like the end of apartheid, women's empowerment will never be given on a silver platter. Those who enjoy the benefits of women's subordination will never willingly set women free. Sometimes those who benefit are actually fellow women—our managers, our in-laws, and our aunties who act as gatekeepers of patriarchy. Do not expect their help. Some may assist you, but you have to participate in and own the process yourself. It's your journey. It's your lived reality. That's why you should never allow anyone who does not understand your background, your challenges, and your pain to silence you!

Power is a broad concept, spanning economic, social, cultural, political, and organisational dimensions. It describes the freedom of individual women to make individual decisions with agency, or to collectively mobilise and organise to empower themselves and behave as they choose.

Invisible power is manifested a lot in gender relationships. That is what I call *gender power*. Gender power raises your awareness of gender discrimination. Women and girls as well as men and boys can possess and practice positive gender power. Women have the power to analyse, stand up, and fight for gender justice. Women can be fair to each other.

Power enables us to recognise gender discrimination in all its forms, beyond the visible facades that men and women put on. This book endeavours to give you awareness to understand the underlying causes of gender discrimination. You can then empower yourself to become vigilant. You can analyse the negative impacts of gender discrimination on individual human beings and choose to take action.

You can become inspired and proactive to do something about gender discrimination. It's my passionate dream that after you read this book, you will encourage many other people, especially women, to read it. That way you will have people to discuss issues with and to work with you on those issues when you have to.

I also hope you become self-actualised to a level where you can say *no* to gender discrimination, whether it's happening to you or to another person.

THE UNFINISHED BUSINESS OF THE 21ST CENTURY

Achieving gender equality is a long-term and continuous process that requires commitment and different actors. One cannot do everything, but every action counts. We grew up being told that it takes a whole village to raise a child. Indeed, my generation was raised by the whole community. But gone are the times when neighbours could find us in the village, punish us and report us to our parents, if they ever saw us playing truant. 'We cannot succeed when half of us are held back.' Practicing gender equity and equality are truly communal responsibilities.

—Malala Yousafzai, Nobel Laureate

In the same spirit, I say it will take the goodwill of entire communities to achieve gender equality. It is our collective responsibility to address gender discrimination. One leader must have been referring to this when she said, 'To achieve gender equality, we need to mobilize not just parliaments but populations, not only civil society, but all society.'

—Phumzile Mlambo Ngcuka, Under-Secretary General & Executive Director of UN Women

I can confidently affirm without fear of any contradiction —that the twenty-first century owes women and girls equity and equality. Anyone living in the twenty-first century should feel the same burden on their shoulders to do something about this disparity. You should be ashamed to die before you win some victories for women and girls' rights in this century. I totally agree with what former US Secretary of State said that, 'I believe that the rights of women and girls is the unfinished business of he 21st century.' This should not be seen as an option. It is women's right to be treated as full human beings, like men. Period!

—Hillary Clinton, American First Lady, Secretary of State

Mother Teresa rightly saw it and said, 'I alone cannot change the world, but I can cast a stone across the waters to create many ripples.' I dare you today to stand up and throw your own stone that will create ripples and unearth this elusive monster called gender discrimination. Let your voice be heard. Stop giving excuses and take action today. Excuses change and build nothing. I will always remember when my primary school headmistress refusing to accept my excuse for coming late to the general assembly. She chastised me and for emphasis she told me that, 'Excuses are the nails that build a house called failure.'

—Jim Rohn, American entrepreneur, author and motivational speaker

We should all rise up and take a stand. The former United Nations secretary-general led byexample when he stated, 'Gender equality and women empowerment have been a top priority for me from day one as Secretary General. And I am committed to making sure that the UN leads by example.'

—Ban Ki Moon, UN Secretary General

When he launched the sustainable energy for all (SE4ALL) initiative, we found it easy to speak up in international conferences and meetings with government officials, to authoritatively advocate for women by highlighting the link between poverty, energy and women's health. We especially spoke of the importance of investing in modern energy for cooking. African women typically collect firewood over long distances, and then cook in smoke-polluted kitchens. They need energy for productive uses, such as for running small and medium enterprises, increasing food production, transporting their harvest, and storing it properly to avoid wastage They need energy for the communal services such as water pumping, health centres, schools, markets, and police stations. Modern energy would not only relieve women's workloads and drudgery but serve as a protective measure when they don't have to walk in pitch darkness.

It is very important that influential leaders, especially male leaders who can easily inspire men and boys, recognise and speak up about the important contributions of African women to the development of the continent. For example, during the 2015 World Economic Forum held in Cape Town, South Africa, it was stated that 'If Nigerian women had the same opportunities as men, they could drive GDP up by $13.9 Billion.' We all need to recognise and appreciate the immense contributions of women.

— Patrice Motsepe, President and Chief Executive Officer of Youth For technology foundation.

I would like to challenge you all to use your influential positions to meditate on these nuggets of wisdom and get your priorities right when it comes to gender equality. 'Achieving gender equality is about disrupting the status quo; not negotiating it.' Its not a women's issue only, because it affects us all.

—Phumzile Mlambo Ngcuka,

I urge every man and every woman to become a disrupter, to go against conventional wisdom, and to colour outside the lines by promoting the rights of marginalised and disadvantaged women. Become a voice for the voiceless! Each one of us can make a difference. As the old proverb says, 'If you think you are too small to make a difference, try sleeping with a mosquito!'

There is no single magic bullet that will totally change everything. It will take communal efforts, consistent initiatives, and prolonged goodwill from leaders at all levels for gender equality to become a reality in this century. Female and male role models are critically needed. 'The best economies in the world have grown on the back of an environment that is tolerant and accepting.'

—Patrice Motsepe, the South African billionaire and founder of African Rainbow Minerals

LET WOMEN BECOME YOUR FIRST CHOICE

There is an interesting case regarding Janet (not her real name), a young woman who was desperate to give her children a better life. She prevailed upon her indolent husband to join her in doing menial jobs. Wages were a pittance yet countless times they were not even paid because he could never keep time. They were hence unable to put food on the table. In anguish,

Janet sought the support of her younger well-to-do brother who, being male, had been favoured by their parents to receive a good education and consequently qualify for a good public policy career.

Given that Janet had not completed primary education and did not have any certificate, her brother chose to get her husband a job instead, since he believed the man should be the breadwinner and head of the family. Because Janet's husband had a Kenya Certificate of Primary Education (KCPE), it was also easier to place him in a job.

Regrettably, Janet's egotistical, lazy excuse of a husband couldn't hold a job anywhere. After several trials, his brother-in-law gave up on him, but was still concerned about the welfare of Janet's family. He subsequently enrolled Janet, maturely, in a programme to undertake the KCPE examination. When she had her certificate in hand, he supported her to get a better-paying job. The boost this little gesture gave the family was instant. Remember, taking action and not taking action are both decisions. 'Whether you think you can or you can't … you are right.'

—Henry Ford. American business magnet

Often our societies and institutions condone impunity for gender discrimination through overt and subtle actions. Many times we are not even conscious we are discriminating women. Janet's younger brother never thought about giving her the first chance. The biggest power one can exercise over another human being is to gain power over that person's mind. The one who believes things are predestined has the attitude that one must simply bear it all. It starts when you develop apathy, telling yourself and others in similar condition. We rationalise that 'after all, that's our culture and it's God's will, so there is nothing we can do about it.'

Your husband, a human being like you, exercises power over you and stops you from working and you believe its God'd will? What about the millions of other women you see going to work every day—doesn't God love them too? You are totally powerless when you believe that you can do nothing but submit to the authority of someone else even as they abuse you.

God's will, for you and every other human being, is for you to go to school, get a job, and enhance your well-being and that of your family. You will then be able to praise God and pronounce his name among nations, nothing more, nothing less—period!

CALL TO ACTION

- Mobilise a team of peers interested in understanding gender.
- Review the 12 types of discimination in CEDAW (chapter four). Identify and list the effects of each form of discrimination on the women and girls involved.
- Imagine one of them was happening to you, or your mother, sister, or aunt. As a group, discuss what you can do to change and ensure such incidents do not happen again in your community.
- Identify which government agency or agencies, you would approach to become involved as a duty bearer, and stop such incidents from happening.
- What three proposals would you take to the agency?
- Find out what your government has done so far regarding these types of discrimination and what more it should do in the future.
- Remember as a person you are a 'rights holder' while your government, as a state is the 'duty bearer.'

CHAPTER 6

Why is Gender Equality So Important?

Gender equality is more than a goal in itself. It is a precondition for meeting the challenge of reducing poverty, promoting sustainable development and building good governance.

—Kofi Annan, UN Secretary-General

Based on what you have read in the previous chapters and on your personal experiences, express yourself creatively. Compose three 'quotable quotes' stating why you think it is important for everyone to understand gender.

1. _____
   _____
   _____

2. _____
   _____
   _____

3. _____
   _____
   _____

It is not easy to explain in a few sentences why gender is so important. You need to have a correct understanding of how you define roles and gendered relationships of power between men and women. You also need to understand the relationship between males and females at a young age, before they are securely set in cultural ways that are not beneficial for the development of a balanced society.

If you do gain this sensitisation and awareness, you will start to find yourself struggling and at odds with the community you live in. The socialisation process prepares us for what we will be in future. Society tries to mediate femininity to the girls, which unfortunately emphasises being submissive and unquestioning of male behaviour and the status quo. Women are socialised to be calm, patient, understanding, unaggressive, dependent on men, soft, and non-assertive. 'The wounded child inside many females is a girl who was taught from early childhood that she must become something other than herself, deny her true feelings, in order to attract and please others.'

—bell hooks. American author, feminist

On the other hand, boys are trained to dominate women, become assertive leaders, and be strong physically and emotionally. No wonder Norah Vincent said, 'There is a time in a boy's life when the sweetness is pounded out of him; and tenderness, and the ability to show what he feels, is gone.' Therefore 'The wounded child inside many males is a boy who, when he first spoke his truths, was silenced by paternal sadism, by a patriarchal world that did not want him to claim his true feelings.'

—Norah Vincent. American writer

If you are an adolescent and reading this book, then you are privileged. You will approach adulthood as an empowered and enlightened human being with new knowledge, skills, and exposure to gender sensitivity, which is critical for you and your future family's well-being.

One day you are likely to get married. You are likely to become a mother or father. You will then take on the enviable parental responsibilities to nurture, inspire, and launch a new generation into the future. You will stand between your vulnerable children and the harsh external environment. You will, symbolically, lock up and release all luck into your child's life. You will be the one who gives both tough love and blessings to your child.

Alternatively, you might model duplicity, anger, malice, and resentment to your child.

> When men and women punish each other for truth telling, we reinforce the notion that lies are better. To be loving, we willingly hear the other's truth, and most important, we affirm the value of truth telling. Lies may make people feel better, but they do not help them to know love.

—bell hooks. American author, feminist

Someone warned us long ago that 'every child has the propensity to learn'. Your child will not only listen to what you say. At a deeper level, you will also be moulding your child's character according to your behaviour. You will determine whether and for how long they will go to school to acquire social and academic skills. It's my hope that you will try everything possible to empower your vulnerable child. Become a mediator for them. Work with other people in the community to empower not only boys but all children.

—Reuven Feuerstein, Israel psychologist

You, younger woman or man of today, are the next generation. We have invested a lot of our dreams in you. We want you to have a proper foundation of relationships based on love, trust, and respect. That is why understanding gender is so important. Gender is about valuing people as full human beings—human beings with unique talents and unalienable rights It is about powerful and unconditional loving relationships that are mutually beneficial and allow society to live in harmony and transform this unequal world.

'Whether the issue is improving education in the developing world, or fighting global climate change; or addressing nearly any other challenge we face, empowering women is a critical part of the equation.' The heart of the gender agenda is to have a society in which there is zero tolerance for gender discrimination, violence, or abuse in any form. It does not matter whether you are male or female. You should enjoy equal rights, protection from abuse, and equal opportunities every day of your life, simply because you are a human being!

—Bill Clinton, American President

Gender is important because it is not only about the roles of males versus females. Even among people of the same sex, there are differences due to personality, age, socio-economic status, personal experiences, and opportunities. Make no mistake: females are not a homogeneous group. They are not at all alike. Males too are not a homogeneous group. Every person has their own specific needs and interests that are unique to them. Any approach should take into account these personal and context-specific differences.

For example, a girl aged 6 years old does not have the same needs and interests and risks as a teenager of 12 who has just entered puberty. A boy of 14 attending high school does not have the same needs and interests as a man of 24 who has just left university, married, and started work in a new town.

Gender is important because it is about giving equal opportunities to women and girls, men and boys to survive childhood, develop, and grow till they are able to participate meaningfully in development processes. It is also about equal access and control over resources for all.

Gender is important because it is upon gender that our success as humanity will stand or fall. We need to develop gender relationships that are soft, tender, and flexible, yet firm, and reliable as a chain. Relationships must be based on respect and dignity even though it could be risky sometimes.

Gender is important because when it is defined in an incomplete and inequitable manner, certain groups of people gain unfair advantage over others. This is reflected in the heavy workloads allocated to women and girls, which makes them face time poverty and drudgery. The allocation of social resources and inheritance favours men and boys. It is reflected in their ability to talk confidently in public and take up opportunities like higher education and leadership positions.

Each group's roles have to be defined very clearly and equitably based on a deep understanding and appreciation of their needs, interests and capabilities in order to live harmoniously with each other. Without understanding the factors on which to base gender roles in a specific context, you can create disharmony in the community. Also, when we do not take time to consider biological differences and cater to specific needs, then we have people who are discriminated, such as those with disabilities, who become socially excluded.

When gender roles are not properly defined, they develop unbalanced, unhappy, and insecure families full of physical, sexual, and emotional violence. Such families make up unbalanced communities and nations. Therefore gender is a very important part of life as a whole. We need to understand it. We need to appreciate and celebrate our differences as females and males.

WANGU WA MAKERI, THE OVER-EMPOWERED FEMALE

My late friend, Lily Mudasia shared an interesting story. Legend has it that Wangu wa Makeri was an empowered female chief among the Kikuyu folk in Muranga, Kenya. She created disharmony because of her tyrannical ways. She oppressed the menfolk, especially the village idlers who quaked whenever they heard her name and the tax evaders who would be harshly whipped, incarcerated and sent to solitary imprisonment. She empowered women to take on roles that traditionally belonged to men. Human beings are known for not liking vacuums. They will endeavour to fill any vacuum they encounter, be it at home, at work, or in the community.

Like all legends, there are various stories about how the mighty chief fell from glory. One hilarious version is that the oppressed men met and discussed their problem. They found what they considered a smart strategy to overcome their subordination—they impregnate all their wives at the same time! During that time of pregnancy, all women became tired and weak and could not play some of their roles. So the men were able to wrest power from their wives and from their notorious chief, Wangu wa Makeri.

Another version is that she was forced to resign when she committed an abominable sin in her community. By the standards with her younger warriors. She added insult to injury when she removed some of her clothes and danced vigorously and provocatively, that's when she was forced to step down from her leadership role. She had defied all the revered traditions concerning the status of respectable old women who are perceived to be sexually inactive. They dress decently without showing their private parts like breasts, stomach, thighs. One wonders what would have happened if she had not made men hostile to her leadership.

This is a good example of an over-epowered leader who had an unbalanced view of gender roles and relationships of power. She made inequitable decisions. Men rightly resented her and her reign of terror. Imagine experiencing a similar leader. What would you do?

When women and girls, men and boys understand and operate in their properly defined and equitable roles, any part of society will be a nice and beautiful place to live. There will be harmony and transparency. Society will develop very well because everyone's potential is maximised. However, when there is imbalance, inequity, and inequality, it makes one group of people behave as if they are more important than the other. We are all born equal as human beings and must enjoy all our endowments equally!

Gender discrimination is a terrible tragedy because there is no group that is better or more important than the other. We complement each other. When we understand the importance of gender, we shall be more appreciative and tolerant of each other. We shall also be comfortable with our biological differences because there is no mistake in life. Males will enjoy their freedom in masculinity and women will be fascinated by their femininity more fully. When they do so, they shall bring forth their best to complement each other and complete the beautiful life around them.

A world without males would be a colourless, unfulfilled, and formless world. A world without females would be a very boring, ugly, incomplete world. Males and females must all have equitable, important roles in society. We must learn to coexist in a balanced way, so that we can harness all the good that is in and around us. Without this balance, we shall continue to exist in the unfortunate, unbalanced situation that exists in most African nations due to gender stereotyping. We shall explore more about that subject in the next chapter.

THE PARADIGM SHIFT

To build a society where discrimination becomes an abomination requires a complete paradigm shift. A paradigm shift is a change in the fundamental beliefs, perspectives, and mindset that men and women have about each other. A major shift is paramount if we are to experience change, live in harmony, and have access to the same opportunities.

At present, generally men are born with silver spoons in their mouth. Later on they are socialised to adopt certain beliefs, values, attitudes, and practices which, over time, become a mindset. This mindset creates a culture of discrimination, favouritism, and subordination which dictates how males and females treat each other.

Gender balance will only be achieved if men rise to the occasion and accept disruption of the discriminatory mindset that creates gender disparity. Women too must disrupt the subordinate status quo. This is not easy because it is something solidly embedded in the African culture, but it is not impossible as we were told long ago, 'Only the stupidest and wisest of men never change.'

Aparently these types of men are too stubborn to change. Those in the middle tend to be more pragmatic to see the opportunies offered by change and create dynamic and vibrant communities.

—Confucius. Chinese teacher and philosopher

Our lived experiences have taught us that the wisest and the stupidest in our society can be really fanatical. These people can decisively lack objectivity in anything related to their chosen stance. They choose and are simply driven by self-interest and short-sightedness. As one leader remarked once, 'A fanatic is one who can't change his mind and won't change the subject.'

—Winston Churchill, British Prime Minister

If you are a man reading this book, how will you describe yourself when it comes to having a paradigm shift on matters of gender equity and equality? Will you look at yourself as a disrupter? Are you a person who endorses cultural myths that drive inequality and fail to advance the well-being of women? Or will you be described as a fanatic? Are you among the wisest or the stupidest? Those of you who are traditionally and culturally brainwashed to believe that men must rule over women, look around you and think about this reality. In which category are you?

You can treat all women with respect and dignity if you look at them as human beings created in God's image with a purpose in life, rather than as sexual objects to conquer, exploit, humiliate, and dominate. One of the most respected sons of Africa, once authoritatively said that 'Men and boys … show our manhood through the way we treat our women, our wives, our sisters, our mothers'.

—Desmond Tutu, Archbishop, Nobel Peace Laureate

Remember, in any relationship, the only person you can change is you! Women should embrace power. Never say that you don't need power. The truth about power is that if you don't have it, then someone else has it, and can use it against you! You have the power to learn and grow. As an adult, you alone have control over your gendered life. You can control your emotions, especially your anger, temper, endurance, and humility towards women in your life.

CALL TO ACTION

- Who has power in your key relationship(s)? Why?
- As a man or woman with power, how do you treat the women in your life? Do you treat them in a great way? In a good way? In a normal way? With respect and admiration? Or in an inhuman way?
- To be man enough you need to re-evaluate your relationship with all the women in your life: those closest to you and even those who are strangers to you.

REAL MEN SUPPORT WOMEN'S EMPOWERMENT

To be man enough, you need to re-evaluate your relationships with all the women in your life: those closest to you and those who are strangers to you. I repeat, know it from me today that 'Real men support women's empowerment.' If your wife, girl children, and female colleagues at work were asked to rate you today, where do you think you will fall? However, some women are also 'socialised' males who discriminate others.

- Would you be rated among the bullies, the weak, and the ruthless?
- Would you be rated among the great, the inspirational, and the compassionate?
- Are you the duplicitous type of man or woman known as a Hyde and Jekyll character? (A person alternating between a good and evil character, in a spannish novella entitled 'Strange case of Dr. Jenkll and Mr. Hyde.')
- Are you the type who loses your temper so badly that as soon as you enter the house, everyone greets you furtively before escaping to hide somewhere and avoid more contact with you?
- How would your employees, like the house girl, maid, nanny, or personal assistant, rate you?

Rate yourself frankly. Then ask yourself:

- Are there aspects of your character and behaviour that you are not very comfortable with, or areas where you are not so proud of yourself as you read this book?
- Do you have areas of your character that you would rather the rest of society didn't see. Know about?

You have a moral duty to respect your wife, your girl children, your house girl(s), your wife's female relatives and friends, female subordinates at work, and neighbours' daughters—period!

If so far you have not done so, then hold deep conversations with yourself, as Nelson Mandela did while at Robben Island. He reflected on his character and purpose in life and made a decision to change. As a human being of flesh and blood like Mandela, ask yourself challenging questions. Remember this too: 'Good questions inform, Great questions transform.'

—Ken Coleman. American radio and television sports caster

Don't you find that amazing! You have the power to challenge and disrupt all the socialised aspects of your character, You can learn, unlearn, and transform yourself into a great man like Mandela. I challenge you today to start taking action about those areas that you think you could improve upon. It's your choice! 'One step at a time … you wonder when and where and how you are gonna make it … one step at a time. Its like learning to fly.'

—Jordin Sparks, American singer and songwriter

CHAPTER 7

Gender and Socialisation

It was easy to persecute me without people feeling ashamed. It was easy to vilify me and project me as a woman who was not following the tradition of a 'good African woman' and as a 'highly educated [unlikeable, insolent] elitist woman' who was trying to show innocent African women ways of doing things that were not acceptable to African men.

—Wangari Mathai, Kenyan environmental political activist, Nobel Laureate

Do you remember that time we were curious about this new huge elephant in the room—the unique animal they called 'gender?' Wangari was one of the fearless activists pushing for environmental protection and women's rights. To our surprise, gender was not about sex, i.e., being physically male or female. Despite all the challenges and life-threatening risks men and women face, gender did not refer to an endangered species or a health condition like Ebola. So what could it possibly be?

Many successful women, especially in politics, confess that, similar to what happened to Wangari Maathai in the quotation above, they have at some stage in their successful careers been derided, admonished, debased, humiliated, and sometimes even stripped naked and slapped in public by fellow male leaders—simply because they are women!

These women are treated like irritating mosquitos. Men use violence on them with impunity, ostensibly to silence what they call 'the bitches' loud mouths'. Men think that such women have strayed into the public realm, a space that must be a preserve for men only. The abusers conveniently forget that these women are legitimate and credible people's representatives who were voted into office. Their voices must be heard and respected!

What an affront men's behaviour is to our democracy and honourable houses of Parliament. So much for being honourable. Are they not behaving dishonourably? Shame upon all of us for electing them to parliaments! Are you now surprised that being honourable or professional does not make a difference, as long as one's gender base is faulty?

We have also seen that the touts (conductors who collect money from passengers in our public taxis and buses often congregating our public car parks and bus terminals) whom we normally dismiss as illiterates, dare to undress women, giving the flimsy excuse that the women have put on short skirts and excited them. As if they are just wild beasts without any self-control! Surprisingly, professional police, who are educated, professionally trained and charged with enforcing law and order, also beat women to the floor, squeeze their breasts, and undress our mothers and sisters for the 'abominable criminal offence' of demonstrating against the ills of their dictatorial, corrupt governments! Isn't that a tragedy for mother Africa?

Boohoo, men in uniform, touts, and (dis)honourables—give us a break!

As if that is not enough, some men use the media to peddle lies and lament that these so-called 'stubborn and uncouth women' dare to defy their power and disrupt the authority of the police blockages. They claim the women need to be punished because they refuse to budge when ordered to keep quiet and disperse. Why? To where? The list is endless. What happened to the right to demonstrate peacefully.

Well, do not be silenced by people who do not know your story. Do not be silenced by people who have never had their child stolen from the maternity ward. Do not be silenced by people who do not know the pain of having a dear child snatched away by death because the hospital did not have electricity to sterilise the vaccination needle or the equipment for emergency obstetric care. Do not be silenced by people who stole money and medicines from the hospital and the national coffers, so that underpaid midwives are rude and disrespectful when you are in labour.

Do not be silenced by anyone who has never felt the pain of seeing a dear child sent to prison on flimsy, trumped-up charges; Do not be silenced by people who have never felt the humiliation of being battered and undressed in front of their adolescent children. Do not be silenced by people who have never lain in bed, listening to their husband conversing with his girlfriend in their local language which you don't know.

Do not be silenced by people who have never known the pain of having an unfaithful partner. Do not be silenced by the man whose zip is ever open, who runs blindly after any skirt, who puts your life at risk of infection from HIV for a one-night stand, who makes you the topic of gossip by silly, mean neighbours who enjoy your plight. Don't be silenced.

Members of Parliament, touts and police officers share two issues in common: *they imagine they have a lot of power, and they were socialised to disrespect women.* Behaving like demons is not the main issue here.

The main issues are:

- *Why* do they think they are untouchable?

- *Why* do they operate with such impunity?
- *Why* do they find it so easy to demonise and humiliate women, in private and in public?
- *Why* don't they respect women's rights as human beings?

Why? Because we as a society have socialised them, as boys, not to respect women. We have trained them that to be called men, they need to humiliate and dominate women. We have placed a lot of emphasis on their sexual parts and sexual prowess to be the signifiers of manhood. We have encouraged them to develop fragile egos based on a masculinity which they fear is not a reality. We have told them to admire 'heroes' who achieved extraordinary feats of violence in the past. They have seen their fathers treating their mothers like used toilet paper

Do you know that at school, next to the urinals, older boys flaunt their nakedness in front of the younger ones as an act of intimidation?

We have falsely taught boys that women are dumb, not gifted, so that whenever they meet an intelligent woman, they want to silence her through verbal violence. They have seen and know that a man can get away with murder as long as the victim is a woman. They have seen and learnt that one can depend on powerful connections to defeat justice. They have seen and learnt that one can claim to kill in the spirit of 'protecting our family's honour', and that claim will be due to faulty socialisation. You have probably used the word *socialise* to mean how you mix socially, talk to other people, and behave around them. If you have a mobile phone or computer, you might use social media like WhatsApp and Facebook to talk not only to friends, but even to foreigners in far-flung places like China. But have you ever understood the power, perversity, and insidious nature of some of our socialisation processes and their negative impact on women?

Socialisation is one of the most important words to learn, understand, and internalise in the study of gender.

It is the process of shaping a person's thinking, values and behaviour - the things they will value as important or unimportant, the skills they can develop, and ways of thinking in order to meet the society's gender expectations, norms, and expected behaviours. In most cases these expectations are different for men and for women. They define your quality, and worth, and status in society as a woman/wife/mother or man/husband/father in a particular society. It also determines the unfair division of labour, opportunities and resources between women and girls, men and boys.

For example, in Saudi Arabian culture, when a girl reaches the age of puberty (around 13 years old) and starts her periods, she is considered to be a grown woman ready for marriage. Her way of dressing has to change. She must cover her whole body so nobody sees it. She must not mix with boys except her own father and brothers, because she will soon get married.

She must obey and follow expected societal behaviour in totality. If she defies or questions it, she will be breaking the honour of her family. And the consequences are dire! No one will be willing to marry her. All her family members will be ashamed because of her behaviour. This can bring negative consequences not only to her but her whole family. She could actually be killed by close family members who feel ashamed and betrayed.

Do you see any problem with this kind of arrangement?

Write your answer here:

Share your answer with a friend and discuss your views.

To a brother, his sister is part of the family's property which, if well taken care of, can be exchanged for dowry when she gets married. Her male relatives therefore feel the obligation to protect their property so she does not lose her value in this exchange. This is a sad scenario. It means that women are made to feel they have no ownership of their own bodies.

Everything they do is targeted to ensure that they retain high value for the time when they are exchanged.

So the way a Saudi Arabian girl is brought up, the kind of training she gets, is about things that wives and mothers are supposed to do. Formal education is important, but domestic training is a high priority to ensure she becomes a good wife who pleases her husband and secures a future. Becoming a good mother to her children is also very important, even though she may still be a child herself when she gives birth.

When she goes to her husband's home, a Saudi girl will have acquired an attitude of subservience to her husband plus knowledge and skills in cooking, cleaning, taking care of babies, and taking care of a husband physically, emotionally, and sexually. Other women in the family will help the girl's mother in this important process of training the girl for 'acceptable' and 'honourable' womanhood.

> One motivation for women's empowerment is basic fairness and decency. Young girls should have the exact same opportunities that boys do to lead full and productive lives. ... The empowerment of women is smart economics.

— President Robert Zoellick- World Bank Spring Meetings, 2008.

In Saudi Arabia quotes like that are not so important if women's empowerment distracts girls from domestic training.

In other societies, such as in Europe or the United States, at age 13 a girl is just a teenager. She is expected to be in high school and to get exposure to different careers so she can choose the subjects she will study later, in college or university. She is brought up to start school at an early age. She is not expected to think about marriage until she is past 18 years old. It is not even legal to get married before the age of 18, because most countries have ratified the UN Convention on the Rights of the Child, which includes an age of consent of 18 years. This is how different societies are socialising their girls to become independent career women at age 18 and above.

Do you see any problem with this kind of arrangement?

Write your answer here:

Share your answer with a friend and discuss your views.

Boy children in Africa are socialised to become 'real men' who can take control of a family as its head. They are discouraged from entering the kitchen, no matter how hungry or cold they feel. They are told that men are always strong and do not cry, no matter how hurt they feel emotionally. They are supposed to beget as many children as possible to propagate the family lineage. That is how a society socialises its boys to become the strong, unemotional heads of large families.

So most mothers in-laws celebrate inwardly and pretend not to know about their son's promiscuity, even though at a personal level they love, know, and feel the pain of their daughters-in-law. This is the pain of having an unfaithful husband and living in fear of the risks of HIV.

Some boys (and girls in some communities) undergo painful but highly valued traditional circumcision rites through which they are initiated into adulthood. They are encouraged to face the knife as 'real' (strong) men who do not flinch with pain as they are cut, and the fresh wound is splashed with red chilli-peppered water, and made to vigorously dance around. They are supposed to be 'strong and manly' and symbolically show that they can withstand any level of pain to keep their community secrets.

These boys become the heads of households. They are the breadwinners who should command power and authority over their wives and children. However, in modern times, many women have encroached on this male space. They earn the family's living, because the economic crisis has rendered many husbands unemployed, helpless, and unable to fend for their families.

Can you imagine how such a reality has affected husbands who were socialised to believe that they must always be the ones with jobs and money? To be strong and be in charge?

Boys are also shown that they are allowed to beat up their wives and discipline women like children if women dare to defy male authority. How easy it is for them, now that they are humiliated, to beat up a wife who has become the breadwinner?

Do you see any problem with this kind of arrangement?

Write your answer here:

Share you answer with a friend and discuss your views.

---&❧ CHAPTER 8 ❧&---

Socialising a Girl to Become a 'Good' Wife

From childhood, a Muganda (singular) girl in Uganda is socialised to be a good wife. She is trained in word and practise to be a hard-working cook and housewife who will care for, and nurture everyone in her family, especially her husband. The Baganda (plural) start the socialisation process right from birth, through the rituals they carry out immediately after birth and the way they breastfeed girls. They dress girls in a specific way and train them to sit, kneel, and look after their younger siblings. Lots of similar parenting styles are used for both boys and girls in early childhood, but once signs of adolescence show, parenting becomes more and more segregated.

The training especially focuses on two spaces - the marital bedroom and the kitchen. They train her to strictly keep her marital secrets; after all, *'ebyomunju tebitotolwa'* (i.e., it is a taboo for her to divulge marital issues concerning her husband in public). They train her to be a caring, loving, calm, respectful, and submissive wife. She is not expected to deny the huband sex. This is well articulated in the common adage that 'a woman never faces her back to her husband.'

Throughout these preparatory processes, emphasis is especially put on a wife pleasing her husband, keeping his honour, and respecting his authority and that of his relatives. At her parents' home, she practises all these teachings first.

She is expected to obey the authority of her brothers. Boys are also expected to practise how to treat a wife by the way they treat their sisters, with kindness and respect. Otherwise he may be cruel to his wife in the future.

In Buganda, a wife is not only responsible to her husband but also to her in-laws and the whole of his community. So whereas the marriage starts as a union between two people it soon transforms it a clan affair. She is taught to greet her husband and elders by kneeling and not looking straight into their eyes. This is a visible symbol of where women belong in Buganda society—at the very bottom!

A girl learns to respond obediently and respectfully whenever her husband calls her. She is coached to charmingly welcome back her husband. It's imperative that she offloads whatever he brings home with appreciative joy and humility. She is told to always show him a happy face because men don't like unhappy women, period! These instructions always have a subtle, competitive message: 'If you don't do all these things for him, you will lose him to another woman.'

A girl's paternal aunt is especially responsible for training her on sexual and reproductive health issues. The aunt begins by training the adolescent girl about menstrual hygiene management. The girls is instructed to bathe very often and thoroughly, especially during and soon after menstruation and birth even after the main flow has stopped. She is instructed how to handle the husband in bed.

From adolescence, protecting a girl's decency becomes very important, for fear of attracting rapists and child defilers. Therefore it's not uncommon to hear a mother or aunt admonishing her if she sits with legs apart or squats. 'If you sit like that, who will ever marry you?' As if marriage is the one and only destiny for all girls. A girl must dress properly, ensuring she has completely covered her breasts and thighs.

It's 'common knowledge in Buganda that if a girl climbs a tree, it will stop producing fruit. So good girls do not climb trees. The truth is, this prohibition is meant to protect and prevent girls from 'indecent' exposure. Girls do not whistle or shout, because a good girl is a cool and calm lady.

MARRIAGE IS MADE IN THE BEDROOM AND KITCHEN.

The Baganda believe marriage love matures like a sugarcane. She is told that marriage is made in the bedroom. Therefore she has to maintain a clean, attractive bedroom if she is to sexually attract and inspire her husband. Girls are strictly warned never to commit adultery or have sex before or outside during marriage. On the other hand, boys are practically encouraged to 'taste' and be promiscuous.

A husband has rights over his wife's body, and he is allowed by society to have sex with his wife any day, any time, at his own whim. I once heard of a man who raised a formal complaint with his wife's aunt (my mother) because his wife dared to defy this cardinal marital rule. Today as an adult, I insolently question that societal expectation on women. What if that wife was heavily pregnant, sick, tired, or menstruating? Should she have just been permissive? It was *her* God-given body, wasn't it?

A lot of emphasis is put on hygienic handling of food when cooking. A typical meal is the complicated Kiganda dish of *matooke* (green plantains) that is steamed in banana leaves, together with another starchy food like sweet potatoes, cassava, rice, or yams. This is accompanied with a sauce made from ground nuts paste, beans, or peas, and leafy greens like spinach or cabbage. She must prepare all this food, ensure that it does not burn, and cook it completely until it is soft and tasty.

The Baganda are a generous people. So as a girl learns to cook, her mentors belabour the fact that food must always be prepared in abundant amounts to ensure the family is fully satisfied and that there is enough left over to cater for potential uninvited visitors. No wonder a lot of effort is put into teaching her how to grow not only enough, but diverse foodstuffs to ensure a big harvest and she is not mean in her cooking, has food security for her family, and employs variety in the meals she prepares for the family.

A wife has to know how to keep a clean, well maintained compound and a well-organised house without clutter. She has to socialise well with the neighbourhood but limit the time she spends with neighbours. Spending time like this could become a basis for not completing her household chores, cooking half-burned food, and worse still commit adultery.

I believe you all agree these teachings are very good. Girl children learn to be loving, organised, generous, and responsible. They are trained to be well-groomed, keep hygienic homes, and prepare tasty dishes. They learn to socialise. They even have a saying: 'When a fire starts at your neighbour's, it will not discriminate. It will burn both your neighbour's and your house. So be your neighbour's keeper.'

The paternal aunt trains the girl to become a consummate hostess. The aunt tells the girl, 'There is no route through your compound. Every one who branches is your visitor.' You should always welcome visitors with joy. Treat them warmly and always to serve them something to eat or drink. After all, the Baganda say a person who leaves your home in a hungry state never comes back.'

THIS IS NO LONGER YOUR HOME ... YOUR HOME IS WHERE YOU ARE GOING

Prior to her final departure, on the wedding day, the girl sits on the laps of her father, her mother and her grand mother. Sitting on their laps is their final show of love and a message that she is still their beloved daughter. They say farewell and counsel her lastly with tips of a successful marriage.

The father could say, 'I love you and will miss you greatly. Go in peace. Love, obey, and respect your husband the way you saw your mother do with me. May all the blessings of your ancestors accompany you.'

Then the mother would add on saying, 'This house will never be the same without you. Go well my dear child. I wish you have a successful marriage like mine. Always love, respect and submit to your husband. In case of any marital issues, ignore the malicious words of neighbours, don't rash to come here but first seek counsel and support from your mother in law. This is no longer your home, from now you are a visitor here, your home is where you are going. Above all trust in God.' Thereafter her bed would be thrown out or destroyed as a symbol that she can no longer seek refuge or rest here but only as a visitor. She is made to carry on her head a bundle of firewood, a pot and knife, to symbolise her responsibilities as a wife in her home. Its such an emotional farewell, most brides leave in floods of tears!

I am greatly proud of my culture. I love and respect it dearly. However, the 'criminal part of my brain,' which is disruptive in nature, has other things in mind. My wish is that my beloved tribe, the Baganda, were as deep in their training of boys as they are of girls. I wish they emphasised great respect for wives.

I wish the Baganda told their boy children that their wives are not children but fellow adults, equal partners in producing and raising their children. Wives should be treated as equal partners for the growth of family income and its overall development. Wives are equal partners during youth, middle, and old age - to love and to cherish, growing up with their husbands and jointly enjoying the fruits of family love and labour.

I wish the Baganda emphasised deep compassion and support for wives in carrying out the household chores. I wish they trained boys to desist from domestic violence. I wish boys unlearned the philandering of their fathers, grandfathers, and great grandfathers. I wish boys were told that philandering affects them negatively too (e.g., the impact on health) and could tear apart their families.

I wish boys were taught housework and to appreciate how repetitive, boring, and tiring it can be for their wives and daughters. I wish boys learned more about childcare and became both emotionally and practically involved beyond buying the basics. I wish all husbands learned to reciprocate whenever their wives fell sick and cared for them, rather than hurtling them back to their parents like unwanted luggage.

I wish girls were taught to be assertive, rather than shy, to build their self-esteem and self-confidence. They should believe more in their self-worth as full human beings with full human rights! Once girls know their self-worth, they will not stand for nonsense. I wish, oh how I wish both women and men equally shared the burden of making their marriage a success or failure. I wish and wish and wish for changes in this stubborn and elusive issue of the gender relations of power!

Do you see any advantages and problems with this kind of arrangement?

Write your answer here:

Share your answer with a friend and discuss your views.

There are many other examples of what socialisation is. There are many methods of socialising people to understand what it means, in a particular society, to be male or female. Ironically, it's women as mothers, aunts, and grandmothers who happily play the major role in socialisation. So if we are seeking transformative changes in the content of any society's unwritten socialisation curriculum, women should become the key change agents.

> If I have a daughter I will tell her she can do anything, and I will mean it, because I have no other intention of informing her otherwise. As my mother did with me, and my mother's mother before her, I shall simply hide the truth from her. I will tell her that despite what others may whisper, there is no difference between her and any boy.

—Amy Mowafi, Egyptian Writer

NOT JUST ANOTHER AVERAGE 13 YEAR OLD GIRL

I know a girl who was socialised in a way that promoted her self-esteem and confidence. Not only did she become curious but also competitiivve. Imagine you are a mother or father and you received the message below from your empowered 13-year-old girl. How would you feel? How would you react?

Hello family, I am currently revising really hard for the science exam I will be taking this Thursday. Last month I did a different science test and hit a breath-taking 96% wich [sic] really shocked me as before I never imagined that someone *like me* would be capable of doing such things, but through time I have developed more confidence in myself as an individual and realised that as long as you have faith and believe in yourself all things are possib [sic] So I beg of you all to please wish me luck. My personal goal is to hit a staggering 100% this time wich [sic] is nerve racking [sic]as I've never gotten above 98% average on a science paper before but hopefully I will change that and show all my teachers that I … (names not disclosed) isn't just another average 13 year old girl and that I take my work very seriously because I am no joke and don't wanna be seen as one either (Thank you bye).

Wow! Wow! Isn't that nice and beautiful?

CONCLUSION

Gender describes culturally and socially based expectations, roles and behaviour of men and women. Gender is socially constructed and is related to how we are seen and expected to think and act as men or women based on the way our society is organised. These expectations are handed down, mostly orally, from one generation to the next.

In most African communities, women are expected to cook, wash, and take care of babies. Men are expected to become the automatic heads of families, while women are subordinates. Men do the 'hard' jobs like being a mechanic or accountant or building. Men also go to bars. Men inherit land. These roles and opportunities can, however, be played by either sex. They are not determined by whether you are male or female. They depend on ones capabilities.

Societal expectations of how a man or woman should be, are mediated through the socialisation process. In Africa, most socialisation is done by parents and extended family members as the first role models. They are supported in the child's day-to-day life by the teachers in school.

They talk to us. They teach us games. They use traditional proverbs, idioms, and similes packed with deep societal meanings. They use stories and fables to model moral characters according to what our society expects from a boy or a girl. They compare us to others and make us very competitive (sometimes negatively) with each other. They dress us differently, in different colours, sizes, and styles, to show us our cultural norms and societal rites of passage.

Socialisation is mainly mediated through local languages, their embedded meanings, and the images that every society uses daily to show its children what is of value and what it perceives as the right things to be embraced by a girl or boy. It also highlights what to expect if you defy these teachings.

Nothing is as powerful in a person's life as what they experience in their early years, like socialisation. It shapes and influences our world view, personal beliefs, values, and perspectives. It also informs us how we should live our lives. If you understand our socialisation, then you can perceive how we think, how we behave, and how we relate to other people, whether of the same or opposite sex, because these are all functions of how we have been socialised during our childhood.

I read somewhere about a psychologist who described the formative years of a person's life as being like wet cement: any impression placed on it is hard to change once the cement has dried up This corresponds to the popular saying, that you can't teach an old dog new tricks. The Baganda also say that 'a tree that was bent in its infancy will snap and break if you try to straighten it when its mature.'

It is high time we developed a new curriculum about gender, a new way of socialisation based on the truth about the abilities of men and women, and about the tenets of human rights for all human beings, irrespective of gender. No one can claim it is not possible, because 'it is only the wisest and the stupidest who never change.' It is unfortunate that most of our beliefs about gender are misinformation and half-truths. 'Be aware of false knowledge, it is more dangerous than ignorance.'

—Bernard Shaw, Irish playwright

It is high time every family, every culture, and every community went back to the drawing board for a new social and cultural dispensation in which our children are socialised differently for a new world that is inclusive. Here, everybody will have enough opportunities and resources to exploit their talents and reach their full potential.

It is the responsibility of every adult to hand over to the younger generation a better world than the one given to them by their fathers and forefathers. We can choose to start learning new cultural values now, and decide to shape the thinking of our children in a different way. We should seek to influence their mindset and lifestyle so that they learn to accommodate and treat each other with mutual respect.

In Africa, our sociocultural values are at the heart of every relationship we develop with each other. I am advocating for a paradigm shift in socialisation. We can choose to learn new things and behave in new ways. Someone observed that, 'The illiterates of the 21st century will not be those who cannot read and write, but those who cannot learn, unlearn and relearn.' Let us all make a commitment to learn new ways of positive and balanced socialisation, unlearn the unequal gender relationships of power, and relearn what it means to live with respect and dignity for each other.

—Alvin Toffler, American writer and businessman

CALL TO ACTION

- Discuss and describe ten things you unconsciously do today because of your socialisation as a girl or a boy.
- Discuss and describe ten things you unconsciously do not do today because you have been socialised as a woman or a man.
- Do you think the next generation should be socialised in the same way regarding those things you do and don't do? Why?
- Draw ten individual images of what comes to your mind when you hear the words 'socialisation' and 'my tribe'. Put a description of your pictures at the bottom.

Things I do because I have been socialised		Things I don't do because I have been socialised	
Girl	Boy	Girl	Boy

3. In this chapter, I described a 'good' Muganda wife. Write or draw two profiles:

- Profile a good wife from your own tribe or community. Research your community by talking to the elders.
- Profile a good husband from your own tribe or community. Again, consult the elders.

Start your research with questions like these:

- What are the qualities of a good wife in our tribe?
- Why are those qualities important to our tribe?
- What are the qualities of a good husband in our tribe?
- Why are those qualities important to our tribe?
- Who usually teaches young girls about a wife's qualities? When? How?
- What are the consequences if a girl/woman/wife behaves differently from her tribal expectations? Give examples.
- Who usually teaches younger boys about a husband's qualities? When? How?

- What are the consequences if a boy/man/husband behaves differently from his tribal expectations?
- Are there any similarities or differences in the way they are handled? Why?

Share your images and profiles with people from another tribe (peers, friends, and community members). Explain that you are doing it for the purpose of learning about other cultures. Discuss the similarities and differences you learn about socialisation.

Remember:

- This is not a competition about which tribe is good or bad.
- Do not make comments or judgements as people explain their culture to you. Humble yourself, listen, and learn.
- All cultures and tribes in Africa have strengths and areas that need improvement in their socialisation processes, and weaknesses in their gender socialisation processes. It is only through open learning and sharing that we can retain the best and discard the worst.

After your discussions, reflect on your learning.

- Highlight what you have learned about the good and bad impacts of socialisation from a gendered perspective.
- What will you do better or differently in the future as a result of your learning? Jot down at least five action points and start implementing them today.

---- ❧ CHAPTER 9 ❧ ----

When Do You Become Gendered?

The emotional, sexual and psychological stereotyping of females begins when the doctor says 'It's a girl.'

—Shirley Chisholm American politician, educator and writer

From the moment your parents discovered that they were pregnant with you, they thought about sex and gender. Some of them even went to the doctor for a scan to find out whether you were a boy or a girl, so as to

prepare to respond to you. They went for a scan to find out whether you were male or female. But that is not what gender is; that is simply sex. As we learned earlier, gender is not about whether you are biologically male or female. Gender is about how you are socialised to be a 'normal' female or 'normal' male in your particular society. That 'normality' comes with lots of deeply held expectations and preferences.

Whether your parents had a scan or waited for a surprise at birth, on the day you were born, your sex was revealed. So what did your parents do?

They thought of names that represented what they thought a girl or boy should be. They bought clothes in colours which they thought suited you as a boy or a girl. The way they carried you and the types of food they gave you had different meanings. The kind of toys they gave you and stories they told you depended on whether you were a boy or a girl. The time when they started positioning you to sit up was gendered. Even the decision to use nappies was gendered. As you grew up, the kinds of games, duties, and chores your parents expected you to participate in were based on gender.

Write down three dos and three do nots you hear parents in your tribe or community telling children based on whether the child is a boy or girl.

Boys do …	Boys do not …	Girls do …	Girls do not …

Did you know there is usually some hidden meaning behind what society allows you to do or does not allow you to do? Try to figure out the reasons why they made the rules you listed above. Ask your teacher, your parent(s), or your grandparent(s) to help you complete the table if you cannot finish all of them.

Here is how I would complete the worksheet for my own society:

Boys do …	Boys do not …	Girls do …	Girls do not …
Boys play football	Boys don't cry	Girls skip rope	Girls don't shout
Boys look after the animals	Boys don't sit in the kitchen	Girls fetch water and firewood	Girls don't climb trees
Boys guard the family	Boys can stay out later than girls	Girls bathe twice a day	Girls don't fight
Boys go to school	Boys don't cry	Girls cook and wash plates	Girls don't thatch houses
Boys look after livestock		Girls play with dolls	
Boys play football		Girls play netball	
Boys curtsy while greeting adults		Girls kneel down while greeting adults	
Boys marry		Girls get married	

CONCLUSION

Gender is a choice. It's reflected in the roles and expectations society places on women and girls, men and boys. Gender is a social construction that one puts on as one puts on clothes in the morning. One can undress when necessary. The definition of gender for males and females is not set in stone. It is dynamic and it changes over time and space, depending on how a person wants to adapt to their changing environment. Each environment will have a different definition of what it means to be a male or a female, and what kinds of roles you play as males and females in order to have a harmonious community in which people mutually respect each other.

I once heard that places do not make people; people make places. A baby is born into this world with a clean slate. There is no cultural influence in that moment. The biggest problem with culture is the fact that it is a *double-edged sword*. It can empower and disempower.

From a gendered perspective, culture tends to disempower women most often. Instead of celebrating a woman's innate personality and capabilities, culture distances her from many things that define her humanity. Culture empowers a woman in a limited way, based only on things that are acceptable in the immediate environment. These things may not necessarily benefit the woman directly, but as long as these are societal norms, the woman is forced to abide by them.

There comes a time where an individual woman must make a choice to liberate herself, alone or collectively with other women, from all societal and cultural stereotypes. She must choose to live a full life, free of gender bias or prejudice. In so doing, she responds decisively to the famous dictum: 'To be yourself in a world that is constantly trying to make you something else, is the greatest accomplishment.' Wow, think of that.

—Ralph Waldo Emerson. American essayist, philosopher and poet

For every female in the world who feels that her true identity, value, and purpose in life has been compromised, my message is simple and straight forward. Do not blindly follow the crowd along the normally trodden path. Its difficult but you will be better off if you make a choice and fight for your rights.

The world at times can be ruthless and heartless. If people are denying you your fundamental human rights, complaining alone wouldn't get you anywhere. If you don't like being a doormat, then get off the floor, dust the dirt off your clothes, and stand up straight. Remember, 'A woman is like a tea bag; you never know how strong it is until it's in hot water.'
You are ther

It takes no effort to follow a crowd, but it can cost you everything to take an independent stand in life. However, stand up and be your sister's keeper. Get up and be your brother's keeper. Do not be afraid to be called a feminist. One person, once asserted that, 'A feminist is anyone who recognises the equality and full humanity of women and men.' You are better off if you make a choice and fight for your own rights. Is that a crime?

—Gloria Steinem American feminist and journalist

The world at times can be ruthless and heartless. If people are denying you your fundamental human rights, complaining alone wouldn't get you anywhere. If you don't like being a doormat, then get off the floor, dust the dirt off your clothes, and stand up straight. 'A woman is like a tea bag; you never know how strong it is until it's in hot water.'

—Eleanor Roosevelt, American First Lady

It takes no effort to follow a crowd, but it can cost you everything to take an independent stand in life. However, stand up and be your sister's keeper. Get up and be your brother's keeper. Do not be afraid to be called a feminist. asserted, 'A feminist is anyone who recognises the equality and full humanity of women and men.' Is that a crime?

—Gloria Steinem American feminist and journalist

CALL TO ACTION

Select and outline your personal path to contribute to gender equality.

CHAPTER 10

Behold! The Socialisation Agents Are Coming!

Socialisation agents are the people and traditional institutions that will affect how you think, value yourself, express your personality, and behave because you are a man or a woman. A child's sense of who they are is a result of the large number of ideas, ways of thinking, ways of behaving, and beliefs that he or she is introduced to. The information that surrounds the child and with which the child engages daily comes to the child from different socialisation agents.

1. GENDER, PARENTS, AND THE FAMILY

> The single best indicator of whether a nation will succeed is how it treats its women.
>
> — Barrack Obama, American President

The first socialising agent is your immediate family. Almost everyone in your family has socialised you. It doesn't matter whether you lived with parents, siblings, aunts, uncles, or grandparents—you name it, they socialised you, and most likely in a similar manner.

From the time their children are babies, parents treat sons and daughters differently. Parents dress infants in gender-specific colours. Parents buy gender-differentiated toys.

If you go to any search engine, e.g., Google, you can search for images of 'boys' rooms'. Do that and write down the colours you see:

_____

_____

_____

Carry out a similar search of 'girls' rooms' images and write down the colours you see:

… …

Did you know that a study of children's rooms has shown that girls' rooms have more pink, dolls, and manipulative toys? No wonder that, when the girls become adults, they are deft at using their hands. Boys' rooms have more blue, sports equipment, tools, and vehicles.

In an urban setting, boys are more likely than girls to take on repair and maintenance chores around the house, such as replacing electric bulbs, fixing things that are broken, painting, and mowing the lawn. These are one-off activities. Girls are likely to have domestic chores, such as cooking, washing, doing the laundry or babysitting their siblings. These are daily, repetitive activities. They are boring and lead to drudgery. This assignment of particular household tasks to boys or girls leads children to link certain types of work to males or females.

Providing care can be both a source of fulfilment and a terrible burden. For women and girls in particular, their socially prescribed role as carers can undermine their rights and limit their opportunities, capabilities and choices – posing a fundamental obstacle to gender equality and well-being.

—Emily Esplen, Feminist, IDS

Have you ever heard the statement 'This is girls' work' or 'This is boys' work'? If you have, can you give one specific example?

Girls' work_____

Boys' work_____

There is a study which shows that parents have different expectations of sons and daughters as early as twenty hours after birth. Once the baby is born and it's a boy, you can hear a proud daddy saying, 'I am lucky I have now got an heir. I am going to take him to the village and introduce him to my father. I will also buy that train set so we can play together. He is going to become an engineer or pilot,' You will rarely hear the father say that he will buy a Barbie doll for his son and play dress-up with him. That is all part of socialisation. Your parent is your greatest socialising agent.

Write down at least five expectations and loaded meanings in this innocent comment by a father about his son.

1.

2.

3.

4.

5.

You spend your earliest years with your family. Socialisation comes through contact with your parents, other family members, and neighbours. You learn by watching the way your father and mother interact and how your brothers, sisters and extended family relatives behave and relate to one another and to you.

The way they talked, the way they dressed, the chores each carried out, the things your parents quarrelled about are all informative. You also learnt from the things that you said or did which prompted a negative or positive response from your parents. This strengthened certain behaviours because of the way they liked them or disliked them and mediated through the rewards and punishments you received. You grew up learning and being rebuked for not behaving in the right manner according to what was expected of your gender roles.

2. GENDER AND PEERS

The second socialisation agent is your peers—your friends. The kind of friends you have will cause you to speak and act in certain ways. They say,

'Birds of a feather flock together' and 'If four of your friends are bullies to girls in your school, who is the fifth one?'

When you come into contact with certain people, and you spend much time with them—in school, in your neighbourhood, communicating over the phone, or on social media—you will pick up ways of thinking, talking, dressing, and behaving from each other.

Friends are a big socialisation agent. Whether deliberately or unconsciously, you tend to become like the people you spend the most time with. Some agents of socialisation, such as the family and the peer group, may conflict with each other, offering alternative goals, values, and styles of behaviour. That's why the Baganda have a saying that, 'Tell me who your friends are and I will describe your character.'

Sometimes when you imitate friends dress in a certain way, your parents may not agree with that. They may tell you 'Stop being a copycat. Good boys don't dress like that' or 'Respectable girls don't dress like that'. You may have a big fight. It's simply because these are two different socialisation agents, and when you choose to conform to one, you may not feel comfortable.

3. GENDER AND SCHOOL

Consider and observe the school toilets:

- How private do they seem to you?
- How comfortable do your peers seem to be as they enter or leave the toilets?
- Look around and notice any activities going on around the area.
- How does the status of the toilets protect the dignity of the girls or boys using them?

These are seemingly normal issues, but they inform you of many things that have to do with gender at school. Schools are a major socialisation agent for your peer group. There, you are exposed to socialisation via the dominant school facilies, female and male teachers' roles and status in the school. You observe who does support work, receptionists, cooks, cleaners, and secretaries. You interact with a diverse range of other students, who will begin to shape your performance, expectations and career ambitions. They will also influence your behaviour.

Do you notice that children from certain schools are more confident than others and behave in certain ways? Do you notice that some schools produce many more girls who are willing to take on science and engineering courses at university than others? What do you think makes this fundamental difference?

Look at who holds which position in the administration of the school. Which teachers normally teach particular subjects, and at what level of class? Then you will see emerging patterns. Look at the pictures used in the educational curriculum and main textbooks. Study the images displayed on school walls. Consider the numbers and genders of children who are prefects and those who are constantly absent from school. Try to confidentially find out the reasons for their absences.

Research the enrolment rates at primary one and age at which girls and boys usually drop out of school, and for what reasons. Again, patterns will emerge. Head teachers, and teachers in general, have ways in which they communicate with their students. Certain character traits rub off.

It is at school that you spend the greatest part of your growing and formative years. As you move into this larger world of friends and mentors, many new ideas are shared with you. Many beliefs and values are instilled in you. At the same time, these beliefs and values are challenged or influenced by those around you. You learn to behave in a certain way because of the things that the school accepts, and to stop the behaviour it disapproves of. To behave in the way they approve can be a huge challenge for you, That is how you slowly become shaped by the character of that school.

Deniz Kandiyoti wrote an interesting article about how schools socialise pupils and replicate what happens at home. The article is entitled 'Peeping through the windows: the elusive agenda.' It highlights how the gender division of labour at home is reproduced at school. Girls alone are made responsible for cleaning the classrooms, fetching water for cooking at school, and so on. Have you observed similar experience in your school?

Observe and take note of the gendered do's and don'ts in your school. Write down which ones target boys and which ones target girls.

_____

_____

Monitor the daily routine in school.

- What do the boys and male teachers do generally?
- What positions of leadership and responsibility do male teachers have?
- Are there any similarities between what happens at school and what happens at home?
- What are the differences?

- What do the girls and female teachers do generally?
- What positions of leadership and responsibility do female teachers have?
- Are there any similarities between what happens at school and what happens at home?
- What are the differences?

_____

_____

School uniforms

Look at the differences between boys' and girls' school uniforms and write them down:

1. Boys' uniforms

_____

_____

_____

2. Girls' uniforms

_____

_____

_____

Textbooks, learning materials, and images on school walls

Pick an illustrated textbooks or other learning images on the walls in school.

- What do the images indirectly depict about the roles of males and the roles of females?
- How does the language used depict the status of men and women?
- What do the shapes, colours, and sizes depict about boys' or girls' use?

Menstrual hygiene management (MHM) and privacy at school
Study your toilets and the activity that goes on around the boys' toilets versus the girls' toilets.

- Do you notice any differences in the number of cubicles for girls compared to those for boys? Why?
- What about the level of hygiene?

4. GENDER, MEDIA, AND THE TOY INDUSTRY

The third socialisation agent is the media. This includes radio programmes, TV shows, music, news programmes, pamphlets, newspapers, magazines, the internet, and social media like Facebook and Twitter.

When you spend time engaged with the media, it influences how you think, talk, and behave. From a gendered perspective, the media is an all-embracing influence in subtle ways on all aspects of a child's life. Remember, our lives are also mediated by the adverts for the goods and services we use.

From an early age, children receive gifts that are gender specific—related to society's expectations of the child's future role—from parents who are already socialised themselves. One British parent recently acknowledged the powerful combination of Christmas toys and the media. She said that she and her husband had never exposed their children to gender-specific colours or toys. They were really surprised because as soon as their daughter could make a choice, she asked for a pink Barbie doll. The mother asked her daughter why she preferred a pink Barbie doll gift, and without hesitation, the child answered that she saw them every day on TV and in adverts for Christmas. The powerful combination of the media and the toy industry socialises children consistently in very passive ways that parents may not recognise.

The media can make or break the value we see in people and their careers by what it publishes. It can produce celebrities overnight and also destroy them within the same breath. For example, every day it tells us what to value or detest about male and female leaders. Find out why the media referenced to Margaret Thatcher (British prime minister as 'the iron lady'

For example, media images focus on women's bodies to send out a subtle but powerful message that the most important things about women is to have a certain type of body. You must weigh less than a certain amount to be considered beautiful. Your hair has to look a certain way. If you don't have that type of body, then you are perceived as not really beautiful. You cannot really be successful in that society.

So you find African females struggling to ensure they have a slim body shape yet naturally they are often curvy. They bleach their skins so they can look a bit lighter and 'attractive.' They choose lengthy hairstyles in order to be appreciated. All this is because they have grown up with a media that sends out subtle messages about femininity and its meaning to their society.

Is it not funny that you do not find such emphasis on body images for men?

The 2016 US elections attracted the whole world. Look at how Hillary's ways of dressing, talking, and smiling were emphasised during elections. Yet Trump could look like anything or dress anyhow and the media would not judge him in the same way.

5. GENDER AND RELIGION

The fourth, most controversial, and most powerful socialisation agent is religion and its ministers. The religious beliefs you have and how much you value them will permanently shape the way you think and behave. Religious beliefs are protected from any challenge, especially if the challenger is from another religion. If you are serious about your religion, you will behave the way that religion advocates. For example, everyone knows that Muslims have to pray five times a day, fast during the month of Ramadan, celebrate both Eid al-fitr and Eid al-Adha, and attend prayers every Friday. Similarly, Christians have specific types of prayer, days to celebrate Mass, fast before Easter, and celebrate Easter and Christmas.

Religion socialises through a strong moral message. It enables you to see and appreciate what is 'right' and what is 'wrong'. You see the world and the behaviour of everyone else from the way religion teaches you.

Some religions insist that their followers dress in a certain way, keep their hair in a certain way, or eat only certain types of food. When you see these behaviours, you know that their religion has socialised them. Religions determine how males and females relate and what their roles should be. So it strongly shapes the gender agenda.

6. THE GENDERED WORKPLACE, THE POLITICS OF GENDER, AND WOMEN'S LEADERSHIP

The workplace is a major socialisation agent. The people you work with and your employer's organisation culture/rules determine how you think, act, and relate to people around you at work. The workplace, like school, is a place where people spend a lot of their adult life/time. However, by the time people go to work, they have already been socialised for many years at home and school. They come to work with different values, ideas and understandings about gender. It is hard to promote gender awareness at work and for people to accept it because of these pre-existing beliefs.

Staff may respond to workplace gender issues in different ways. The majority tend to ignore gender issues and say these do not matter. Others claim they have no problem with policies about gender roles, but they do not know how to deal with them. Those in leadership roles may pretend that they do not understand gender's importance. A few may passionately push for gender to be put on the agenda of the organisation. A few others may actively resist it.

Because of these varying responses, a number of gender-sensitive issues can come up. Women can be very vulnerable in the workplace. Some leaders could use their powerful positions to exploit women sexually. They are expected to work at the same capacity as men at all times, even when they are pregnant or having difficult menstrual cycles. Women are also expected to give 100 per cent of themselves to their husbands, families, and extended families.

***

Through all of these socialisation agents, people learn and practice gender-stereotyped behaviour. As children develop, these gender stereotypes become strong beliefs and influence the way the child or later on as an adult understands the world around him or her.

CONCLUSION

What is gender? It is the way society defines what the role of a male or female person should be.

Gender definition depends on how you have been socialised by family, peers, school, workplace, media, and religion. The socialisation agent with the biggest influence is the one that will make you think, behave, and relate in a particular way.

For most children, the mother is the most important socialising agent. That's why I believe if we are to nip patriarchy in the bud, we should not only focus on men. Women are the initial gatekeepers of patriarchy. Of course fathers also participate, but mothers play a greater role.

Gender does *not* mean you are a male or a female. As one of the greatest writers once wrote, 'One is not born a woman, one becomes a woman.' I completely agree with her. Each one of us is socialised to become a certain kind of person and to behave in a certain way. At the end of the day, we are the sum total of the people we have interacted with, the environments we have lived in, the beliefs we have embraced, and the choices we have made. All these are consequences of our socialisation.

—Simone de Beauvoir, French writer

Nicholas D. Kristof wrote that in the nineteenth century, the central moral challenge was slavery. In the twentieth century, it was the battle against totalitarianism. I reaffirm that in this century, the paramount moral challenge will be the struggle for gender equality around the world.

In the African context, everything seems to be a gender issue. Unfortunately, issues surrounding gender have sabotaged the advancement of the continent in areas of skill development, equal opportunities, and self-actualisation. I therefore believe it is time for all stakeholders from every major socialising agent to come together, take a common stand, and say no to the gender equality gap.

I take this opportunity to challenge every religious or community leader to answer this call of destiny: step forward and make a public commitment. Ask yourself, 'If not me, who? If not now, when?' In the words of Phumzile Mlambo Ngcuka, 'Africa must close its gender gap in order to succeed.'

One American President once said that, 'All great change in America begins from the dinner table.' Given that all societies sit at a table or mat to eat, but women and girls remain in the kitchen, let's start there. It is high time women and girls join everyone else at the table and mat to eat. Let families include topics of gender equality and discrimination in their daily conversations. Both parents, being joint leaders of the family, should show the way from an early stage.

—Ronald Reagan, American President

If parents socialise their children positively in matters of gender, then when those children grow up, they will not depart from that school of thought. It is said that the strength of a nation derives from the integrity of the home. Whatever begins in the family either transforms or destroys the world. So the best place to start advocating for gender equality in this world is in the family. 'Family means no one gets left behind or forgotten.'

— David Ogden Stiers, American actor

Equality, like charity, starts at home since, 'Everything depends on upbringing.' If you are a parent, you are the shapers of society's values.

—Leo Tolstoy, Russian writer

If you give your boy child positive exposure to gender balance, he will grow up emotionally intelligent, kind, and compassionate to women and girls. He will not shame you with brute violence. He will be a stable man who is confident in his masculinity. He will value and respect all people because they are human beings, and he will behave accordingly.

If you give your girl child positive exposure to gender balance, she will combine her compassionate nature with calm self-confidence and self-belief. She will fully exploit all her potential and talents as a human being. Ultimately the whole society will benefit. You will be proud of her.

Peer pressure potentially shapes or breaks a child. As it was once observed, 'We are the average of every 5 people we hang around with.' We therefore need to inspire our children to build healthy relationships with one another based on strong values and attitudes, irrespective of their gender, because relationships rule the world.

—Jim Rohn, Enterprener, author and motivational speaker

I believe schools should introduce gender equality in their regular curriculum subjects. This way students will look at gender equality as something constitutional and important—something that they will fight to uphold. Schools are well-placed to shape the attitudes, beliefs, and values of our children, making them better citizens of the world. When I watched Nelson Mandela's very inspirational film, *Long Walk to Freedom*, I reconfirmed that he believed that education is the most powerful weapon you can use to change the world.

WHOEVER CONTROLS THE MEDIA, CONTROLS THE MIND

The media is also very powerful. It has significant leverage to influence not only decision makers but the general public also. That's why someone observed, 'Whoever controls the media, controls the mind.' Adding to this thought, Malala Yousafzai, the charismatic activist for girls' education, said that, 'What is interesting is the power and the impact of social media.' So we must try to use media in a good way to create a more beautiful society.

—Jim Morrison, American singer, songwriter and poet

Our recent history has taught us that the media, especially social media, can also bring a revolution to an entire nation. We saw it during the Arab Spring uprisings that connected people nationally and globally and toppled three hitherto very powerful governments in Tunisia, Egypt, and Libya.

Malcom X had foresight when he said, 'The media is the most powerful entity on earth. They have that charismatic power to make the innocent guilty and to make the guilty innocent because they control the minds of the masses.'

—Malcom X, American Muslim Minister and human rights activist

I challenge media owners and managers, especially editors, to take it upon yourselves to responsibly use your immense power to leverage and advocate for gender change. 'Whoever controls the media, the images, controls the culture'. Be at the front line of gender balance and equity advocacy. I urge you to run special campaigns, special newspaper features, and positive portrayals of women as normal, full human beings. The media is a strategic partner that can close the gap of gender inequality.

—Allen Ginsberg, American poet and philosopher

Similarly it has been said that the power of religion can both guide and destroy society; hence religious leaders are some of the most influential people in the world. We often respect and want to follow what they tell us to do. They are in the vanguard of forming our values and morals, and consequently our conscience as human beings. Some of their values like those of love, peaceful co-existence, humility, endurance, and compassion can be adopted everywhere to promote gender equality. If they use that power well, they can make a gigantic difference when it comes to gender equality.

I humbly urge all religious leaders, who counsel us before marriage, to step up the plate and take the lead in advocating for gender balance and equality in our families and communities. More often than not, people unquestioningly follow instructions from their religious leaders more than they are influenced by their own families and friends.

Every company is guided by its policies, procedures, and regulations. I believe if all company Boards of Directors become aware of and adopt affirmative action policies to address historical biases against women in leadership and employment equality, our working places will become safer than they are today. They will become nice and beautiful places to work in, for both men and women who spend a lot of their waking hours at work. And, I hope, we would benefit from a feminist style of leadership that supports everyone irrespective of sex

CALL TO ACTION

Go back to the above six socialization agents. Look for every important gender word that has been used and fill in the puzzle below:

R	I	W	Y	L	I	M	A	F	U	B	E	H	A	V	I	O	U	R	I
R	E	E	K	M	Z	X	M	I	F	Q	Z	X	B	U	H	J	W	Z	N
F	J	L	H	Z	P	A	R	E	N	T	S	X	V	F	O	O	D	M	S
G	N	D	I	S	N	X	I	W	S	Z	M	V	Y	W	X	C	X	X	T
B	B	T	N	G	S	O	C	I	A	L	I	Z	A	T	I	O	N	N	R
F	H	G	F	F	I	C	H	I	J	X	W	U	A	W	Z	B	Z	C	U
A	U	P	L	G	K	O	N	E	Q	J	O	J	P	M	U	S	I	C	C
C	Y	E	U	T	H	I	N	K	I	N	G	G	P	U	A	V	Q	B	T
E	G	E	E	T	K	V	K	U	W	K	O	O	R	W	Q	N	M	S	I
B	V	R	N	E	H	H	S	B	O	I	I	D	O	F	T	T	H	A	O
O	C	S	C	H	O	O	L	D	R	J	J	K	P	I	B	A	H	K	N
O	I	Y	E	T	T	R	E	G	K	G	H	J	R	Z	P	X	S	A	Q
K	P	I	D	O	L	K	N	K	P	W	W	X	I	E	J	B	V	C	X
Q	W	E	I	R	T	I	H	J	L	S	T	A	A	H	B	I	R	D	S
I	U	D	Y	T	N	R	W	Q	A	X	X	V	T	B	H	G	J	I	Q
O	A	P	O	E	B	N	M	A	C	Z	G	T	E	C	T	Y	U	J	E
R	I	O	T	T	E	A	C	H	E	R	S	T	J	H	H	B	X	Z	I
Q	W	S	E	R	T	Y	U	U	I	Y	P	I	R	I	O	I	W	S	B
I	I	P	T	A	L	K	I	N	G	M	B	J	K	A	L	P	N	R	R
L	O	L	K	J	H	G	F	D	S	N	H	A	Q	Z	I	C	S	G	A
Z	X	C	V	V	C	H	A	N	G	E	X	X	B	S	D	N	R	H	B

Find these words: 1.Religion 2.Socialization 3.Workplace, 4.Shape, 5.Facebook, 6.Listening 7.Watching, 8.School, 9.Friends, 10.Appropriate, 11.Change, 12.Peers, 13.Talking, 14.Thinking, 15.Instruction, 16.Teachers, 17.Influenced, 18.Behaviors, 19.Family, 20.Parents, 21.Barbie, 22.Train, 23.Food, 24.Radio, 25.Music, 26.Birds, 27.Baby

CHAPTER 11

Does Gender Justice Equal Women?

We are talking about inequality in all its forms—in influence, access, agency, resources, and respect. We would argue that inequality, in one form or another is coded into just about every one of our social ills. Research demonstrates that extreme inequality weakens economic growth and undermines the social cohesion of societies.

—Darren Walter, president, Ford Foundation

In this chapter, I would like to discuss why we must amplify the voices of half the world — Women and girls! Their voices have been silenced for decades. I want you to heed Chris Hani's rallying call during apartheid and become angry—angry enough to rise up and fight for gender justice and women's rights!

You will see outrageous facts and figures. But beyond the statistics, I hope you will see the suffering human beings and understand the underlying causes of gender injustice. You will understand why some people, apart from you, are already so angry about gender discrimination and the resultant inequality.

In most countries, especially in sub-Saharan Africa, women comprise more than 50 per cent of the total population. It's appalling to see the results of research on gender parity in our socioeconomic and political systems. Women's majority numbers miraculously disappear!

Is this by accident? No. It's not a miracle; it's man-made! It is by design, and due to socialisation, inequality is rooted deeply into our social conscience and subconscious. We tend to take gender inequality for granted, burying our heads in the sand like ostriches. Some argue the inequality is God's design.

In my fight for gender justice at work, staff often asked me to explain why the majority of gender activists were single, elite, and divorced women, and why activists focused on issues concerning women mainly despite the suffering of many men who are widowed and divorced. 'Is gender synonymous with women?' they would ask.

The answer is a resounding *no*!

'Then why are gender activists usually women? And why are those women so angry, bitter, and aggressive? Is it because they have no men?' The implicit arrogance and meaning that women's happiness depends entirely on men, could be infuriorating.

My answer, nevertheless was, 'They are like that because society has not been fair to half of its population—the women. Women are angry and tired of being treated as less human, as second- or indeed third-class citizens in their own countries!

In 2002, Dr Sylvia Tamale, a renowned Ugandan gender and human rights activist, affirmed, 'They are sick and tired of being sick and tired.' Women are angry and exhausted due to their lived experiences of gender discrimination, frequent violence, and inequality. These are pervasive despite the work of many activists.

—Sylvia Tamale, Ugandan professor, and human rights activist

To appreciate the depth of this anger, you need to learn some realities about gender discrimination. You need to have the facts at your fingertips. Usually gender activists are well informed, but sometimes they find it hard to lay the hard facts on the table—facts that they know and have lived.

Humanity requires both men and women, and we are equally important and need one another. So why are we viewed as less than equal? These old attitudes are drilled into us from the very beginning. We have to teach our boys the rules of equality and respect, so that as they grow up, gender equality becomes a natural way of life. And we have to teach our girls that they can reach as high as humanly possible.

—Beyonce Knowles-Carter, American singer, songwriter and actress

When I hear the stories of those they call 'angry and bitter' gender activists, I also hear the eternal voice of Chris Hani, who, while fighting for social justice in South Africa, called upon his protégés to become angrier than him if they were to liberate South Africa. You cannot fight injustice without passion. And often your passion is misconstrued as anger and negativity by the people who are reaping benefits from the unjust system. I believe the same is true today for those who want to stand up to fight against gender discrimination and for women's rights.

However, there are far more women than men who have, at a very personal level, experienced gender discrimination. That experience, that lived reality, has inadvertently spurred more women than men to become gender game changers and activists.

The United Nations and its secretary-general are often in a privileged position with a global view and knowledge. This helicopter view makes the secretary-general deeply aware of what rights are enjoyed (or abused) by different societies in the world. The 1997 and 1998 Human Development Reports drew a fundamental conclusion when they said, 'No society treats its women as well as its men.'

—Human Development Reports – 1997 and 1998

Every year the HDR reports produce evidence that shows almost all countries in the world have fallen short of UN mission to ensure that everyone, irrespective of sex, is entitled to he same rights and freedoms—core principles for the very foundation of the UN.

Of course, the rights abuses are diverse and context-specific. Governments or duty bearers in different countries respond differently to those abuses. Developing countries had uniquely higher levels of gender injustice than developed countries. Scandinavian countries like Sweden and Norway have the best practices with regard to gender equity and equality.

---- ❧ CHAPTER 12 ❧ ----

So Why Gender Awareness? Why Females?

Because females are the ones who suffer the most gender-based oppression in society, women tend to respond most strongly. A leader once affirmed, 'Freedom is never voluntarily given by the oppressor; it must be demanded by the oppressed.'

—Martin Luther King Jr., civil rights fighter

In many cases, campaigns about gender justice are synonymous with women's rights campaigns. This is not by accident. The reality is that whenever and wherever one compares life indicators of women and girls with those of men and boys, the women and girls fare badly. Women and girls are worse off. So if gender justice is about fairness and balancing the scales, then emphasis must be put on adding weight to the women and girls' side of the scale. Think about this.

Even so, there are some aspects in which men and boys are worse off than women and girls. Take, for example, high mortality during armed conflict. More men and boys die and are deliberately targeted. This is also an area in which men and boys are targeted with unique sexual violence. Women and girls are also marked for gender-based violence and are used as weapons of war, to lower the fighters' morale and defeat them.

Women and girls need inspiration. At university, I studied many great literary works that portray women as losers and tragic victims of their own circumstances—women such as Anna Karenina, Madame Bovary, and

Hedda Gabler. But as an adult, I now realise there are many incredible women with great stories of success, defiance, resilience, and persistence against all odds. They are successful women *who should inspire us.*

That's why I believe education and media are important socialisers to influence - because they capture women and girls' minds in very subtle ways. That's why we should encourage and support many more women to write 'her-story'.

Women need to read stories of survivors and conquerors. They need inspirational quotations from women such as Mother Theresa, Princess Diana, and the American poet and civil rights activist Maya Angelou. These women used the unique qualities of their femininity to transcend gender discrimination and limitations, to add value to humanity. For example, Maya Angelou (1928–2014) is credited with publishing seven autobiographies, three books of essays, and several books of poetry and plays. Isn't that an incredible legacy to humanity? What will yours be? Do something, now!

Angelou was on the spot to encourage all oppressed people to have the courage to fight injustice. Surely women's gender journey is full of injustice and pain. But that pain can be confronted and changed. Some of the ways to ensure that women and girls live happy and beautiful lives is to build their knowledge and skills, enabling them to access and share information and services in the following key areas:

- education from primary to secondary to higher levels, acquiring skills for productive employment
- good nutrition and hygiene knowledge and practices

- employment and entrepreneurship, so they gain in income
- reproductive health and services, so that they survive pregnancy and birth
- access to productive assets like land, advice, support and loans for their businesses and farms.
- protection from direct violence and the subtle threats of violence

Of these, protection is at the core of women's empowerment. Irrespective of age, status, and location differences, domestic violence is a key threat to all women's efforts to live with dignity. In Africa, many married women live with the threat of polygamy as a subtle strategy used by men to bar women from exercising choices and participating in development processes.

Consider this reality: low education affects the ability of many girls in Africa to understand and relate with the world around them. This in turn affects their ability to practise healthy living through proper nutrition, healthcare, and hygiene practices for themselves, their families. They will struggle to contribute effectively both to the workforce and at home.

Women are not dumb. They have simply missed out on equal opportunities since time immemorial.

Lack of proper levels of education among girls also affects how they will perform economically. Not only will they miss out on good jobs, they will have less access to productive assets like land, equipment, and loans which can improve their incomes. Echoing the words of Christine de Pisan., someone said, 'I want to be honest. And if I do that, we all know the problem here isn't only about resources. It is also about attitudes and beliefs. It's about whether fathers and mothers think their daughters are as worthy of an education, as their sons.'

— Michelle Obama, US First Lady

In most African cultures, girls do not inherit anything from their families, because the families believe that the girl will get married and go away to become part of her husband's family. Once she is in her husband's family, she cannot inherit anything there either. The property goes to her male children, whom the clan expect will marry, bring women home, and increase the family.

The patrilineal system places greater value on boys than girls. Property inheritance goes directly to those boy children and not their mother because she might leave her husband and go back to her parents. Her husband's family does not want her to leave with his property. If she is to keep any property when her husband dies, she must accept to be inherited as a wife to one of his male relatives!

So it is difficult for girls and women to gain ownership of productive property, unless they get their own money (usually through education and employment) and buy it. Can you imagine how hard it is to change this situation? Isn't it something you should know about at an early age so you can be part of the positive change for equality?

Illiteracy and lack of education affects women and girls' productivity, ability to add value to their income-generating activities, and lifetime earnings. Their weak position exposes them to various types of abuse, including violence, threat of violence, intimidation, humiliation, and poor wages for their work.

Many women and girls in the developing world are malnourished and in poor health due to lack of proper education about hygiene, nutrition, and basic farming skills. And because of their role of giving birth and caring for children, girls and women have a more difficult time when it comes to further education opportunities and promotion at work.

Take time and reflect on women's day-to-day realities. In practice, gender discrimination is deeply embedded in our societies and clearly exhibited in our statistics.

> Of the approximately 1.3 billion people living in poverty, it is estimated that 70 per cent are women, many of whom live in female-headed households in rural areas.
>
> —Sustainable development goals: factsheet

Trust me, once you get a deeper understanding of gender discrimination and take a stand, you will also find yourself justifying why the fight for gender justice needs to focus on women and girls. You will know that the scale is tilted in favour of men and boys. For example, 'Nearly two-thirds of the world's 780 million people who cannot read are women.'

— Global Citizen

You will have a burning desire to balance the scale because women and girls have similar rights to men and boys by virtue of being human.

--- ❧❧ CHAPTER 13 ❧❧ ---

Gender, Agriculture, and Food Security

Women do two-thirds of the world's, receive 10% of the world's income and own 1% of the world means of production.

In some countries like Chile and Lesotho, women lack the right to own land. All title deeds must include the name of a man. In most African countries, women have access to till the land, as long as their husbands are alive. Should their husbands die, they lose the access and have no claim upon or ownership of the land on which they have sustained themselves throughout their lives.

Becoming a widow in Africa is horrendous for most women, especially those in rural areas who have little education and whose livelihoods depend on agriculture. Not only do they have to bear the trauma of losing a cherished husband, they lose their land, and sometimes their children too as the family property is reclaimed by the relatives of their late husbands. Lucky are the few who have mature and compassionate sons to support them.

Overnight, widows become extremely vulnerable and are pushed into a corner. They may become homeless, abused, and destitute. Some are hounded out of their homes without their young children, on the pretext that they are witches who killed their husbands. The underlying reason is to grab the property they occupy.

Some women rationally accept the indignity of being inherited by their late husband's male relatives, who are usually already married. These women face the longer-term risk of being infected by HIV and enduring polygamy, which often entails abuse from the existing wives. From a widow's weak perspective, this is safer than becoming displaced or homeless.

All this happens because in most cultures, women only have access to land through their male relatives and husbands. Their situation is similar to that of squatters without ownership rights to the land they till all their lives.

Many women stay in abusive marriages for fear of losing homes or livelihoods. They convince themselves that they are securing their children's future and economic well-being. Land is one of the most important assets in Africa. Having land rights often means that one has access to credit in formal banks. Most families, businesses, and economies in sub-Sahara Africa depend on agriculture.

> The women we see daily tilling the soil with the hoe, [referred to] as smallholder farmers, are 85-90% responsible for household food production and contribute as much as 60 percent of labour on family farms in Sub-Saharan Africa.
>
> —OHCHR, 20TH anniversary

Male and youth migration to cities, in search of cash income, is leading to what economists refer to as the 'feminisation of agriculture' and/or the 'feminisation of poverty'. Women are increasingly left alone in rural villages, acting as single parents with sole responsibility for childcare, food production, and management of land, animals, and on-farm activities.

> 'Women are less likely to own land and usually enjoy only user rights – not owner rights! - mediated through a male relative.' Their lower access to education, financial resources, and inputs such as improved seeds and fertilisers means they also have less access to improved technologies and bumper harvests.

Globally, less than 20 per cent of landholders are women. In many poor countries it is less than 10 per cent. did some research and revealed that women are only 5 percent of registered land owners in Kenya, for example.

— Deere C.D. & Doss C.R. (2006)

Despite the fact that women comprise 70 per cent of smallholder farmers— the backbone of Africa's food security—agricultural extension services do not optimally reach women. This negatively affects women's food production. 'The gender differences in access to land and credit affect the relative ability of female and male farmers and entrepreneurs to invest, operate to scale and benefit from new economic opportunities.' Very often women have no control over income from their farm labour. If that is not discrimination, then tell me, what is it?

Gender inequality is a major cause and effect of hunger and poverty: it is estimated that 60 percent of chronically hungry people are women and girls

— WFP Gender Policy and Strategy.

CHAPTER 14

Gender, Energy, Time Poverty, and Health

The issue of saving women's time and effort seems not to receive the attention it deserves. This might be attributed to the fact that decision makers and planners are not fully aware of the situation regarding women's physical labour.

Until recently, when the Sustainable Development Goals (SDGs) were developed, energy had not been prioritised. Yet it is critical in fighting poverty and reducing gender discrimination. For example, in Africa, we eat hot food most of the time, no matter the weather. The majority of our food is cooked over wood or charcoal fires, but do we ever reflect on what this means to women and girls?

Boys and men do not have domestic obligations in cooking; they may help, but it's an option for them to collect firewood and water. The responsibility is on women and their primary assistants— the girl children.

Access to energy services and basic household equipment would reduce the time spent by women on basic, mundane, and repetitive survival activities. With energy support, girl children would have time and energy to do their homework in the evenings and reach school on time in the mornings

The burden of biomass fuel use is a major aspect of most poor women's lives. It absorbs large amounts of time in heavy work and it can have negative effects on health. Although this problem has been recognised for thirty years, very little has been done about it.

Did you know that lighting permits home study and extends the 'daylight' for girls to do their homework after carrying out household chores? Lighting also increases the safety and security of women and girls, especially in heavily populated, narrow streets, if they have evening classes and have to travel at night.,

> 'There is no way we will come out of poverty if we divorce women from the energy debate.'
>
> —Josephine Ngumba, Kenyan energy entrepreneur

Access to energy and internet, enables women who missed out on education to access internet and take up education by distant learning/e-learning to develop themselves. Also low level female teachers and their students could access and use educational media and communications in school, promoting distance and e-learning education that is crucial for them, given their childcare workloads and limited mobility from home.

GENDER, CARE WORK, AND WORKLOADS FOR WOMEN AND GIRLS

> In Uganda, women refugees collect firewood 8.3 times per month, and girls aged 17 and under collect wood 7.2 times per month. Time spent per trip is 3 hours and the average distance travelled is 5.7 km.
>
> —UNHCR Uganda, 2014

Women and girls take responsibility for survival tasks we all need to sustain households and the community. Providing care to the family, the sick, and the vulnerable, at home and within the community, is one of the jobs girls and women undertake. This is why women and girls should be celebrated as the heroes of Africa when it comes to care. For example, the importance of care became apparent during the AIDS pandemic. These care roles are extremely important and fulfilling.

Unfortunately, sometimes the women caring for others are sick or pregnant. That's when care roles become a huge burden on women, who often feel extremely tired and sick. Despite this, they do not get the necessary support from male members of the family. Where did our husbands lose their compassion?

THE DRUDGERY OF COLLECTING FIREWOOD AND WATER

It's in care that gender discrimination is most manifested, daily and universally, across Africa. The most challenging issue about care work is that it's physically challenging, tiring, boring, and repetitive. It's unfair that women look after everyone else, but when they fall sick, their husbands quickly bundle them off to their parents, consequently relegating the care role to her elderly mother.

As I pointed out earlier, in Africa women are expected to provide hot and well-cooked meals. Preparation of staple root crops, grains, and legumes takes more than an hour of intensive pounding, grinding, and cooking. Then the food is served, and once everyone has eaten, women clear away and wash up. Firewood is another challenge.

> In camps in Chad, women travel an average roundtrip distance of 13.5 kilometres to collect firewood, spending on average 5 hours and 30 minutes per trip roughly once a week.
>
> —UNHCR Chad, Annual Report 2014

There are a few women and girls, the lucky ones, who have access to a grinding mill or water pump. Still, they walk long distances and queue for long periods to use these facilities, which often leads to fights among them. In Kenya, the average weight of a woman refugee's wood bundle per trip is 20 kg (44 lbs). They collect firewood 5.6 times per month, spending 7 hours per trip and covering 9.7 km. In Doro Refugee Camp, South Sudan, it takes women and girls on average 3–4 hours roundtrip to collect firewood.

—UNHCR, Kenya Annual Reports, 2014 and —UNHCR, Sudan Annual Report, 2014

Women and girls' care work is often not counted in statistics, yet it is an opportunity cost for girls' education and adult women's other productive work and self-development —which is their right. Hence care work limits women's productive time and ability to focus on their development.

Jobs in the care sector are highly female dominated. These jobs are notoriously low status and are badly paid. Look around on the status of teachers, community carers and nurses. They often have very low morale and motivation. 'This is partly due to gender ideologies which portray care work as unskilled – as something which comes 'naturally' to women.' These ideologies may be wrong because some men enjoy this role.

—BRIDGE, Institute of Development Studies (IDS), University of Sussex

'I'm a male care worker and, I'll be honest, it wasn't a deliberate choice. I'd worked in local government for more than 20 years but came to a crossroads of sorts when my mother died, my partner left and I lost the house we'd been sharing. I fell into a career in older people's care and don't regret it one iota.

—The Guardian, Social Care Network blog

Most girls drop out of school as soon as they become adolescents. They are withdrawn to assist their mothers with childcare and other care work. For example, if a family has a terminally ill or hospitalised member, a girl child is normally the preferred choice to stop schooling and care for the patient. As a result, most girls do not proceed for tertiary education, where they would acquire strategic knowledge and skills for employment.

This ensures that as adults, women are trapped. They will populate the low-cadre jobs, often as casual workers. These jobs have no security, are not unionised, are low paid, and are often at the bottom of an organisation's structure. The heavy care burden placed on women and girls at home, in the community, and in employment sectors simply reinforces their low status in society.

> Did you know that almost every day, women and girls walk incredibly long distances and carry heavy burdens comprising children, firewood, water and food?

Care obligations also create obstacles to women's full and meaningful participation in the public sphere. This makes it difficult for women to enter debates about social policy, stand as representatives for decision-making bodies, or even exercise their right to vote. The result is that women's specific priorities are often overlooked by the male-dominated institutions responsible for making public policies and allocating budgets. Even when care activities are paid, the work remains undervalued.

> Did you know that many of the tasks that women and girls carry out are repetitive and demanding in terms of time and energy? The activities are tiring and stressful, and sometimes negatively affect health. These tasks include cooking in polluted kitchens, which affects their eyes and lungs.

Some care jobs expose women to risk as they move alone along isolated paths and through forests and rivers in search of water and firewood. They are exposed to wild animals, like crocodiles on riverbanks and carnivores and snakes in the forests. They are also at risk of rape and murder by human vagabonds.

> An evaluation of the Dadaab firewood project in Kenya found that on days when households were fully supplied with firewood, rapes decreased 45.2 per cent.
>
> —UNHCR, Kenya annual report 2014

Like the fight for gender justice, international development can be tough, emotionally draining, and controversial. Despite initial consultations, good initiatives can shock staff badly. I was horrified when I worked with some pastoralist communities in north-east Uganda and northern Kenya.

Did you know that pastoralist women in some parts of the arid and semi-arid areas of Africa silently suffer from miscarriages as a result of drawing water from deep underground, harvesting tanks we set up to alleviate their suffering?

Women end up in fights at the low-producing water sources. These women, because of where they were born, suffer extreme forms of discrimination, not only in their gendered lives but also from poverty, climate change, and marginalisation within governance systems.

Drudgery has come to be the universal and sadly acceptable daily reality of the majority of women and girls in Africa. Surely something can be changed. Men and women can share roles better or identify innovative ways of alleviating the burden.

CHAPTER 15

Gender, Education, and Training

> If it were the custom to send little girls to school and teach them all sorts of different subjects there, as one does with little boys, they would grasp and learn the difficulties of all the arts and sciences just as easily as the boys.
>
> —Christine de Pisan (d. 1430), author in the French royal court

We all know that acquisition of knowledge, skills, and exposure are fundamental for any person's empowerment. Education is crucial for women and girls' empowerment because it enables them to transform their lives and status in society, and consequently reduces gender disparities in the long term. Acquisition of education therefore is a foundation for transforming women's livelihoods and their acquisition of wealth.

The World Bank has been vocal in articulating that women and girls' education is good economics. It boosts a country's productivity and catalyses economic growth and development. Education is also critical to reducing maternal and child mortality, as an educated woman is more likely to develop and practise health-seeking and preventive health behaviours.

Many development reports about girls' education in Africa reach consensus on how we as a society deny education to our girls. I was once privileged to read a research report for the British Council titled 'Gender in Nigeria report 2012: Improving the lives of girls and women in Nigeria'. I was totally mesmerised by how representative the findings were.

The results were the sum total of what was happening in many countries in sub-Saharan Africa where I had lived and worked. It showed that despite all the above benefits of women and girls' education, it is not prioritised by their families and governments. The best most families do is to send their young girls to school through the primary levels. As soon as girls reach adolescence and can be exploited economically and sexually as house girls or child brides, they are withdrawn from school.

The reality is that, for girls, attendance in the primary grades does not translate into excellent academic achievement or direct transition into secondary school.

We still experience relatively low enrolment rates into secondary schools, coupled with high dropout rates and low completion rates by girls. Even these low enrolments tend to fizzle out as girls approach tertiary education levels.

Many girls face insurmountable challenges as they transition into secondary or tertiary education. Parents find the cost of learning unaffordable. They would rather use their meagre resources to educate boys. Girls suffer further difficulties in menstrual hygiene management, child marriage, child sexual violence, teenage pregnancy, low-quality education, safety concerns, violence at school and at home, heavy household chores, and low future perceived benefits.

Since girls do not join secondary schools in large numbers, and those who join have to overcome several obstacles, it's not surprising that there are very low rates of girls' admission to university. There are major concerns about their underachievement in exams, which is linked to their low attendance rates compared to boys.

GENDER AND GIRLS' SCHOOL DROPOUT AND LOW COMPLETION RATES

Girls' attendance, completion, and dropout rates in Africa are alarming due to several factors. As they become teenagers, they become valuable at home for the assistance they give to mothers who have to work. Some work at school and at home, and thus are tired and fail to do homework. This leads to punishment—often corporal punishment—at school, irregular attendance and poor performance.

Some parents genuinely can't afford the high cost of school, which involves formal and informal charges for user fees, books, uniforms, food, and sanitary towels. Family poverty, sickness, and death often lead to inability to pay. Girls face pressure to earn an income by becoming house girls for richer relatives, hawkers, and sales girls in shops.

The long distance and perceived dangers on the way to school can be major barriers to girls' attendance. This is especially true in Muslim communities, which enforce mobility constraints on women and girls to maintain their purity. Other communities just disapprove of secular education or have a preference for allocating scarce resources to boys' education.

Menstrual hygiene management can be a nightmare due to extreme painful cramps, heavy bleeding, lack of access to sanitary towels, lack of water at home and at school, and poor sanitation facilities at school. Girls are sexually exploited by older students, teachers, and sugar daddies, who subject girls to early sex, rape, and defilement in return for money and small gifts. Girls become pregnant, leading to expulsion from school and early marriage.

Violence and threats of violence at home and at school can put off some girls. Parents and teachers may use corporal punishment, giving all types of excuses. Older boy students may emulate teachers' violence. They can enforce 'no-go' areas and other types of humiliating rules against girls, such as uninvited sexual advances, catcalls, and belittling comments. This aggression leads to a loss of self-esteem and confidence.

Puberty comes with its own issues. Some girls refuse to control their sexuality and prefer early marriage. They cannot wait for the start of adulthood and adult roles. Unfortunately, reproductive health lessons are handled poorly at the primary levels.

Early entrance into secondary education benefits girls. Girls can concentrate better in girls-only secondary schools. They benefit from having female teachers for role models, support, and counselling during adolescence. In most schools, there are more male teachers at upper primary levels, and also in science and maths subjects.

CHAPTER 16

Gender, Reproductive Health Services, and Rights

THE CAIRO CONSENSUS

Early pregnancyand chilbith have severe consequences for adolescent mothers including complications at birth, obstetric fistula and death, often linked to unsafe abortions

—Advocates for Youth

Gender is a Choice

In 1994 there was a major international event that was critical to women's health, reproductive, and sexual rights: the Cairo Consensus. Population growth was the top-ranking issue. It was positioned as a development issue linked to poverty, patterns of production and consumption, and threats to the environment.

Focus was put on the low status of women, who were seen to be the key to sustainable development. Development and humanitarian goals were highlighted beyond demographic targets.

- No call for population stabilisation was made, but governments were called upon to provide universal access to a full range of safe, reliable family planning and related reproductive health services.
- Key areas of focus included health, the role of the family, aging, migration, urbanisation, research, and technology.
- Media coverage was dominated by the abortion debate and the reality of the pervasiveness of abortion.
- Women's access to reproductive health services, including family planning, was highlighted as a critical issue for women's survival. Maternal services in Africa, however, continue to be de-prioritised because of the low status of women.

One woman dies in childbirth every minute.

—UNICEF

Isn't it shocking that access to a midwife seems like a luxury to many women in Africa? We lose many mothers in Africa due to preventable causes. This happens because of a shortage of trained midwives and emergency obstetric care services in health centres.

> Did you know that we are losing many African mothers to the human papilloma virus, transmitted through sex, that increases the risk of cervical cancer? Yet the virus can be screened for via Pap smears, and also vaccinated against.

Don't you think health education matters?

> A demographic and health survey of Kenya in 2014 showed that 18 per cent of younger women aged 15–19 years have given birth or were pregnant with their first child. This had a great overall impact on women's education achievement.
>
> —Kenya, DHS 2014

CASE STUDY: GENDER AND REPRODUCTIVE HEALTH SERVICES AND RIGHTS

Modesta was a young woman hardly into her teenage years. Her parents made arrangements for her to marry a rich but much older man, who already had four girl children near Modesta's age. She treated the girls as her sisters. They often the played skip rope and dodge ball, to the dismay of her elderly husband.

Modesta became pregnant five times, but each pregnancy ended in the stillbirth of a girl child. Her sixth pregnancy was of a boy, to the immense delight of her husband, who wanted a male heir. However, it was a very complicated pregnancy and birth. Modesta almost died due to high blood pressure and high gestational blood sugar. Her life was saved through a caesarean section.

The doctor quietly advised her to consider preventing future pregnancies, as next time it could be more dangerous. After the birth, Modesta continued to suffer from high blood pressure and diabetes.

One day as she was going to church, she saw a flier at the local council office. It announced that a family planning team was coming to the village to offer contraceptive services to any woman at the health centre during the coming week. She told her husband about it. His response was that only prostitutes block conception or abort foetuses, because they don't know the father.

Nonetheless, a friend convinced Modesta that contraception was good for her health and well-being. Modesta asked her husband to accompany her to the health centre, but he declined, saying he still needed a second boy child. After much soul-searching, Modesta confided in her eldest stepdaughter, who was empathetic and advised her to seek the services quietly. On the final day, Modesta plucked up the courage, covered her head, and went to the clinic.

However, Modesta was politely chased away by the nurses. She was told that she looked young, and that services could only be given if she brought along her boyfriend, father or husband. In essence, services could only be provided with a man's consent. Modesta was in a catch-22 situation: her father had died a few months before, and she did not dare broach the subject of family planning to her husband again.

Modesta therefore conceived again. Her blood pressure kept rising. She died at 20 years old, during childbirth, which had come early at seven months' gestation. Her son survived.

Her mother and brothers removed Modesta's 14-year-old sister from school and offered her to Modesta's husband as a new wife to help him look after Modesta's young children. When asked by a census enumerator how he felt about losing Modesta, the husband responded, 'Modesta was a very good and obedient wife. I loved her a lot. But, you know, the Lord gives and the Lord takes away.'

CHAPTER 17

Gender, Water, Sanitation, and Hygiene

It is ironic that women and girls who spend all their time collecting water are severely affected by its lack. Consider the life of Zabina; she lives in one of the informal urban settlements in Nairobi.

Zabina eloped from her impoverished home in rural Kenya at age 14. Her soon-to-be husband and homeboy, Yobu from Kakamega, in western Kenya, was aged 17 at the time. He had left home at age 9 to live in the city, and only came back to get a wife. When he came back, he was considered to be extremely rich by village standards. He had a unique, long, green car. It made a horrendous noise whenever he drove past Zabina's home. Everyone would come out to see it and envy the homeboy who had made it in the city. But no one knew for sure what he did or how he had got so rich so soon. Other people from the village had gone to the city only to come back not only sick with HIV, but more impoverished than their poor relatives in the village.

'Such is the mysterious generosity of God,' commented Oscar, the village joker. 'He donates to you squinted eyes and feet facing opposite sides. All at a go!' Watch it, he will go away with a very beautiful girl from here.

Many girls in the village lusted for Yobu, and the boys envied him. They talked endlessly about him when they went to collect firewood or water.

Then the unbelievable happened. Yobu saw Zabina on the road. She was coming back from the garden, hoe on her shoulders, firewood on her head, dirty, no shoes, and torn clothes! He did not seem to notice though.

She felt ashamed, shy, and timid. He greeted her with an air of familiarity. He invited her into his shiny car. She entered reluctantly, thinking he had made a terrible mistake. He must have thought she was Miriam, the village beauty. But no! He was clear it was her he had stopped for. Within a few minutes, he was proposing marriage and promising to take her to the city. He was all over her.

In no time, it was done. He had taken away her virginity!

Zabina was totally shocked, confused and disgusted with herself. She was covered in blood, saliva, and sweat mixed with farm dirt. Yobu dropped her behind her widowed mother's home, next to a banana plantation. He promised to take her to the city if she agreed to elope with him. He was not yet ready to be formally introduced to her parents, as he had important and urgent business in town.

All this was too much for Zabina. She dashed into the plantation, imagining the whole village had witnessed her defilement. Fearing that her mother was home, she checked her out and made a mad dash to the temporary shelter they used as a bathroom.

Fortunately, there was water in a small five-litre jerry can. She bathed, even though she felt like she would never be clean again. No one ever found out what had happened to her.

Six weeks later, she was gone—gone with Yobu to the city. Her mother had gone to an early morning mass and found her gone. As she left, Zabina waved, Bye to poverty! Bye to the chilly early mornings in the shamba (garden)! Bye to dirt and hunger! Bye to the lousy, sweaty boys in the village! She missed her mum a little bit, but not her impoverished rural life.

They reached the city at dusk. The place was abuzz as if there were bees in the air. So many people were crowded in a small place, rushing in all directions with all types of big-sized goods, some in hands, others on heads/shoulders, some being pushed on bicycles and on huge carts.

Yobu opened a small storeroom, similar in size to the one at her mother's home where goats and chicken stayed at night. Zabina was happy to get away from the crowded space outside but was shocked by mouldy, urine and beer stink inside the little space. It was a dump, stinking of sweat, urine, and beer. What business did rich Yobu have in such a place? That was her first dilemma! Little did she know this would be her home, her prison, and her hell on earth for the next fifteen years of her young life.

Zabina had been forced to elope with Yobu because her first encounter with him, inside the green car, had resulted in pregnancy. She was carrying not one child but girl twins. When Zabina discovered she was expecting twins, the jester's naughty saying rang true in her mind: 'Such is the mysterious generosity of God. He donates to you squinted eyes and feet facing opposite sides. All at a go!'

At the age of 14 years and 10 months, Zabina became a child-mother. She delivered at home, her only help coming from her not-so-sober but kind neighbour, who disappeared every evening and came back in the morning.

Zabina had long suspected her neighbour of having a secret relationship with Yobu. But this was no time to think of that when Zabina was being torn apart by excruciating labour pains. She had no money to go to the clinic. The nurses there had wanted to admit her before because she was so young, with narrow hips. They feared for her safety during delivery.

Yobu, the coward that he was, mysteriously disappeared the moment labour pains started. He was a kind man, such a darling, but too frightened by his relentlessly impoverished reality. Zabina had soon discovered that he had no money to his name. He had 'temporarily borrowed' the green car he had used to woo her—without the owner's knowledge or consent. He had come knocking loudly on the ramshackle cubicle where Yobu and Zabina slept on their first night, bitterly complaining. He only cooled down when he was taken to the petrol station where Yobu had parked the vehicle for safekeeping. He checked it, touched it, went round and round three times until he was convinced the vehicle was intact.

The story was that the owner had left the car with Yobu to take to the garage for repair. The owner himself had gone upcountry by bus to see his sick mother. He could not afford the fuel to drive so far. When he came back after two weeks, he was told Yobu had disappeared with the vehicle the same day he left.

In this way, Zabina learned that Yobu had used this opportunity to lure any gullible village girl into marrying him. He was just a poor car washer, but he was cunning too. Sometimes Yobu was surprised that his scheme to seduce a village girl had worked. He now had a wife and soon he would be called 'Ssalongo', the virile father of twins!

—Name for a father of twins

Zabina's home was, of course, nothing to be proud of. The rooms were close to each other, full of holes, and very narrow. She could hear everything going on in the next family's house. Depending on her level of curiosity, she could just peep through the holes and monitor whatever was going on next door—well knowing that some other neighbour could be peeping at her also!

There was no water in the slum. There were no bathrooms, so one was forced to wash inside the house—hence the dampness and the all-enveloping smell in the rooms. You can imagine the challenge when Zabina was menstruating or recovering from childbirth. To add insult to injury, she had no place to dispose of sanitary towels or afterbirth.

Many people in the slums were in different stages of becoming alcoholics or drug addicts. Toilets were few. Those that existed were in a state of disrepair, extremely dirty, and overcrowded. Many people freely defecated anywhere they could squat.

No wonder Zabina developed a stubborn bladder and bowel infection—probably the result of holding back her urine till nightfall, because she loathed the dirty toilets.

Darkness had its benefits and challenges. She could squat anywhere next to the house and ease herself or bathe. She could not go very far—there lurked in the darkness gangs who could pounce on her and rape her. She would be lucky if they did not gang-rape her, luckier still if they did not infect her with sexually transmitted diseases.

There was no privacy in the slum, whether to bathe, use the toilet, dress, or have a family. There was no dignity in the slum. There was no space to dispose of dirty water or blood. There was no protection from neighbours. There was no place to hide

So after the birth, Zabina wondered what to do with two hungry hyperactive children to care for in such a cramped room. There was nowhere to hang the clothes she washed. Where would her children crawl? That was her second dilemma. There was no space to play in the house, and the alleys were so dirty. The roofs were full of waste from neighbouring houses—the so-called 'flying toilets'. People without toilets defecated into little polythene papers and throw those away on top of their neighbours' ramshackle houses.

What if she went back to the village? Would that be better? Could she face her widowed mother, who had stayed on after her father's death to look after and protect Zabina, and tell her why she had repaid her by eloping with the neighbour's miserable son? That was Zabina's third dilemma.

It took her another fifteen years to finally make a choice. It was fifteen years of endless torture, silent suffering, and tender caring for two beautiful daughters—daughters who would finally determine Zabina's fate.

CHAPTER 18

Gender, Inheritance, and Strategic Participation in Politics

Mr J. J. Otim was a successful and popular member of Parliament for twenty-five years. He had stood for five elections and was always re-elected with an overwhelming majority. Then he died suddenly in a car accident, leaving a huge legacy and gap.

He had written a will, sharing his properties equally among all his children: three older girls from his late first wife, and two younger sons from the surviving second wife. When the family lawyer read out the will, Mr Otim's older brother contested it, saying that in their culture, girls did not inherit property. He suggested the girls could inherit from their own husbands when they got married.

This brother connived with other clan elders to go against Mr Otim's wishes and give all the property to the two sons. The brother also 'inherited' the young widow.

Later in life, Mr Otim's eldest daughter, Akim, who had studied law, decided to follow in his footsteps by standing to become a member of Parliament in his former constituency. She hoped to leverage the goodwill, networks, and personal relationships with her late father's voters. She also hoped to assume power and put right the unfair distribution of her late father's property.

Akim failed miserably in the election! Most women, who had all along voted for her father, did not give her their vote. They said her place was at home, cooking for her husband and children, and not prostituting herself in Parliament.

***

African women's participation in politics is difficult. As girls grow up, they get little social interaction and public exposure, unlike boys. After school, girls are expected to rush home to take on household chores like fetching firewood and water, cooking, and looking after their younger siblings.

In the meantime, their brothers are socialising, roaming the whole village, and playing games like football. This gives boys a fair chance to acquire leadership skills, including negotiating, resolving conflicts, and public speaking. Women and girls' mobility is strictly controlled in most African communities, initially by parents, then later by husbands in conjunction with in-laws.

Lately, participation in elections has become quite costly. Since women do not inherit, they have no capital or collateral to acquire credit, so their participation in politics is financially constrained. It's made worse because, with political pluralism, most political parties are dominated by men. They hardly nominate or fund women candidates to represent the parties. Patriarchy is often played out not just at home, but in our governance institutions as well.

We consequently end up with very few women who are experienced, influential, and able to manoeuvre through the filthy political landscape. At home they face résistance from their husbands, neighbours, and in-laws. Fellow women do not vote for them. It is especially tough for women from upcountry to be away from home consistently for three months during parliamentary sessions.

Most women MPs are expected to stay with relatives. No such expectations are placed on men. If you are a young woman parliamentarian, still of reproductive age, brace yourself for a turbulent journey! First, most African parliaments were designed for men. They have no crèches, making it virtually impossible for mothers to get care for their babies during parliamentary sessions.

At the same time, no one trusts a young woman to be surrounded by so many men and remain faithful to her husband. The reverse is not expected to be true. So, in most cases, a young woman faces the unenviable choice between a stable marriage and family, and a political career

---※ CHAPTER 19 ※---

Gender and Employment

Nations that invest in women's employment, health and education are just more likely to have better outcomes. Their children will be healthier and better educated ... So this is not just the right thing to do for us to hold up these women, to support them, to encourage their involvement: this is a strategic imperative.

—US Secretary of State Hillary Clinton

In 1870, the average female teacher in America earned $12 a week, while male teachers earned an average of $35 a week. Even if a woman did the same amount of work, she would get a payment that was only one-third that of a man. Do you think this is fair?

It has not changed very much in many African nations today. You will find that a female employee will get paid less than a male employee when they do the same job. If you do not take interest in learning more about gender you will not know how to change this situation. Later on you will have a rude shock when you start working.

CASE STUDY: GENDER AND AN INTERVIEW PANEL

Distinction means treating people differently on the basis of their diversity: for example, treating a woman differently from a man because they are of different sexes.

Diana and Badru were good friends of the same age, from the same village. They trained together as engineers at Nairobi University in Kenya. Diana was the best in her class their final year. She scored a distinction and was applauded for her achievement by their academic registrar.

Diana and Badru attended the same interview for the same engineering job after university, at a huge flower farm in Nanyuki. Before the interview, they met and exchanged ideas about the job description and candidate specifications. It was clear to them that Diana was best suited for the job, as she met all the requirements and exceeded some of them.

The job was, however, offered to Badru immediately after the interview.

When Diana requested feedback on her performance during the interviews, she was informed that although she had performed very well, even better than Badru, the panel felt that Badru was best suited for the job because, naturally, engineering was a man's job. Badru was more likely to be stable in the job than Diana, who was young and would soon get married and get pregnant. This gutted Diana, as she had no intention of getting pregnant or married for the next five years.

Out of guilt and a sense of allegiance to his friend, Badru commiserated with Diana and hesitated to accept the job offer. Then he met the company CEO, who convinced him that although Diana had performed very well in terms of intellect and required competences, she did not seem very confident and was too young to take on such a demanding job. And the panel couldn't ignore the fact that she would most likely become pregnant within a year.

Badru listened intently, and his ego rose. He convinced himself that as a man, he was better for an engineering job than Diana. He quietly accepted the job, without informing Diana, and cut off all interactions with her.

***

In 1941, the United States passed several pieces of legislation which put an end to the marriage bans that prevented married women from teaching. Before that, married women were not allowed to teach. Once a woman married, she had to resign from her job.

In 1975, the UK Employment Protection Act made it illegal to dismiss someone on the grounds of pregnancy and established maternity leave. Before that, when a woman got pregnant, she was dismissed from her place of work. Can you imagine if you had just got a promotion and then you got pregnant?

The situation is still the same in many companies in Africa today. Don't you think you ought to know a little more about gender equality in order to ensure you do not do this when you become an employer?

CHAPTER 20

Gender, Sports, and Entertainment

Did you know that participation in the modern Olympic Games, established in 1896, was limited to male athletes? Imagine all the thousands of women who had talents in one type of sport or another, and were denied the opportunity to participate. Some people felt this was not right, so they campaigned for women's participation. What happened?

1900: Women were allowed to participate in the Olympic Games in tennis and badminton only.

1912: Women competed in swimming events for the first time. The first women's swimming gold medal was won by the Australian Sarah 'Fanny' Durack, who won the 100m freestyle.

1928: Women competed in Olympic track and field events for the first time. However, so many collapsed at the end of the 800 metre race that the event was banned until 1960.

Imagine if this race had never been allowed for women again? International sports superstars like Olympic gold medallists Maria Mutola of Mozambique and Pamela Jelimo of Kenya, as well as hundreds of other women, would never have had an opportunity for greatness because their talent was running 800 metres and even longer distances.

The gender awareness campaign for equal opportunities for males and females to compete in Olympics started more than one hundred years ago. In 2012, it finally bore fruit, and now women from all nations have the opportunity to use their potential in sports to its maximum, just like men.

2012: Qatar, Brunei, and Saudi Arabia sent female participants to the London 2012 Olympic Games, meaning every national Olympic committee had sent women to the Olympic Games. The women brought glory to their nations not only for being the first participants, but for winning medals, showing just what great potential there is for women in sports.

Today, we in Africa can put down our own history as we join thousands of voices across the continent to highlight the importance of gender balance. As you learn, begin to put into practice the areas of gender balance you will recognise. In addition, change your mindset regarding any negative thoughts you may have had in relation to gender roles for males and females.

---- ❧❦ CHAPTER 21 ❦❧ ----

Gender and Violence against Women and Girls

> One out of three women and girls worldwide is estimated to have been a victim of domestic violence or sexual abuse.
>
> —UN Women

Violence against women in all its forms needs very urgent attention. We all have, as human beings, a responsibility to stop it in its tracks. The unfortunate thing is that most violence is committed within the realms of our homes, the places meant to be the safest for any woman or girl. Violence is often committed by people close to us within intimate spaces.

GENDER-BASED SEXUAL VIOLENCE AGAINST WOMEN AND GIRLS

There are different types of gender-based violence. There are harmful practices committed against women and girls systematically, including female genital mutilation. Child marriage, femicide, and infanticide damage the physical well-being and emotional self-worth of women and girls. Cultures usually regard such practices as necessary, sacred, or beneficial, despite the fact that they are cruel and reinforce women's marginalisation and gender inequality.

During armed conflict, violence against women increases dramatically. Men and boys also face unique and systemic gender-based violence aimed at damaging their well-being, creating trauma.

No matter who is affected, sexual violence is harmful to our sense of human worth as rights holders, and this damage lasts a lifetime. It is psychologically very dangerous. We should all curse it and dismiss it from our cultures. Unfortunately, support often focuses only on the visible, physical wounds and ignores the insidious emotional wounds that gender-based violence leaves behind.

Recently I got hooked on a BBC programme that showed a team of six very courageous child footballers in the UK who had been affected by childhood sexual abuse and exploitation. The producers unearthed how the abuse had happened to the footballers as young innocents. These men, now in their fifties, literally broke down on camera as they narrated their experiences. They had found the courage, as survivors of a heinous crime, to say *no* to sexual violence and the very loud silence around it. They not only told the truth but also shared very personal struggles as they individually and silently dealt with their demons.

As is the case for many women and girls, the footballers had their innocence stolen by coaches and managers, which is to say the very people who were meant to have protected them against sexual predators. These mentors had used their privileged access to children and positions of power to abuse the young footballers. One survivor expressed palpable anger and regret for his failure to inform his parents at the time. Unfortunately, the parents were now dead. Tears of anguish rolled freely on his face.

That's what violence does to all of us—it creates fear, anger, trauma, loneliness, dashed dreams, and careers broken!

Often for young girls, violence is carried out by people they know and trust, including teachers, friends, and neighbours. Sometimes the violence is so horrendous that it defies all understanding of what a human beings are capable of. This is especially true when violence comes from parents.

INTERGENERATIONAL SEXUAL ABUSE

Take the story of Madeline and Gigi. Madeline was a housekeeper living in the servant quarters of a house owned by Emmanuel. He was a rich, highly respected, and religious man who was also head of the fathers union. One day, he found her mopping his bedroom. He attacked and raped her brutally. He threatened to kill her if she ever told anyone.

Madeline conceived and gave birth to Gigi. Emmanuel refused to acknowledge paternity despite the child's immense resemblance to him. Madeline kept silence about the girl's paternity and quietly continued with her employment.

When Emmanuel's suspicious wife asked him he beat her thoroughly and threatened to throw her back to her parents' poor sty, and the wife kept quiet. His two university sons also suspected. They asked him their questions, and he threatened to cut out their inheritance from his will. So they kept quiet too.

Then one day when Gigi was 14 years old, Emmanuel lured her and defiled her too! That's when Madeline decided that enough was enough, she went to police and spoke out the truth. Emmanuel is currently in prison.

This is a very sad story that has haunted me ever since I learned about it. It may stop you in your tracks.

> If you have been complaining to God for having only one pair of shoes, remember there is someone without even feet.
>
> —Jimmy Katumba, Ugandan singer

When I try to internalise such tragic events (and there are many horrible stories these days), I feel immense pain as a mother who has raised four amazing boys and a fascinating daughter. I realise that a man like Gigi's biological father was once someone's adorable baby boy. He was breastfed with tender love by his mum. His parents sang soft and soothing lullabies to send him to sleep. He was a toddler they lovingly escorted to school, holding his hand and enveloping him with security and parental love. They launched him into adulthood with huge dreams and expectations.

Then one day, he turned into this miserable, demonic, sorry excuse for a man who had contempt and zero respect for Madeline and Gigi, simply because they were women. What happened? Why did he see them not as human beings but simply as sexual objects? I am filled with fear, because he could be anyone's son!

I hope that by the time he raped Gigi, his parents were both dead and buried deep in their graves. Otherwise, how would they comprehend the fact that their son had not only raped his vulnerable housekeeper but his own daughter too? If those parents were alive, how would they respond to the demonic cruelty that the dictatorial regime of patriarchy had inadvertently bestowed on them through its absolute lack of accountability? The patriarchy supports impunity for men as long as a man is in leadership.

What about you, as a mother or father?

- Do you abuse, demonise, and denigrate each other and fight in front of your children?
- Do you know that sometimes words can be more violent than physical violence and can leave very deep psychological wounds that are incurable?
- Do you find it tolerable when your children fight among themselves or torture each other?
- Do you show zero tolerance when reprimanding a child who is hurting another?
- Is your home a no-violence zone?

Realise today that you are planting the seeds, watering them, and fertilising the plant of the future, which is called *violence*. As Wangari Maathai would proudly assert, 'When a seed is planted, a forest will grow'—period!

—Wangari Mathai, nobel laurate

> Did you know that according to UN Women, violence against women is the most pervasive human rights abuse?

Lucky are the children who have never witnessed violence at home between their parents. Blessed are the children who were counselled early by their caregivers to be kind and compassionate to each other. Such children will grow up very conscious that violence breeds violence. They will have the conscience to understand that even though violence against women is universal and endemic, they shouldn't be the beasts to mete it out to the world.

In 2002, I read an inspirational rallying call from a prominent gender activist from Uganda which I am sure resonated with *all* women then and, sadly, would still resonate with all women today. She made a presentation at a vigil commemoration as part of 'sixteen days of activism against gender violence.'

When I read it, I found it so inspirational that I wrote it down. To me she had summarised gender violence in all the forms I had heard of, observed at close quarters, and learned about as I grew up. I am sure she was absolutely right when she said she believed she was speaking on behalf of all Ugandan women.

Throughout the world, violence and discrimination against women and girls is practised *with impunity*. This violence severely constrains their ability to enjoy their human rights and compromises their sexual and reproductive health. Sometimes, men and boys are not spared from violence either, especially, during times of conflict and as stepchildren.

> In 2005, UNICEF found that 97 per cent of women aged 15 to 49 had undergone female genital mutilation.
>
> —UNICEF

Do you know of any examples of women, girls, men, or boys experiencing violence? Please share your own experiences and those you have heard about. Discuss them with friends and fill in the table below.

155

Examples of violence against women and girls

Examples of violence against men and boys

***

> The best protection against rape, stalking and domestic violence is to raise men who both understand that women are different, and would never dare take advantage of this difference.

—Wendy Shalit, American conservative writer

1853: The American Aggravated Assaults Act was passed, to increase penalties for wife beating. Before that, if a man beat his wife, nobody could do anything about it because she was 'his property' and he could do with her anything he pleased. Many women suffered severely because of violence in their marriages. Some even died. Yet nobody could do anything until this law was passed. How different was this compared to slavery?

Discrimination against women and girls begins at conception, especially in parts of India and South Asia, where there is a huge preference for sons. Girls are perceived as huge financial burdens for families, who have to bear costly dowry demands.

Approximately 5000 women worldwide are burnt to death in murder disguised as 'kitchen accidents' ... India alone experienced almost 7000 dowry deaths in 2005 and the majority of victims were aged 15-34.

—UNFPA

1900: Two-thirds of American divorce cases were initiated by the wife. A century earlier, most women lacked the right to sue in court and were hopelessly locked into bad marriages. Many died due to torture and beatings by their husbands. But 1900 changed all that, at least for women in the USA.

Do you know that there are tribes in Africa in which it is still legal to beat your wife? They believe that women and small children have the same mind, so they should all be beaten when they do anything that the husband or his relatives think is wrong.

Don't you think you ought to know if this is something that is happening in your culture? Don't you think you can change it if you begin to raise awareness and learn more about the importance of gender awareness?

1976: The UK Domestic Violence Protection Act is passed. It gave police more powers to arrest spouses and increased the courts' protection of battered wives. Women could now get the police to remove violent spouses and go to the courts for sanctuary for themselves and their children.

CHAPTER 22

Violence Breeds Violence

A VICE PRESIDENT'S CONFESSION

I greatly respect Dr Speciosa Wandira Kazibwe, a surgeon and politician, who was married to an engineer. She was Uganda's first female vice president. She he silence on domestic violence during an International Women's Day speech. She confirmed that domestic violence has no boundaries. It has no respect for ones power or authority. She was Africa's highest ranking woman politician, a vice president of Uganda. But she used to return home each night to a violent marriage. 'I am a reference book for other Ugandan women. Everyone thought my life was perfect.'

—Specioza Wandira Kazibwe, vice President, Uganda

She had a professional husband, a meteoric career, and money. Her children were doing well at school and university—and yet she was miserable in her marriage due to abuse. Finally, she felt she had had enough of living the life people expected her to lead. She had broken her silence about what was really going on. Her hope was that others would find the courage to say *no* to the violence that is in so many homes but is rarely spoken about. That is courage. That is compassion. That is responsibility!

VIOLENCE AGAINST A TELEVANGELIST

In 2007, popular televangelist preacher Juanita Bynum broke her silence about domestic violence committed by her husband, a Bishop! Domestic violence has no boundaries and no respect for religious status. She encouraged many religious women suffering from domestic violence in their marriages to speak out and let their voices be heard.

VIOLENCE BREEDS VIOLENCE: THE AUDACITY OF HOLDING YOUR OWN AGAINST ADVERSITY

Our children, girls and boys, are often caught up in the middle of relentless violence both at home and at school. Do you ever wonder why so many people turn into violent spouses and parents? It is because that is the only lesson they ever learned from their parents. They are tuned in to daily violence like watching a favourite soap or football match!

Men learn to batter women into silence. They talk to themselves saying, 'Batter her every day and every week! Batter her every month! Batter her year in and year out! Afterall she is my wife, and I paid a high bride price for her. Batter her until she learns to respect me 'as a man'! And, if those stupid children of hers dare intervene, I will batter them too! After all I am their father; they are from my loins, they need to respect me without question.' That is the mindset of Team A.

However, there is Team B whose mindset is hyperactive too. Team B says, 'Nag him, abuse him, and belittle his manhood every day until he goes crazy! Abuse him until his manhood is shrivelled like a carrot! Ridicule him! Make him jealous! Compare him with other men until he goes crazier … craaaaazy!' What a mindset warm up altercation before the physical blows even start?

It's an old saying that children are to be seen and not heard. Our children are silent witnesses as well as victims of vicious cycles of resentful, vengeful marital anger. Children are often messed up and live within a complex web of insidious sexual, physical, and emotional violence practised by their

159

own parents. They become anxious, depressed, and traumatised. They go through all the emotions of fear, anger, and bitterness. Sometimes this emotional trauma turns into violent retribution or suicide.

Unfortunately, mental health issues are hardly acknowledged by our communities. Nor do our governments prioritise mental health as a major issue to invest in and address.

'STAND UP, MAN UP, AND BE PRESENT!' EVE'S LEGACY TO HER SON

While still working in Uganda with a national women's organisation, I listened to an insightful story of domestic and school violence, as told by a prominent medical doctor friend of mine, whom I will call Zack (not his real name). His story of the violent relationship between Thomas, his father and Eve, his mother, is not unique to Uganda. As I found out later when I led a regional programme in Nairobi, Kenya, it could have happened anywhere in East Africa.

One Monday morning, Zack woke up in an elevated mood. He knew it was going to be his day. He checked his school timetable and was pleasantly surprised to confirm that he had a double lesson of science as his first lesson. Science was his best subject. In the science lab, he could get lost in chemical observations and daydream. In science he went through a journey of personal discovery which he relished. During those science lab tests, he forgot his incessant pangs of hunger and the family destitution that led to so much deprivation and suffering at home.

THE INTERRUPTIVE NATURE OF SNEAKY FEAR AND FOREBODING

In such a buoyant mood, Zack dared to dream. This was the only time he could successfully mute the stealthy, desperate fear that his seemingly flourishing educational journey was just an illusion. The more his parents fought, the more tattered his dream of education became. The fearful voice that seemed to be permanently perched on his shoulder like a parrot told him that some fickle accident was around the corner, waiting to happen. That voice was so powerful that he dreaded the day it would snuff out the luck in his life.

He connected that indefatigable voice to a famously sad day—the day an accident claimed Diana, Princess of Wales. Diana's short but eventful life was eulogised in the song 'Candle in the Wind' as a jewel, a rose, and a very important light which had been snuffed out too soon, too early. Zack wondered if that be the fate of his education.

In the meantime, he decided to focus on planning how to enjoy the upcoming science lessons. Lab lessons were best. The mighty Bunsen burner spewed fire as the students stood by, mesmerised by the incredible changes that happened when a few chemicals were mixed and exposed to heat. For Zack, these were highly illuminating moments!

Briefly, Zack remembered a momentous day almost a year before, when his mother had offered him unsolicited advice in a very mysterious way. Whereas he knew his mother's name, he could never address her as Eve. It was traditionally forbidden and considered a disrespectful way of addressing a mother. So to him, she was always 'his mother.' Why was he thinking of that event now? Could it be a warning from some invisible power? Was it a bad omen about his mother? No way. His mother had looked happy and expectant as she ushered him out this morning.

He recalled the events of that earlier day as if they had just happened yesterday. He had come home during lunch break, running at a terrific speed, and had failed to acknowledge his mother. She had been lying on a mat, resting under the shade of a tamarind tree, feeling dizzy, hungry, and tired after her exacting farming routine. She was shocked to realise that Zack was in a state of blind fear, so panicked that he had not even greeted her as her usual humble and obedient son. What had freaked him out so much?

She looked back at where he had emerged from and saw a gang of boys of his age, carrying sticks and stones. They were now retreating, having lost him, and were arguing animatedly among themselves. She recognised three of them as neighbours' children. They were children of her friends; children she had helped deliver because their poor parents could not afford delivery at a health centre. Her services were affordable; the family usually just offered her a goat or chicken in appreciation.

She waited for Zack to come back and apologise, but he didn't. Eventually she realised he was not coming back. She forced her frail limbs up and went to find out what trouble he had brought on himself. She knew he was short-tempered and easily got tempted into francas. He was a proud boy so he must have been totally unnerved if he had had to fly like a cowardly dog with its tail between its legs.

LISTEN TO YOUR CHILD'S FEARS: BULLYING IS NOT A JOKE

As Eve, walked to the back of the house, an uncanny thought came into her mind. A few nights before, Zack had confessed to her that a certain muscular bully in his class kept picking on him. But he had only mentioned one boy, not a gang! As Zack spoke, he had been shaking like a leaf. He could hardly hide his anger from her. She had silently observed him initially, questioningly.

Eventually he calmed himself and took control over his anger. He knew very well that his mother despised people who acted in anger so he looked away in shame. She never hesitated to remind him to control his anger whenever she saw him lose temper or heard him fight with his two very stubborn younger sisters. 'Calm down. Take control now or you will make regrettable mistakes,' she would counsel him. 'Remember that every time you lose your temper, your enemy wins hands down!' He would also overhear snippets of her wise counsel as she mediated between young couples who had had bulldog fights.

At school, the bully boy, whose name was Wassajja (big man), would pick up Zack's inevitably dirty books because he would place them on the dirty mat over the dusty mud floor, to do his homework at home. He carried them in a flimsy polythene shopping bag (for lack of a decent school bag). Wassajja would maliciously pour all his books on the classroom floor and

162

ask the rest to comment on how 'clean, and neat the clever boy was.' He made incessant vulgar jokes at Zack's expense, to impress the girls. He made Zack the laughing stock of the whole class, daily. Zack couldn't count how many times he had lost his temper and almost fought Wassajja, but for his mum's sake stopped himself in time.

His younger sisters taunted Zack and spurred him on to fight the bully boy or to stop going to the gym after school. The girls were highly socialised in issues of masculinity and femininity. They told him that they thought he used the gym to avoid household chores, and lamented loudly to their mother that it was very unfair, because they got very tired with school and housework and missed out on play also.

Eve had shown some sympathy initially. But, seeing the manipulative behaviours of her supposedly innocent daughters, she reluctantly joined the chorus to dismiss Zack's concerns about bullying by Wassajja. She told him that the next time the bullying happened, he should go back and 'fight it out like a man'. She reminded him that, after all, he was going to the school gym to build his muscles.

Now, having seen Zack chased by the gang, she regretted that flippant advice. Quietly, she found him squatting behind the house his head in his hands, in lonely misery. After unobtrusively observing him for some time, a torrent of tears came rolling down her face. It had once been a very beautiful face but now it was haggard—ravaged by childbirth, fear for her children's future, daily hunger, the unforgivingly harsh hoe, and daily torture from her erratic, brutal, and alcoholic husband. She was an embodiment of the local saying that, 'He who never saw his mother in her youth, wonders why his father had wasted bride price (dowry) on her.' She approached Zack, sat down, and hugged him, before she tenderly wiped away his tears with her dry, roughened hand.

She stretched out her legs and gestured for him to sit on her lap as he used to do as a toddler. He hesitated. As if he were still her tender toddler, she pulled him up to sit on her, even though he was now too heavy for her dog-tired, weary bones.

Sure enough, he heard a *click* as he sat down on her. Filled with embarrassment, Zack tried to stand up again. With her usual tender yet firm unconditional love written all over her face, she pulled him back, saying it was all right; since he was her son, he could not break her bones. Chuckling, she added, 'Don't you know that an elephant never gets weary of carrying her own tusks?'

Zack laughed loudly. When she saw that he was now completely relaxed, she urged him to tell her why so many boys had threatened to kill him.

CHILDREN CAN BECOME BLOODTHIRSTY TOO

Zack narrated how the boys, led by the Wasajja, had waylaid him on the road after school. They wanted to punish him because their teacher had commended him in class and called him the school's leading star. They had initially pinned him to the ground and beaten him with their bare hands. Then Wasajja had instructed them to pick up sticks or stones or anything that would teach him sense. They had jumped off him into the neighbouring bushes.

Zack who was more athletic, also jumped up and ambushed the weakest of them, connecting some powerful blows to his head and chest. When the weak boy collapsed in a heap, Zack had sought out another foe. That was a big mistake! For by this time, the rest were rushing back, angered at what had befallen their comrade in crime. He tried to disengage from them in vain. They were too many and hit him everywhere like a dangerous snake, without an iota of human mercy.

'MOTHER LUCK'S MIRACULOUS ESCAPE

The blows from the huge sticks literary dazed Zack into sense. He regretted beating the weak boy as he became bloodied all over. His tears mixed with his blood and their sweat. His bruised body was a sight to behold! He silently prayed, sought their mercy and was desperately hanging onto his senses when he saw his golden chance to escape. There was a surprise arrival of a team of boys from an upper class.

Zack's ancestors had a saying: 'A surprise has no respect for a hero.' Everyone pulled back temporarily. Zack wanted to make an appeal to the new group of boys to intervene on his behalf, but common sense won the battle. He warily stood up and suddenly, without any hesitation, or giving any explanation, he took off like a bullet. He surprised even himself at how fast he made it to the safety of sweet mother home.

At this stage of his story, Zack's mother was quaking, envisioning what could have happened to her son if those older boys had not appeared. She apologised to her son for her earlier reckless advice to 'go back and fight it out like a man'. Even though he was no longer a boy, he was not yet a fully grown man. He had no feet to stand on in such a situation. He was just her baby boy, pretending to be a man in a heartless, violent world.

She told him to shut his eyes and imagine that they were on a meteoric journey of discovery together. She told him to concentrate and listen, then repeat everything she would emphasise. She said the journey required both of them to dream big, to be creative, to be dynamic, and to be exponentially successful. 'I want you to transform yourself into different characters as we go along.'

She said this would be her once-in-a-lifetime teaching of the most important lessons about human fickleness and mental agility. She had learned them long ago from a kind British nurses' trainer during a course.

***

EVE'S LEGACY

When exposed to adversity, different people react differently. Imagine that a carrot, an egg and ground coffee are all dropped separately into three pots of boiling water. Each would respond to the hot water differently;

Shrivelled carrot and soluble salt

Like a carrot, some people are completely defeated when they are boiled or when salt is put in the bright hot sun. They became soft, slippery, weak, and shrivelled. Does this signal a cowardly failure in the face of a formidable challenge? Why did they allow the heat to take over their lives and render them so weak and vulnerable?

Hardened egg

Other people became embittered and hardened by life's negative experiences, like a hard-boiled egg—but only on the surface! You only have to tap the egg once and it literally bursts, showing its soft and tender egg white and yellow yolk. Does this mean that some people we fear, who showed the tough exterior at first, are mere pretenders?

These are dangerous people in our lives. We may rely on them, only to be profoundly disappointed when we need them. They are even more dangerous if we mistakenly believe them to be our friends. They are often camouflaged like a chameleon or a venomous green snake in the green grass. They are bitter, they are envious, they are malicious, and they are devious but put on a facade. They monitor us as their fascinating, clueless prey. They use their charm to tighten their grip and sink their poisoned fangs deep into our subconscious.

Behold! Deadly piranha ahead

Another metaphor for these people is the piranha. The piranha is an omnivorous freshwater fish found in South American rivers. It is known for its powerful jaws and sharp teeth, which can strip the flesh from a human body so totally that all evidence is destroyed. By the time a piranha-friend starts on you, you have nowhere to hide and no escape. You will be eaten up and rendered extinct!

Remember, you have been the host to a person like this. They have been hiding their deepest fears and malignant weaknesses deep inside your body. So you fear for them, worry about them, and cater to their needs to protect them from harm. You share with them your own deepest fears, dreams, strategies, and plans, which they pretend to cherish. Little do you know that you are giving them free fodder to plot your downfall.

Could it be true that they were harbouring a stomach full of green, bitter bile that they are now emitting slowly into you? Could they silently be feeling miserable and full of malice? The egg exhibits a tough meanness. But surely as day turns into night, such people are pathetic cowards. They are worse than the soft, weak carrots. They are scumbags of this earth. Give them a very wide berth like a ship to ensure your own safety and manoeuvrability.

Versatile coffee

The third group of people react to adversity like coffee powder. When coffee is put in hot water, it does not shrivel or become paralysed with fear. It's not a victim but a victor. It mixes and spreads its wings wide, but has no poisonous fangs. It knows that anger is wasted energy, like burning firewood or charcoal: despite the initial raging flames and superhot charcoal, the end is dead ash.

So coffee reacts amazingly by linking and integrating lovingly with everybody in its path. It does not separate but socialises. Coffee people are like the aggressive, foraging safari ants found in Eastern Africa. A single ant follows others of its status as the colony incessantly moves. Coffee moves likewise as it seamlessly mixes with the dominant water. It forges ahead and creatively changes the colour of the water and the fragrance of the steam.

What an amazing story of a good fight. It's a story of change, inner strength, and defiance. It's a story of abundance, of integration of new forces, and of amazing resilience and tenacity. Like a river, it follows the existing course. It exhibits a flexible, disruptive versatility. Coffee people are usually amiable, compassionate, generous, inspirational, and intellectually stimulating. They do not give in easily. They will step up to the plate and devise creative strategies. They are flexible and will fight whenever, wherever, and whoever in search of their rights.

Coffee people, though few in number, are the celebrated, legendary, and iconic figures of this earth. Similar to Wangari Mathai, Princess Diana, Nelson Mandela, and Steve Jobs, they don't fear change and can go where angels fear to tread. They dare to dream, and as a result, they disrupt the status quo.

***

Zack's mum ended their journey of discovery by asking him to think and repeat all these messages to her. She wanted him to know that life is about adversity and personal choices. She told him to always decide what to be when faced with adversity.

'You will always have to take on managed risks.' she continued. 'Deadly fear and mediocrity, driven by sickly low self-esteem and anger, are like malignant cancer cells deep inside your body. It will affect your whole body. Remember that uncontrolled anger is wasted energy. It's like putting a Band-Aid on a cancerous wound. It never works. In the long run, that bitterness will kill your character, integrity, and personal values. You will become a faceless thing, drowned in your own bitter venom. Meanwhile the bullies will take advantage and maximise your anger to render you even more vulnerable. You will act irrationally.

I repeat, Eve added for emphasis, 'Decide what you want to be, then devise your strategies accordingly. As I see it, today you initially had a chance to escape but your anger and murderous desire to revenge made you act irrationally like a frightened rabbit caught in the full headlights of a car. You also seem to believe you are alone in this despicable and callous world. You are not alone! First, the Lord our God, the one we believe in, is always around. That is why we pray to him. Using Psalm 35, we can ask him to contend for us and fight those who are fighting us. He does not sleep nor slumber. So never muck around. Tradition also counsels us that 'God helps those who help themselves'. So whenever you are trying to run away from danger, as you cry out for God to help, you must also increase your speed.

'Second, remember that people will always speak behind your back. They will gossip, laugh, jeer, undermine, and try to pull you down. Whatever they say, that is their business. It's none of your business. The bullies will sometimes confront you directly and say bad things about your body, your manhood, and your status in life. Stay calm—very, very calm. Manage the situation. Act *deliberately*. You can ignore them, walk away, and treat them with the contempt they deserve. 'Our ultimate freedom is the right and power to decide how anybody or anything outside ourselves will affect us.' What you can never afford to lose are your temper and self-control in the face of adversity. That is the only way you cab really be a man, who shows up, and mans up.

—Stephen R. Covey, writer, leadership

'Lastly, you are not alone. Ignore them. Your detractors are simply an add on, like salad on the main dish, you enjoy the grand child with your child. Its none of your business. Remain true to yourself. Do not worry. 'No one can hurt you unless you allow them.' They will always meddle in your business, and you cannot stop people talking. Ignore them. It will also pass.'

'Many people who talk about you do not even know the real you. People who cannot feel your pain or joy have no right to judge you. Ignore them. The truth of the matter is that the majority of those who talk negatively about you, recognise you because you have something better in you. They silently envy and admire to be like you. Don't give them your precious time. When they realise they can't be like you, they will want to pull you down. Defy them!'

TAKE CONTROL OF YOURSELF

After some silence, Eve continued, 'Do not get confused. I am saying, Never allow anyone to take over your life. No one has power over you until you give that power to them.' Do you remember that book we used read together with your sisters? Remember what they did to Mandela? They hurt his body tremendously, but they could never reach his mind. That was his shield and buckler against the terror they unleashed in his life for twenty-six long years!

'So ignore the pokes and insinuations. Don't waste your time or energy on smaller people than you, on their insults and condemnations. Whenever they jump into the gutter, remember, you are above that muck. Emulate our hero, who said, 'When they go low, we go high!' Step up!

—Michelle Obama, US First Lady

'Zack, my son, you are a very humble, likeable, bright, and compassionate young man, a natural leader. Utilise those strengths that I, your mother, and other people admire so much in you. Surround yourself with a small but supportive team of reliable friends. Our people say, 'It's when all teeth work together, that they can chew meat (Agali awamu, gegaluma enyama).'

—Ugandan local proverb

'Bullies target loners or try to isolate their targets. Push back! Be a consummate socialiser with people of similar values but better talents. Get people around you who will add value to your character. You don't always need to fight your enemies physically. Many times you can use some wisdom and tact. You can disarm and outwit your enemies and win friends when you rent space in other people's hearts. Offer people unexpected kindness, respect, forgiveness, compassion, integrity, and loyalty.

'Zack, sometimes I see you weighed down by thoughts and fears, as if the whole world is on your back. Just stop it, trust in God, keep silent and watch him work mightly for you. Don't worry about me. Don't worry about your education. I promise you that as long as I am alive, you will always have food, some clothes on your back, and the education you desire. I have started some important conversations with a few very trusted friends. Your education is safe.'

Then Eve looked around furtively. She spoke quickly, as if in a hurry to complete her message before someone interrupted her. 'Zack, you are my firstborn child. Unfortunately, that comes with a burdensome responsibility, because you are my hope for the future. I will rely on you and only you in the future—to rescue and protect me and your sisters from the vagaries of this marriage. I am sorry to thrust such a heavy burden on your young shoulders.'

She looked down, silently contemplating the burden she had just put on her young son. She looked up after making a final decision and continued, 'I am confident you are a sturdy boy. You may bend and sway a bit, but I have brought you up well. You will be a hard-working, sensitive, and compassionate man. You are flexible like the tamarind tree in front of our house. You will always sway but not break! That's why I am proud of you.

'Try to appreciate and use those talents and strengths. Become witty and strategic. Use various tactics to defy the obstacles in your path. Choose what you want to be. Do you want to become a weak, soft-bellied carrot? Or a tough egg whose insides are laced with yellow malice and envy? God forbid!

'Or will you be the warrior-like, versatile coffee?'

She looked him in the eye, waiting for his answer. Seeing him hesitate, she urged him further. 'Today you had a near-miraculous escape. Another time, Lady Luck might not be on your side. Choose, my dear son. Now! Because you cannot afford to procrastinate or to be running all the time. There will always be other, probably worse bullies inhabiting your world. Unfortunately, this world we love so much is not ours alone. It's like we are living in a den full of both harmless and venomous snakes, waiting to attack from all directions!'

MANAGE PRESSURE AND KEEP GOING

'You will undergo extreme pressure and be expected to perform under duress. So continuously enhance your leadership and influencing skills. Learn to work well with other people and pull your weight if need be. Take care to protect your character and values always, especially your respect for women and other vulnerable people. *Never, ever lay your hand on a woman, because the day you do, even if I am dead, I will come back to haunt you!* Mark my words very carefully!

Build your mental strength. Be disciplined and never quit! Never! I said *never quit*, no matter what! So keep going. Keep going, boy, until you achieve your goals and dreams. Nothing, I repeat *nothing* is impossible,' she concluded.

Overwhelmed with emotion and at a loss for words, Zack passionately nodded. At that moment a silent message passed between son and mother.

Smiling affectionately, Eve stood up, wiped off the dust, and without a backward glance, went to cook the family dinner. She was content that her abnormally lengthy, illuminating, but hard-hitting speech and layered attitude to life she had temporarily left Zack speechless She was sure that his silence would evolve into deep contemplation, analysis, and decision-making.

> A strong woman knows how to keep her life in order. Even with tears in her eyes, she still manages to say, 'I am ok' with a smile!
>
> —Joyce Meyer, televangelist, WomenWorking.com

It would be an understatement to say that Zack was surprised. He was awestruck and totally dumbfounded! He felt his heart expand to the bursting point. A sudden flow of warm blood rushed to his head in his pride for this 'new' mother. He had always loved her deeply, but he had in the past looked at her with pity, as an unlucky victim for whom he felt great sympathy and love. Whenever he had pitied her, he had wanted to cuddle and protect her.

Today, he had transcended those feelings of care and protection. He wanted her to fly. Today he had discovered that this new mother was a woman beyond Eve, who didn't need protection but a mixture of understanding, appreciation, respect, pride, and love. This discovery was joyous and fantastically liberating for him. It made him question all his views about her. Like someone peeling an onion, eyes watering, he focused and put enormous effort into looking at each layer and understanding who she really was inside.

He was proud of and grateful for her limitless underlying virtues, values and strengths. She was humble, compassionate, and generous. She was intelligent, stimulating, and inspirational. She had a huge, loving heart. This was clear from the number of couples who frequented her home to seek her wise counsel on marital issues.

The more he peeled away her layers, the more he wondered why his father did not appreciate the gift he had in this unassuming woman. Interestingly, as Zack shifted his pity for his mother, it went directly to his father. Zack imagined a diabolical force standing between his father and his angelic wife—a force that was leading his father relentlessly to disaster. It seemed the man would have no peace until he lost his good wife.

Simultaneously, Zack felt that there was a complex puzzle to decipher about his mother. 'How can this seemingly fragile woman exhibit such a remarkable reservoir of strength and intelligence? How and why did she allow a mere husband to treat her so miserably, like Hurricane Katrina? What happened in the past to break her backbone—for her to become this flimsy doormat who cannot stand up to her own idiotic tyrant of a husband?'

He tried to remember at what age she had become this enigma—in her own words, a boiled, soft carrot that silently cried herself to sleep, yet who never moped around. The next day, she would be up at dawn, minding her own business.

Yet his mother was not a hard-boiled egg. She had a beautiful body and heart on both the inside and the outside. She was a resilient and inspirational motivator to her children despite her tragic marriage.

So who was she?

And why was she still sticking in such a violent marriage? Why? Why? *Why?*

He shook his head in dismay, concluding, 'Some things about my mother cannot be explained.' But even as he contemplated this enigma of the woman he called his mother, deeply but uncomfortably seated in his subconscious was the instinctive knowledge that his mother was not an utter weakling. Neither was she a fool. She had made a rational and common maternal-altruistic choice. To protect her children.

On this issue of her children, she had decided to follow the crowd instead of the lonely untrodden path in defence of her children. She had placed her pride in motherhood first. She was confident and had unwavering faith in the rights of her children. She had exercised her rights to beget children. Her role as a mother was no longer to practise her rights, but rather to practise parental responsibility—to love and nurture her children as she mediated between them and their harsh environment.

Zack was mature enough to understand the brutal fact that his mother had sacrificed her life, her dreams, and her future because she was a mother at heart first.

Zack's father also knew that the children were his trump card to stay married to this wife whom he seemed to hate and loveat the same time, since the family lived in a patrilineal society (where relationships are based on the fathers lineage, for example the children's surnames, main home to grow in and inheritance of land). If Zack's mother were to leave, tradition dictated she would have to leave her children behind with the unreliable father.

Zack deeply appreciated the fact that, as a result of his mother's sacrifice, he and his sisters had benefited from the stabilising effect of staying with their biological mother in their formative years. They had not experienced the wrath and malice of an insecure stepmother, as had millions of silently suffering stepchildren.

Nevertheless, Zack wondered whether his mother had properly counted the cost of the pain she had endured and the emotional suffering of her children. Were these things really worth her precious life? What were the long-term implications of the consistent violence to which she had exposed her children? That knowledge really made him feel guilt. It made him feel restless. But he had no answer.

Deliberately, Zack extracted himself from these depressing questions. He stood up, and unconsciously, he emulated the actions of his mother minutes earlier. He brushed away the dust and straightened. He made the sign of the cross, prayed for his mother's health, and walked away.

At the same time, he puffed out and beat his chest. He shouted out loud as if to convince himself. He made a solemn personal vow: 'I will not allow her to die, I will never let her go like a beggar, however I will never make reckless choices like those of my mother. I will always defy adversity. I will never make reckless choices like those of my mother. My mother's choice was good but not sufficient to liberate us from the evil effects of a violent father. The results are not worth the cost of her life. I am going to be an indomitable challenger—like coffee, always!'

The following day, Zack started to develop his first life plan. He noted down the qualities of a few friends he trusted and respected. He ensured they were a mix of boys and girls and came from rich and families as well as poor families like his. All had strong characters.

With guidance and daily feedback from his mother in the background, Zack studied his friends' likes and dislikes. He assessed their characters and values to confirm what he admired in them and whether he would enjoy more of their company. Then he made deliberate overtures to seek closer friendship with about six of them. He would, for example, smile at them, greet them respectfully, and offer to do hard homework with them. He sought their company as they walked to and from school.

Initially it was tough to get the girls' acceptance. Everyone suspected that he was looking for intimate relationships. Nevertheless he persisted and even learned to embrace rejection without taking it personally. He was pleasantly surprised, after some time, to confirm his mother's wise counsel: 'My beloved son, learn this from me today: love begets love. Persistence pays.'

He linked his new friends together and created opportunities for them to spend quality time together. They participated in a few social, energetic activities like music, dance, drama, and football. They became his inner circle of friends.

From that moment, he ceased to be lonely. He was no longer suffering silently. He could talk to someone about his issues. Life seemed to have started working for him. Whenever Zack was down, anxious, unhappy, guilty, threatened, or overwhelmed by poverty, he remembered the advice from his mother.

He would begin by asking himself, 'Who am I? Am I a carrot, an egg, or a packet of coffee?' Most times he chose to be coffee. His group became very popular with the teachers because they modelled good behaviour, had strict discipline, and followed the ethos of the school, including keeping time and wearing the right uniform neatly. The group never got involved in bullying and excelled in class. Other students asked to join the group, but they maintained a strict vetting process.

Zack sometimes praised himself, singing and shouting loudly for all the world to hear: 'I am flexible coffee, abundant coffee, versatile coffee. I am the warrior and conqueror of the world. I am the leader. When I lead, others follow. I am the greatest in the world, like Muhammad Ali. I challenge and change everything in my path like a tornado.'

One of his best friends asked him one day, 'Zack, are you OK? Man, it seems to me that you are losing your marbles and talking to yourself in tongues. Are you trying to confuse me? Are you born again? Or do you just want to convince the world of your unstable mental state?'

Zack told him not to worry; he was safe and sound. He reassured his other friends that he had a personal, great song. The song had strong calming properties. It was his personal miracle lullaby, his way of reassuring himself that whatever challenges he faced, they were not life or death—none was insurmountable.

He told them that the most important story about his life was not that he constantly fell down. The most important thing about him was that every time he fell down, he lifted himself up, dusted himself clean, straightened his posture, and moved on, again and again!

Wasajja, the bully boy, let him be after smugly approaching him one time. Before Wasajja could start his normal tirade of sarcastic abuse, he observed a steely, fearless look in Zack's dark eyes, coupled with menacing flexing of arm muscles. That was when Wasajja knew his bullying days were finished. He retreated like a spineless dog with its tail between its legs.

***

Which brings the story to the day, a few weeks later, that Zack went to school in exhilarated expectation of his science lesson. Zack felt animated like a real strong man, a legend like Muhammad Ali. He was nimble-footed, dancing around and punching imaginary opponents. Despite his small stature, he had toned-up muscles.

Although he had gnawing pangs of hunger, he felt he could handle any feat. He was versatile coffee. He was ready to defy his enemies and change the negative spaces created by the bullies who loitered around the school.

He wanted to do a wee before class, but common sense made him hold it in. The bullies lingered around toilet areas while most teachers were at assembly. 'Those idiots!' Zack muttered. 'They will eventually smell like toilets themselves!'

He shifted focus instead on the upcoming science lessons, where all the bigger, loud, uncouth but less intelligent bullies that made life at school a constant torture– would be cowed and become invisible. Hopefully, the final exams would begin the following month. Zack was confident to score at least a minimum of 95 per cent - he was always a step behind his teachers, his classmates claimed.

He envisioned the day the head teacher would announce the term results at the school assembly. With all the hard work Zack had put in, he knew it would be another happy day to his life. He had remained attentive and industrious in class. Conscientiously every night, he had placed his feet in a basin of cold water and drunk many cups of sugarless coffee to stay awake, simply to revise and complete his homework on time. He had a consistently excellent record of school attendance. No wonder Zack had certainty of coming out on top!

Zack imagined a very positive future for himself. He hoped to become a highly celebrated intellectual, an inspirational leader, a revered treasure of the nation. Perhaps he would work as a senior civil servant in a big government office, with a four-wheel-drive government vehicle. He would own a huge bungalow, living with his elderly mother and giving her everything she had given up to parent him and his sisters.

On this day, there was to be an assembly to read out the names of students who had excelled in the recent mock examinations. Zack knew he had to be one of them. Six months from now, Zack visualised himself being announced as the top student in his class. He wanted to earn the best marks not only in his year group at his school, but in the whole country.

He imagined reading a feature article about himself in the district magazine. His portrait would be published in all the national newspapers, with colourful headlines to describe his potential: 'Zack the National Intellectual Giant', 'Zack the Contemporary Genius', 'Zack Is Every Teacher's Daily Puzzle', 'Zack, Our Ingenious Forensic Surgeon', and so on. What a fantastically pleasant feeling that would be!

He increased his pace to a quick trot. He practised proudly and confidently striding up to the podium to collect his report card. Later, he would collect his result slip from the proud head teacher. It would be like an Academy Award. Everyone he respected, including the district local leaders, head teachers, teachers, students, and all parents from the neighbouring schools, would give him a standing ovation. 'Oho! Who am I to make every one stand up? Me?' he wondered.

But the premier applause would come from his beloved, humble mother. As usual his father would be declared AWOL (absent without official leave), like a deserting member of the armed forces. That did not bother Zack, not at all. He knew who mattered. It was that beautiful, unassuming, but highly-prized woman who loved him unconditionally. She would certainly be there, rolling in tears of utter happiness. Well, this time he would not try to stop her from crying. She would have earned that blissful emotion. His eyes would seek hers out of the sea of other people's eyes in the huge audience. He would put a seal of approval on her pride as a mother and on his joy too.

He knew that on that momentous occasion, all the nasty bully boys who had made his trips between home and school so miserable for so many terms would shrink. Their penises would shrivel inside their fake uniforms like the carrot. He was sure they would not dare look him in the eyes, knowing their shameful results. They had spent most of their time torturing other boys and seducing younger girls instead of paying attention in class. A few egg-like ones might try to stare him down, but he would not cower. Deep inside, he knew they would be hurting and fearing the wrath of their parents.

It was a shame he would not be around to see their punishment directly, but that day would mark his payback time! That would be his moment of fame. That was going to be his 'coffee' moment. He increased his pace even more, a spring in his legs, happily punching the air, singing and whistling.

CHAPTER 23

Gender and the Tyranny of Corporal Punishment at School

You can never negotiate with fate. Suddenly, as Zack neared school, he felt a few heavy drops of water hitting him from above. Looking up, Zack realised that in his eagerness to reach school, he had missed the freak weather signs. It was about to rain!

The wind and dark clouds gathered ominously, and there were rumblings and flashes from the sky. It was growing dark. Agitated, he realised the Monday morning assembly would be held indoors, and most likely the awards announcement would be postponed. What a shame! He put his polythene bag, full of his books, on his head and made a final dash into the nearest classroom.

He took a deep breath and composed himself before he proceeded to the main auditorium for the assembly. Somehow the change in weather had negatively affected him. His mood had dramatically shifted from very excited and anticipatory to sombre like the freakish weather. He walked ever-so-slowly to the auditorium.

In the auditorium, the other students were talking excitedly. The head teacher, Mr Kibuule, entered and cleared his throat. One thousand pupils and fifty-two teachers quieted expectantly. That was the power of his authoritative presence. He was a surprisingly small man but projected an aura of formidable power, authority, and respect. He did not need to shout to make his intentions known.

Today he was very smart, wearing a black suit with a red tie and a white shirt. He was a dark-eyed and dark-skinned man with jet-black hair, and he stood straight like a reed, despite being in his late seventies. He looked a little intimidating as he walked through the rows of children. He was holding the familiar yet infamous 'big black book'.

When Zack saw the black book, he instinctively jumped back as if someone had suddenly thrust a poisonous snake in his face. His stomach did a massive somersault. All his dreams flew out the window. Everything good came crashing down like a pack of cards tumbling one on top of another.

He frantically sought out his group of friends and gravitated towards them. He breathed in and held on to his stomach, which was making funny noises. He remembered the carrot, egg, and coffee story and tried to reign in his fear. He reminded himself that not only was he a boy, he was a coffee too.

He had minimal success at self-control. His inherent fear of corporal punishment came to the fore instead. Try as he might to be a coffee, Zack felt agony and desperate fear. He had seen enough violence at home in his short life on this abominable earth. Many times at home he had hidden behind a curtain or door, observing as his so-called dad brutally hit his mother's body like a housewife pounding ground nuts. The big black book was to Zack the epitome of violence at school.

He knew the negative outcomes of readings from that big black book. It was not only a mixture of missed lessons and lab tests, but also of unforgettable, excruciating body pain from unjust corporal punishment for things he had neither done nor had the power to address!

Zack surmised that the head teacher was well aware of the power he held, as the man pompously and lingeringly opened the book. He cleared his throat and started to ever-so-slowly call out the names of the children who had not fully paid their fees.

181

Zack would forever remember that day as one of the most humiliating moments in his life.

THE LONG WALK OF SHAME

He knew the head teacher would call out his name and announce to all and sundry how much Zack still owed to the school. It had happened before. In most cases, Zack had one of the highest amounts owed. As if that were not enough agony, he had to make the long walk to the podium to receive a five lashes from the cane and to pick up a permission chit—not a good report card! His plight would be made even more painful when the children loudly clapped and booed him.

The chit gave the student permission to go out of school immediately, as if he were a thief. It also had a categorical warning written in bold capital letters, telling his parents not to send him back until he had all the remaining school fees. The school treated school-fees defaulters as mercilessly as if they had committed an atrocious crime.

Given that his surname was Zungululu, Zack knew his name would be called towards the end. And as sure as night follows day, he knew he was in for a very long wait at home before he could resume school. He lost hope.

As usual when in a fix, he started daydreaming and mentally making caricatures of his teachers and close friends as carrots, eggs, and coffee. Then his incisive brain began asking questions. 'Why were so many of us born in such a deprived, godforsaken village? Why do we suffer from hunger all the time, despite digging so much? Is this what they call karma?' For surely, it felt like they must have committed some heinous crime in a past life for God to be punishing them now.

And this was an eternal punishment with dire consequences, collectively for all pupils and teachers in the school. It was only a month from final examination time, and the school was sending them home. Did it not care that the majority of suspended students would miss sitting for their exams this year?

Zack knew that for almost half of the children sent away, this day marked the end of their desperate attempt at achieving basic education, bringing an abrupt end to their dreams of a career in a government office. And before they left, they had to submit to the torture of the cane.

Zack whispered to his friends, 'Why do they beat us like beasts for school fees? We are not our parents.'

'Maybe it is because the cowards fear to cane our powerful dads,' responded a girl named Rebecca.

A boy named Jack had other ideas. He whispered cheekily, 'The dirty bastards enjoy ogling girls' thighs like yours, Rebecca.'

'You are a dirty bastard too,' retorted Rebecca before walking off.

Zack said bluntly, 'When I grow up, I swear I will pay them back!'

Actually, his own dad was not one of the powerful dads that Rebecca had referred to. His dad was a giant physically, but constant abuse of crude *waragi* (a locally made, highly toxic whiskey) had ravaged his physique. He looked haggard and swaying when he walked. His red eyes were fierce and withered.

In Zack's community, a man's power was measured by the number of wives and children he had, plus his material assets, like a car and a house. It was very desirable to have a house with an iron roof, many rooms, big windows, grilled front door, and indoor kitchen with modern appliances. Such a man could host powerful relatives and friends.

Of course, such wealth didn't mean the man's children and wives were happy. Some of Zacks classmates were more unhappy than Zack, despite their material well-being. Some were orphaned due to AIDS and the recent wars. Many of the men had wives who were as young or even younger than their eldest daughters and sons. They mistreated the stepchildren.

In contrast, Zack's dad had a ramshackle bicycle, a two-roomed house made of mud and wattle with no concrete floor, a tiny compound, one wife, and three children, only one of whom was a son. This placed the family lineage at risk. Zack's dad was as poor as the church mouse!

Zack heard his friend Jack's name being called, and this brought him back to reality. Jack's fees and balance was less than his. He looked around and saw the slowly dwindling line of pupils. His unfortunate turn was due. Most of his friends had gone. He wondered if he would meet them outside school.

He braced himself for the physical pain. It was acceptable for the girls to cry, but 'boys do not cry or flinch in fear' was the unspoken motto of his community. Some manipulative girls really made a scene. Their skirts flew up, and they wailed and screamed wildly, holding on to the teacher for long, unacceptable moments. The teachers seemed to enjoy such moments immensely. You could see the smiles on their faces, as if they were daydreaming.

When his turn came, Zack bent down, pulled in his buttocks, and braced himself, again, for the incisive pain of the coiling cane He breathed in and tucked in his tummy. He tightened his buttock muscles, but still the searing pain was too much. To his utter dismay, he shouted loudly and pleaded with the teacher for forgiveness.

He knew he had committed a cardinal sin. For sure, the nasty bullies would use this experience to tease him as a nanny and weakling in future. His teacher wore a wide grin, relishing the power he wielded and the pain he was inflicting. Zack felt betrayed and inconsolable. Tears ran down his face. He got angry and wished he could physically take on the teacher— smash his face into the ground, rub that silly grin off his face, and step on him in victory.

But then the image of his admonishing mother appeared before him, and Zack deliberately tempered his anger His tender-hearted mum had never tired of counselling him to manage his temper. She told him that every time his opponents saw his anger, they knew they were winning the battle. 'You know, Zack?' she would plead. 'Violence breeds more violence.'

Instead he shifted his thoughts, hoping for that elusive day in the distant future when he would go home and come back to school the same day, paying all the fees at once. Were it possible, then he would show his teacher that he was also powerful and not a joke.

But reality hit him again. He knew his damned father would laugh off the school chit and say he had no money to waste on vagabonds. Zack was almost certain that the fees were going to become another heavy burden placed on the already bent back of his mother. She would most likely seek casual work on other people's farms to get the school fees. God, the amount of guilt he felt was unfathomable.

In the meantime, Zack decided he would work on the farms with her. If they both earned money, perhaps he would not miss the exams—as he had missed the science lab today! He feared that some invisible, diabolic person had placed a jinx on him and he would never complete his education.

Head bent, Zack forgot about his friends. This was his personal battle, alone. He dejectedly walked towards home. He did not want to talk to anyone else. This was a moment, like many others in the past, when he would creep into his own wretchedly dark and deeply disturbed shell.

Try as he might to hold on to his sanity, he could not avoid contemplating his shattered dreams. He dragged his feet, pulling his polythene bag closer. He felt like used toilet paper or a deflated balloon.

CHAPTER 24

Mother, Mother, Mother, Where Are You?

As Zack approached, he noticed a raucous commotion in front of his home. There was a rowdy crowd that was increasing in size every minute. People were running in all directions. Some young boys had climbed nearby trees, strategically positioning themselves to observe everything below. Women were shouting; some were wailing and running in different directions. As he came nearer, he started asking neighbours and friends what was going on, but they avoided direct eye contact.

In the middle of the crowd, he saw people trying to separate two men who were fighting viciously, as if their lives depended on it. The heavy breathing, groaning and discordant noises from them made him think of what a journalist had once referred to as a 'tornado riot' among prisoners who had tried to escape from a high security prison. One of the fighting men was dark-skinned. The other was light-skinned.

Presently, the dark, lanky man threw and sat on top of the light-skinned one's legs, which were spread-eagle. The dark one tried to strangle the one below, who was wiggling and bobbing his head like a cornered lizard. Zack crept forward ever so slowly, fearing the worst. Instinct told him his dad was involved. He must be involved. For a moment, Zack felt some pride, and a smile spread over his face. For once his dad was beating his opponent.

Despite being a famed weakling in the village, his dad had a tendency to incite the neighbours' wrath by using vulgar, abusive language. He goaded them into drunken scuffles for no apparent reason. Zack almost admired his father for his unique talent of richly mixing funny, crude, lewd, vulgar, and obscene words against his perceived enemies until he could provoke them into a fight.

Sure enough, Zack confirmed the worst—the dark-skinned man was his dad. But where was his mother?

God forbid, the light-skinned person was not a man after all. It was none other than his mum. 'Mother?' Zack shouted. He struggled to squeeze through the maze of excited people to get to her.

This level of anger, Zack had never seen coming. Despite numerous fights, his parents had contained their brawls within the walls of their miserable bedroom. What had made the difference today?

HAS MY WIFE DARED TO BEAT ME?

Zack inadvertently looked at his mother's nakedness and immediately averted his eyes. As if by a magnetic pull, his gaze met hers. Her usually timid-gentle eyes became wild—blazing, fiery, and intense.

That's when she gave her husband an unimaginably heavy punch directly in the face. Blood spewed out and splattered all over him and her. He seemed momentarily stunned. Could his wife have beaten him? She easily slid away from under him.

Standing up in a bent manner, she struggled to run away and cover her nudity, but it was too late. Zack and his younger sisters, who had left school earlier, had already seen everything. Zack had a fleeting idea that in the moment when they made eye contact, his mum had decided to heed her own advice and become coffee, despite her gendered socialisation. She had committed the 'abominable' act of attacking and overpowering her husband! She was fighting back and would no longer be her hubby's punching bag! But God, what a price she had paid—and for so long!

Like a completely naked rugged doll, she stumbled around dazedly, looking for something to hold on to. A woman friend finally removed her headwrap and managed to cover the bottom part of his mother's body with it. (This versatile piece of cloth is called a *leso* in Kiswahili and is commonly used by women in East Africa for multiple purposes: as a baby carrier, headdress, skirt, apron, sweater, blanket, and so on.) But they were only partially successful in covering her very small breasts. Meantime, some cruder neighbours happily made unflattering comments about her private parts.

It was truly a horrifying and humiliating scene for any mother to go through or any son to hear. For a boy child to see his mother's nakedness was one of the community's greatest taboos!

Zack was sweating profusely and walking around in circles like a zombie. He saw his mother coming towards him. To save her decency and avoid embarrassing her further, he turned his back and blindly ran off, deep into the nearby coffee plantation. This act of instinctive compassion would be the biggest mistake of his life.

He wandered, dazedly wailing. Despite feeling hollow and famished, he started retching violently, as if a powerful force inside him wanted to expel his intestines. But he only spewed forth slimy saliva. Probably he was simply disgorging himself of the grotesque image of his mother in utter distress. Finally, feeling beaten, burned-out, and drained, depleted of all strength, Zack gratefully slipped into deep slumber.

After a long while, Zack woke up. He felt cramped and disoriented, suspended in time. When the day's events started to sneak back on him, he fervently prayed to God to spare him. He wished he could die, but remembered it would kill his mother. He was extremely lonely, tired, weak, and confused. He felt deep anger, frustration, and sadness.

He lay down in the dust and grass, looking up at the setting sun. Coffee branches formed a canopy over him. He was in total anguish. He sat up eventually, shaking his pounding head, arms hanging down dejectedly. He wondered where he was and what had become of his adored mum.

WHY DO MEN BEAT THEIR WIVES SO OFTEN - LIKE CHILDREN, LIKE HORSES?

As usual, he had numerous questions but few answers. Was she badly injured? Would he find her home or in hospital? Had the neighbours finally stopped the mother of all fights? Had someone managed to completely cover up his mother's nakedness? How would he ever look her in the eyes again, given what he had inadvertently seen? Why had she tried to come towards him in her nakedness? Had she expected him to give her refuge and protection, as she had prophesied earlier? What was she doing now? He knew she was not one to sit moping or feeling pity for herself. Why did she not run away, back to her parents? Her marriage was a farce, a comedy, a badly acted tragicomedy.

Why did men beat their wives so often—like children, like horses? Even for Zack, a child, being beaten or threatened at school was painful and humiliating. What was it like for a mature, respectable mother with grown-up children? Did men beat their wives in anger because the men had been coerced to pay exorbitant dowries? Was that the real cost of a mother?

How many times had his dad beaten his mum while Zack was at school? What would he say or do if the nasty bullies heard about the fight and taunted him at school, using unsavoury descriptions of his mother's private parts? Why did society not summarily deal with domestic violence? Why, why, why? He felt trapped in a web of questions with nowhere to run to.

He then started the blame game, putting himself in a virtual corner—rationalising, beating himself up, feeling guilty for not protecting his mother as a man. As the eldest and only son, he knew he had the responsibility to protect his mum and young sisters. Yet he had run away and vomited like a frail mouse.

He vowed that no matter what happened, he was not going to become a carrot. He was also not going to pretend to be strong and hardened like the egg, while being a grieving weakling inside. He swore once again—this time in reverent hope, like Noah building his ark—that one day he would save his family. He would become coffee, overcome his father's brutality towards his mother, and totally change their home environment.

He vowed that today would be the last day his father laid his hands on his mum, and he would make the message very clear to his dad. If his dad dared respond sarcastically as usual, Zack would beat him to a pulp. Thank God he had been practising in the school gym. He now had a six-pack. As a reminder, he did a few press-ups in preparation for the invisible war.

He stood up and, like a man on a mission, he walked home, ready for the confrontation with his father.

Upon reaching home, he found neither his mother nor his father. His two petrified sisters were cowering in a corner, holding on to each other. They explained that their mother had told them that she was very sad and sorry, but she had to leave. She had no option but to return to her parents' home. She emphasised the fact that she loved them a lot and always would.

Amid new sobs, his sisters told him that after the fight, their mother had been followed by a small, rowdy crowd. Feeling shame because he had been beaten by a woman, their father had run back home. In a frenzy, he had thrown all their mother's belongings out into the compound. Suddenly one could see dresses, skirts, half-slips, and knickers scattered everywhere. Children and neighbours competed to gather them up. (Zack discovered later that the redeeming factor in all this was that almost all the clothes had been washed, ironed and folded up by his mother. After threatening to kill her if he found her in his house again, their father had unsurprisingly lounged off to his local pub.

The children were left to pick up the pieces of their lives. They gathered their mother's meagre belongings in a basket and consoled her. Bruised but still defiant, she finally stopped crying and resolutely told them she was going to stay with her now-widowed father for the rest of her life. When the girls begged her to take them with her, she explained that unfortunately, theirs was a patrilineal society, and children belonged to their father's side. Society as a whole would castigate her if she tried to take away her children from their hapless father.

Thereafter she had sat silently on the veranda, sad and in deep thought, hugging her girls very strongly, as she waited in vain to say goodbye to Zack. When darkness came, they heard drunken voices at a distance. Their mother had hugged the girls again and then reluctantly disengaged from them, saying she did not want their father to find and humiliate her again. She beseeched them to look out for each other and accept Zack's leadership and counsel as their elder brother. She made them vow they would pass her deep love to Zack.

Their spineless father had come back home briefly. Upon finding their mother gone, he had said nothing but skulked off again to another bar. He would most likely not come back to his bereft children that night. Rumour had it that he slept around with the women who sold *waragi* (crude, highly potent local brew) and food in neighbourhood kiosks.

For their mother, that was what had finally broken the camel's back, causing the crisis in their already turbulent marriage. Friends had offered to monitor him and to escort her to fight off the other women. But she had respectfully declined, saying she couldn't stoop so low and give credence to the other women. Keeping quiet was her chosen way of treating rivals with the contempt they deserved.

In any case, she was not the only wife affected. Many other women suspected their husbands had meandered the same way. She, like them, feared contracting HIV—the fate of most married women at the time.

When their mother learned of their father's illicit liaisons, she had initially given him the 'silent treatment'. When he persisted, she escalated the punishment by refusing to clean his clothes or warm his food when he came back very late at night. He still didn't stop, so she denied him further conjugal rights and had a blood test for HIV.

He initially scoffed at her, saying she would come begging for him now that she was old and ugly. But when she didn't submit to his erratic desires, he tried to rape her 'as a husband'—after all, he said, he had married her traditionally.

By this time, things had gone so wrong she would cringe when he touched her. The attempted marital rape was also thwarted by the determined and now very disgusted wife. He felt his manhood had been wounded. That was when he had resorted to heavy drunken bouts of domestic violence, late at night or after the children left for school.

This day's scuffle had started as such. She confronted him with the HIV test results—she had tested positive. He became so violent that she was taken aback. Instead of acknowledging responsibility, he accused her of infidelity. The violence had spilled outside the bedroom, to the dismay of their young children and neighbours. The children learned later that their father had deliberately undressed her and spread her legs to degrade her dignity totally. Such cruelty and vengeance left the whole village incredulous.

The three abandoned children huddled together, crying, on the mud floor of their unhappy home until sleep took over. They rolled onto the dirty mat without any cover. They thus provided a hefty meal to the mosquitoes.

If they thought they were unhappy at that moment, then they didn't see what was coming. That night, using her torn red dress, their mother committed suicide. She was just 45 years old. People gathered from near and far to bid her farewell. Everyone asked why and why and why?

The children were astonished their mother had had so many friends. The villagers were ashamed. They could not explain why they had witnessed ever-increasing violence against such a good-hearted woman and never intervened.

Sadly, because of her suicide, their mother was not supposed to get a decent burial. She was instead meant to be beaten with a cane. They would dig a pit below her, cut the rope and burry her in the position she fell in. This would punish her even in death, and hopefully discourage other people from doing the same. However some of the elders, who had heard what transpired the day before, quickly conferred and agreed to defy their culture and bury her. There was thunderous applause when they announced their decision. Eve, Zack's mother, had achieved a cultural change and dignity in death which she had failed to get during her lifetime.

After the burial, people made eloquent nostalgic speeches about Eve, Zack's moher. The elders asked the children to say something if they wished. At first, Zack thought he couldn't manage it. Then he remembered her good counsel to him a year ago to be strong and never quit. He reversed roles: this time, the mourner was the son. He quoted her words: 'My beloved son, Zack, always remember this …' He paused, and everyone thought he was lost. But he continued, 'Violence breeds violence; that's what my mother counselled me last year …' When he finished the story, there wasn't a dry eye among the mourners, irrespective of gender.

Volunteers came forward, offering to raise the children. Again the elders made a huddle. They told the volunteers that after hearing what Eve had said about violence, they could not tolerate her orphaned children being abused or separated. They spontaneously opened a fundraising drive and put all the money in a fund they called 'Eves Purse,' which anyone could access and add money whenever they desired. They asked every mourner to consider themselves joint carers for the children of Eve. That was how Zack and his sisters secured education up to university level.

In telling me this story later, Zack conceded, 'My mother emasculated me. I cannot beat or rape any woman, much as my weak masculinity might wish to. She promised she would come back and haunt me if I did. I just can't, I swear I never will. My biggest regret in life is that I am now OK, but I never even bought a handkerchief or a headscarf for my mother, to say thank you! The world can be such a cruel master.' He sobbed uncontrollably. I was puzzled. I didn't know what to do for such a deeply hurt man who was so strong - looking, at least on the surface.

CHAPTER 25

'It's Not Funny!': The Spectre of Gender-Based Violence against Men and Boys

When you speak about domestic violence perpetuated by women against men, especially in Africa, the first, spontaneous reaction of most listeners is laughter and disbelief. A male friend of mine told me once that it was 'almost comical'. It's unimaginable. We have been socialised to believe that men are invincible, strong, and virile. They can't be beaten and pushed around like women, much less by women. Most domestic violence is practised against female victims by male perpetrators.

Violence against men is hidden in the closets of our bedrooms. It is surrounded by cultural taboos. We neither see nor talk about it. Woe to any man who submits to it. Society ridicules him as a weakling, a nanny, a cowardly dog which has folded its tail between its legs. That is our blueprint reaction to domestic violence against men.

This does not, however, mean that men and boys are free from domestic and other forms of violence. For example, when still young, boys as well as girls are victims of corporal punishment at home and at school. In some homes, it's like a crime to be a stepchild, especially if one is unlucky enough to be the firstborn boy child living with a stepparent. A stepmother especially fears that one day this child will inherit the property of her husband, at the expense of her biological children. A stepfather fears that one day this boy will grow up into a man and fight for his mother's rights.

Many stepmothers work to break any good relationship that could have existed between the father and the boy. Such children are often overworked, beaten, and starved. Their school prospects are blocked and lies are fabricated against them. The goal is for the fathers to hate them and kick them out of their homes. No wonder they constitute the largest population of street children.

When I lived in Kenya sometime back, the whole country was sometimes in stitches over media discussions of the way a particular community of men was being 'disciplined' by their wives, who had become frustrated by their abuse of alcohol. These men were so drunk so often that they could neither provide for their families nor fulfil their marital obligations in the bedroom.

The most horrific physical and sexual violence has happened to men and boys during armed conflict. History is littered with such ghastly violence.

***

Previously, I mentioned the construction of masculinity for boys and femininity for girls as we socialise our children to play their male or female roles in the future. Ask two other friends to tell you what comes to their minds when you mention 'femininity' and 'masculinity'. Write down the synonyms and examples they give you. Based on these words, write definitions for:

Femininity:

Masculinity:

I also mentioned earlier that gender is about power and domination. Do you see any aspects of power and disempowerment in the constructions of femininity and masculinity?

Constructions of masculinity and of power predict men who are strong, hard-hearted, and stubborn. They do not show emotions or cry. Kindness and compassion towards others is looked down upon and despised. Kind men are silly weaklings who command no respect in society. Some compensate with alcohol and wife battering.

Men are supposed to be the undisputed heads of families, securing their families' basic needs and protecting them from harm. This is symbolically reflected in some African societies in the way men and boys walk behind their wives and sisters, often holding a stick to fend off enemies and wild animals.

On the other hand, society's construction of femininity idealizes a woman who is beautiful, well-groomed, agile, coy, and submissive. Women are supposed to be chaste until marriage and to symbolically keep the purity of their clan or family. That's why in some communities in South Asia, families react aggressively to suspicion of loss of virginity before marriage or of committing adultery during marriage (unfortunately, even if the woman is raped). A woman may be beaten or killed because of the perception that she has destroyed the family 'honour'.

In Africa, female mobility, especially among women of reproductive age (15 to 45 years old) is severely constrained, for fear they will commit adultery. As a woman grows older, she acquires a new status in society and is increasingly released from these barriers. In the meantime philandering by men is actually supported and admired; hence their insistence on 'freedom'.

Violence against boys and men during armed conflict is driven by male desire to subdue opponents, possess their power, and ultimately dominate them. This dominance is enforced cruelly in an environment of fear, mostly at gunpoint and under threats of violence, coercion, and duress.

I have read about men's genitals being tied to a motorcycle that is driven away, ripping them off. No wonder the conquered live in fear. The environment is tense with fear, and one cannot freely give consent.

Major forms of sexual violence carried out by men against other men and boys include but are not limited to:

- rape by other men, sometimes using dangerous objects to injure the genitals
- enforced sterilisation and/or castration
- damage to sexual parts, including mutilation, beating and electric shocks
- parading prisoners naked in front of others
- forcing prisoners to commit sexual acts on each other, including incest
- enforced masturbation, sometimes with dangerous objects such as deadly snakes

It is reported that in almost all conflicts in all parts of the world, men and boys have been sexually abused. Unfortunately, due to the universal gender socialisation, most are very reluctant to disclose that they were abused. As men, they believe they are supposed to protect others, not be subordinated themselves. The few who report will often narrate their stories as if the atrocities happened to some other person, not themselves. Consequently, most abused men and boys miss out on opportunities for health support and psychosocial rehabilitation. This horrendous violence is often brushed under the carpet by our very powerful gendered attitudes, beliefs, and taboos about masculinity and femininity. These wars leave our communities full of people with untempered mental health issues. We are all not safe.

> The Rome Statute of the International Criminal Court (ICC) defines sexual violence as 'rape, sexual slavery, enforced prostitution, enforced pregnancy, enforced sterilisation, or any other forms of sexual violence. It is a crime against humanity.'
>
> —The International Criminal Court

Male violence is never critically assessed or analysed in the way female rapes and forced pregnancies are. Sexual violence against women is aimed

197

at power and domination by defying a society's chastity and diluting its pure blood, hence conflicting its lineage. Rape is a way of throwing mud at a society's dignity and defaming it.

Women's femininity is targeted through mutilations like cutting off their noses, lips, ears, breasts, and buttocks, which culturally symbolise feminine beauty, womanhood, and sexual attraction. When this happens to a society's womenfolk, the society is truly conquered, because its male protectors are no longer able to protect their women's chastity, and provide for their precious families.

So when the conqueror demeans, despises, and rapes either male or female members of society, the conqueror communicates a very powerful, dangerous, gendered message to the women in that society: 'Your so-called "male defenders" have been emasculated. They are now nannies just like women, because we have turned them into females either physically or psychologically!'

Of course, the consequences are dire. The defeated army is humiliated and demoralised. It has been pushed into a corner. When it fights back, it is very ruthless as it has nothing to lose. I understand that's why some military strategists believe that when you surround an enemy, always leave them some outlet, a cornered army becomes desperate.

If a society is totally defeated through sexual violence, the defeated society is demoralised and a new order is established. Wow, the things human beings can do to each other in the name of power and domination!

Humanitarian responses are necessary but not enough. International NGOs and UN agencies, through peacekeepers, counsellors, and medical practitioners, often focus all their energies on the familiar, more comfortable, less controversial gender issues of female sexual violence. If this violence is against women, so it is expected! It is sad that sometimes the perpetrators of sexual violence are UN staff who are meant to protect the civilians.

Do you know that in Africa, sexual violence against men and boys is reported to have happened in armed conflicts in Liberia, Sierra Leone, Sudan, Burundi, Rwanda, Democratic Republic of Congo, Nigeria, Uganda, Kenya, and South Africa? It is therefore pervasive. It is outrageous. It is heinous. It is abominable. It is a dark, bloody spot on Mother Africa!

REAL MEN AND VIOLENCE

There is a diverse range of reasons why people stoop so low as to abuse each other sexually, but the most dominant reason is to subdue by the exercise of power and control.

In many cases, domestic violence is exercised upon women by intimate partners. It is often accompanied by its twin, sexual violence. Sexual violence is seen as the ultimate capitulation of a victim to the perpetrator.

During armed conflict, the tables are turned on men. The perpetrators are fellow men. In most cases, the perpetrators are strangers. In some countries, women have also used their sexual powers as an act of defiance. I read somewhere that women in Palestine decided to produce as many children as possible to replace their men who perish in war.

Violence comes in different forms. Domestic violence does not have any boundaries at all. From top political leaders to peasants, there are countless unreported cases of domestic violence against women. The steps taken over the years show that there is greater and greater awareness of this challenge.

Violence against women is violence against humanity. History shows us that no significant change was ever achieved through violence. Those who ruled by the sword died by the sword. Violence has never brought any lasting peace—not in the past, not now, and not even in the future! Some damage caused by violence may be irreversible.

Remember, most of the great souls, iconic figures, and legends that we celebrate today rose to fame through peaceful means during violent times—the likes of Mahatma Gandhi, Martin Luther King Jr, and Nelson

Mandela. One of them said, 'I object to violence because when it appears to do good, the good is only temporary; the evil it does is permanent.'

—Mahatma Gandhi

When a man attacks a woman and violently beats her, it makes him wrongly feel in charge. In reality, it simply reveals the smallness of his mind, the pettiness of his reasoning, and the immaturity of his judgment. A real man doesn't need to beat women, he should simply reason with them.

Real men understand that violence is an illusion. It is a short-term illusion of a solution for a long-term problem. Before acting, 'real men' take time to think. They never engage in any form of violent activity, be these physical, sexual, or verbal. They think of the causes of the problem and the consequences that such barbaric acts could cause in the long term.

I repeat: real men live life with their consciences awake. They desist falling victim to bad temper or unreasonable short-term anger that sparks violence between a man and a woman. The shorter the temper of a man towards a woman (or man by a woman), the higher his stupidity in other human relationships. That's why Pope Francis, in his wisdom said, 'Even today we raise our hand against our brother … we have perfected our weapons, our conscience has fallen asleep, and we have sharpened our ideas to justify ourselves as if it were normal we continue to sow destruction, pain, death, violence and war leading only to death.'

—Pope Francis

It is a shame that in this century, we still have men who believe in violence against women and girls. Real men show real manhood in the way they relate to the women in their lives. It is high time for societies to have a paradigm shift on how they treat women. It is time for men to convert, say *no* to old habits, and embrace new ways of treating each other with dignity, humanity, and mutual respect.

I read that Nelson Mandela went to jail believing in violence, and twenty-seven years later his colleagues realised how he had slowly and carefully honed non-violent skills. These incredible skills were the ones they needed to turn around one of the most vicious governments the world has ever known.

Our socialisation processes divide us into first-class and second-class citizens. Men should never be socialised to live life with a sense of high entitlement, because this leads men to have unfair and unreasonable expectations about women. In the event these expectations are not met, relationships often turn abusive, like that between Zack's father and mother.

A man should never live with the attitude of 'You owe me.' Women owe men *nothing*. All human beings have been created equal by God, in the image of God, to honour him and to be a blessing to one another. Mathew Henry said, 'Women were created from the rib of a man to be beside but from under his arm to be protected by him, near to his heart to be loved by him.'

—Matthew Henry, Minister

After scrutinising gender discrimination in our society, I would like to make a fundamental appeal to all sober-minded men (and women) to be allergic to violence against women and girls. Step up to the plate and make your voices heard. To the men who are part of these regressive practices, I say it is high time to convert. Treat women and girls with the full dignity they deserve. Strong men support women's empowerment—period!

Some time back, I worked as the director of a national women's NGO. An ingenious activist had pinned a poster on the door to my office. It read, 'Strong men support women's empowerment. Are you one?' It got some amazing reactions.

A strong man cannot feel threatened by his spouse's advancement. He steers clear of threats because to him, a threat against his wife or child is the same as an act of violence. Where do you lie?

A real man doesn't slap, bully, threaten, or exploit any woman, even the lowliest housemaid. He knows how to keep his self-respect and maintains his wife's self-esteem.

A real man busts his ass to feed his family. He fights for them. If he has to, he dies for them. He treats his wife with respect every day of his life. He treats her like a queen—the queen of his home and revered mother of his children.

Let men be real men, not copies!

CONCLUSION

Facts don't lie! It's my assertion that the huge disparities in the way resources, workloads, opportunities and decision-making powers are divided among women and men is not an accident. It is a systemic and institutionalised process of gender inequality in all our societies.

There are significant underlying causes of these differences. Achieving gender equity and equality is another big struggle for social justice. It is the same struggle that led to the abolition of slavery, defeat of colonialism, and dismantling of apartheid. Unlike apartheid, which was limited to South Africa, these inequities seem to be global and accepted across the world.

Remember also that addressing issues related to gender always raises people's emotions. Gender is a controversial and divisive issue. It is therefore a very difficult and long-term issue to deal with. It should be tackled from different angles and broken down into age-gender communal realities. It cannot be dismantled by an individual. This must be a collective effort of older men, older women, younger men, younger women, and children, because each group has different lived realities when it comes to gender inequality.

I presume that, having read to this point, you have discovered or reconfirmed for yourself that the fight for gender justice is based on how men, women, boys, and girls:

- must treat each another with dignity, fairness, and respect
- must have equal ownership and control over productive resources, like land, labour, and their own bodies

- must have access to equal opportunities in life, like going to school and getting a job
- must be treated fairly, irrespective of gender, age and class, as human beings with human rights
- must each be treated individually as a person born with inherent self-worth, potential and immense talents
- must have compassion towards each other and willingness to support those who are vulnerable, poor, and/or less able, including everyone in decision-making processes

CALL TO ACTION

Now that you have got some insight about why gender tends to negatively affect women and girls, observe the world around you.

- Critically assess the difference between the lives of women and girls versus the lives of men and boys. Read newspapers and magazines, and note the positive and negative portrayals of men and women.
- Observe events like community meetings, sporting matches, birthdays, weddings, and funerals. What are the gendered differences at such events? Identify areas where change is important to achieve gender justice.
- Write down five differences you see in the lives of men and women that show there is gender discrimination embedded in our traditional rituals, taboos, and myths.
    1.

    2.

    3.

CHAPTER 26

Gender Stereotyping Rebranded

I want every little girl who's told she is bossy, to be told instead that she has leadership skills ... I am not telling women to be like men. I am telling us to evaluate what men and women do in the workforce and at home without a gender bias.

—Sheryl Sandberg, Facebook

The family is the most important unit of society in which gender differences, roles, and relations of power are first taught to girls and boys. Mothers, as the major caregivers, are critical developers of both positive and negative gender stereotypes. A *gender stereotype* is a widely held but fixed and oversimplified view or idea about males and females. Stereotyping involves putting individuals into a common group without noting any differences. Such groupings are often depicted as if they never change.

For example, saying that all boys like football and all girls like Barbie dolls is an act of stereotyping. This saying is not true. There are very many boys who do not like football and very many girls who don't care about Barbie dolls. Gender stereotypes often emphasise a negative message related to gender roles, behaviours, and physical appearance. Apart from their role in reinforcing gender discrimination, stereotypes are also the basis for racial and religious discrimination and prejudice.

Stereotypes usually exhibit deeply seated biases about particular groups. They sometimes depict what we admire, but most often they are a sign of what we dislike or fear in that group. Most stereotypes are heavily loaded with innuendo highlighting sexual, tribal, or racial prejudice.

For example, when you hear people talk about tribes in their country, they say things like, 'People of tribe A like money. They are thieves.' Or they might say, 'People of tribe B are very lazy.' Similarly, you may hear somebody say, 'Men are violent' or 'Women are moody and emotional.' That is not a true representation of the whole group.

It is mainly mothers who train their children. They may train their children to complement each other in their gender roles, or they may encourage old, unhelpful traditions that no longer function in modern society. Fathers, too, as key caregivers and role models, play a role in mediating positive and negative gender stereotypes. Both parents can influence their children to have negative stereotypes.

INSPIRATIONAL AFRICAN WOMEN GENDER DISRUPTERS

African women require role models, giants in the gender sector, on whose shoulders to stand to disrupt disempowering gender myths, attitudes, and beliefs. Unfortunately, many women's stories are never written or told. Many are never disseminated to populations beyond their local context. We only get to know women who take on extraordinary feats at the international level. We may also get to know women who dare to take up strategic political leadership. But we all know there are heroes in every village whom we rarely see. Think about the community health workers who move from house to house to care for bedridden patients. What would we do without them in the fight against HIV and AIDS?

That is why I appeal to every woman to tell 'her-story'. We need to learn from human stories of failure and success. We need to emulate women's resilience, persistence, and resistance to discrimination. We need to hear from those who successfully broke through the glass ceiling and sat on governance boards and senior leadership committees. We need to share the extraordinary feats of African women in politics, in the military, in sports, and in all socioeconomic areas.

Kimberly Anyadike was born to Nigerian parents and named the first African American teenager to fly across the United States, setting an exemplary record at the age of 15. Kimberly achieved this feat in 2009. She intends to become a cardiovascular surgeon after her college education but has a passion for flying aircraft. A cardiovascular surgeon with a pilot's license—what an immense achievement that would be!

Nicola Adams, 29 years old, was the first-ever Olympic gold medallist in women's boxing. In 2012, this black British woman fought her way past a yearlong injury to knock out another female boxer.

Wangari Maathai, one of Kenya's most illustrious daughters, was an indomitable environment activist, a founder of the Green Belt Movement, and the first African woman named as a Nobel Peace Prize laureate, in 2004. She was felled by cancer. An outstanding scholar of English and literature in East Africa said this of her:

Wangari Maathai was an exceptional person. My admiration for her was, is and shall always be unreserved. 'Brilliant scholar, inspiring teacher, dedicated researcher, she humbled all of us petty, self-important 'dons' by remaining a truly grassroots woman. As much at home with the mashambani (grassroots) 'Wanjiku' (smallholder woman farmer), as she was with the topflight scientific celebrities.'

—Professor Austin Bukenya

Nkosazana Dlamini-Zuma, a South African politician and anti-apartheid activist, was in 2012 elected chairperson of the African Union Commission, making her the first woman to lead the organisation.

Ellen Johnson Sirleaf of Liberia was elected in 2006 as the first female elected head of state in Africa.

Other notable African women include:

- Anne Kansiime: cross-culture comedian
- Rebecca Kadaga: the first Ugandan woman speaker of parliament
- Lupita Nyong'o: Academy Award-winning actress
- Margaret Kenyatta: relentless fight for women's maternal health
- Winnie Byanyima, CEO, OXFAM International; global INGO leadership
- Winnie Mandela- anti apartheid freedom fighter
- Graca Machel – child rights advocacy

CONCLUSION

Gender stereotypes are all in the mind. One decides whether one will break barriers in terms of what women can or cannot do. Every human being was created with some capacity to achieve almost every goal they desire to achieve. As the examples in this section have shown, you can work toward becoming anything that you want to become. As one celebrated actor said, 'No matter where you come from, no matter who you are, your dreams are valid.'

—Lupita Nyongo, Oscar winner

CALL TO ACTION

- Form two competitive groups at work, in school, in the village, etc.
- Let each group carry out some research and develop its own list of African women gender disrupters.
- Let each group write descriptions highlighting the extraordinary feats their disrupters achieved.
- Let the two groups exchange their lists.
- Identify similarities and differences. Are there some disagreements? Why?
- Discuss and write down in your book what you have learned (a) from the research process and (b) from your findings.

CHAPTER 27

The Impact of Gender Stereotypes

Gender roles are a social construct. When we attempt to assign strengths and weaknesses to either gender, we literally cut our potential as the human race in half.

—Unknown

The following story shows how people have assumed that certain roles and characteristics should be found in females in general, and certain roles and characteristics should be found in males. People are impacted by their negative and positive gender stereotypes.

ILLUSTRATION OF NEGATIVE IMPACTS

Flora was born into a family of nine children: eight boys and only one girl, i.e., herself. She was the fifth-born in the family. In her culture, boys traditionally tended cattle and girls helped in the home. But Flora and her family lived in town, and everybody had to attend school. There was no herding of cattle any more.

When her mother left home for work, she would come to Flora, who was aged 12 at the time, and say, 'You know you are the mother in the house now. You have to make sure everything is in order. Ensure lunch is ready by 1 p.m. and your younger brothers bathe when they wake up. Fetch some food for your older brothers, because I do not have time. I have to rush out, but if I find anything wrong, it will be your fault.'

Flora was just like a junior mother in the house. She had four older brothers who could equally well have helped with all those chores, but her mother said it was a girl's duty to learn and help in household chores. Boys could not do such 'girls' work'. Above all that, Flora still had to study for school and was expected to pass her exams with flying colours every time.

As if working alone were not enough, the boys never acknowledged her or said thank you after she had done all the work. Instead they would come in after playing with their playmates and make dirty the house she had just mopped. She would serve them food, and they would leave the plates scattered all over the dining table, expecting Flora or her mother to clear away. The home always looked cluttered and messy. As soon as Flora finished her work, she would quickly sneak to her clean bedroom. That was her haven of peace.

What happened? Flora's mother had a negative gender stereotype about the roles of girls and boys. For her, girls did all the housework and boys sat around, played, and waited to be served. Flora was the only girl, and having eight boys in the house was a big burden. Yet all those boys were strong, clever, and able to share the work.

Write two things you do not like about the way gender roles were defined in Flora's parents' home:

1.

2.

ILLUSTRATION OF POSITIVE IMPACTS

Throughout my life, I have never stopped to strategize about my next steps. I often just keep walking along, through whichever door opens. I have been on a journey and this journey has never stopped. When the journey is acknowledged and sustained by those I work with, they are a source of inspiration, energy and encouragement. They are the reasons I kept walking, and will keep walking, as long as my knees hold out.

—Wangari Maathai, Nobel Laurete

As she grew older, Flora vowed to change the roles of all the members of her own family. She would not make the girls slaves while the boys sat around and became unhelpful, irresponsible males. Flora got married and was fortunate to have six children: four boys and two girls.

Their culture did not allow boys into the kitchen to do household chores. Flora had seen how her brothers had become helpless like little babies when they left home. They struggled to pay for an expensive life of buying cooked food because they had never learned to cook. They could not keep their university rooms, and later on their own houses, clean or tidy. They had to spend more to hire people. They were desperate to get wives who would help them with all of what they considered to be 'women's work'. It was not easy. When finally these brothers married, their wives struggled with overwork and little rest because these were not very responsible men.

The so called culture of leaving boys to do nothing and learn nothing of value in the home had taken a heavy toll on her brothers. Flora wished that they had learned from an early age and discarded all of the foolish and unhelpful notions that made them so unproductive on the home front.

With these experiences in mind, Flora trained all of her children to learn every chore in the house. She put a big message on the kitchen door, which said, 'Strong men empower and support women.'

Everyone in the home knew they had a responsibility to do housework. Flora hired a maid only until the little ones started kindergarten. As soon as each child became 5 years old, they began to help around the house with little duties. By the time the last-born was 7 years old, every child had a specific day of the week when they did different household chores.

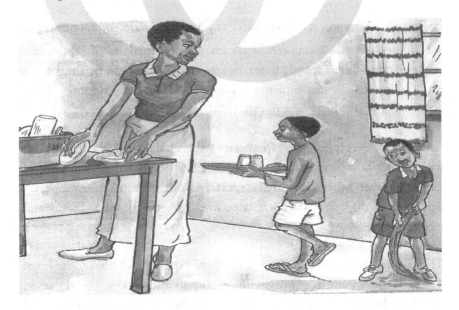

Flora made sure she monitored them. Their dad used mealtimes to reward the children who had done their chores well and on time. For example, he would offer more meat from his plate. He would also reprimand those who had exhibited negative behaviours like laziness.

The children divided up the household duties into manageable chunks, including cooking, washing the dishes, washing the bathroom and toilets, sweeping the compound, and washing clothes. None of them was exempt from duty. Even the little one had learned to carry her own plate to the kitchen by the time she was 4 years old.

Although Flora's husband was a little shocked at the beginning and concerned that his sons would become weaklings, he was pleasantly surprised at how very responsible and mature his sons were becoming. They knew the value of working and the cost of running a house. Neighbours always commented to him about the well-behaved boys in his household. Some even encouraged their daughters to play with them, with the hope that when they grew up, they would marry each other. He was proud of the kind of sons he was raising.

Flora was a happy and relaxed mother. She ran a highly organised home and her children were always courteous to each other. She had time to try out new cookery styles, different ways to arrange the living room, and fix the garden. Her children hardly had time to get into trouble like other neighbourhood boys and girls. Tardiness was not tolerated; hard work was encouraged.

As a result, everyone truly appreciated the challenges of carrying out daily chores and supporting each other. They developed a silent code of reminding each other to say 'that important word'—thank you. Whenever a member of the family tried to escape work or be selfish, the other would reprimand them.

The family always created space for girls to be girls and boys to be boys. The girls spent their free time styling their hair and playing board games. The boys liked active games, so they spent their free time wrestling and playing football. Positive competition developed, not based on gender roles, but on their abilities, creativity, and talent.

What happened? Flora developed a household with positive, balanced gender roles for her sons and daughters. Everyone respected each other. She had learned from her negative experiences in her father's house and had decided to make positive changes in her own home.

Write three things you admire from the way gender roles were defined in Flora's home:

1.
2.
3.

Gender stereotypes can be reflected in the family home, in the school, in the workplace, in the community, in media, and in our places of worship. These are what we refer to as the six gendered spaces (see chapter 10). As the old saying goes, it takes a village to raise a child, I strongly believe that it will take the good will of all stakeholders to overcome gender stereotypes in our communities. I challenge all mothers, as the greatest socialisation agents, to rise to the occasion and inspire families into a world full of equality.

> Equitable, open and inclusive information and communication societies must be based on gender justice and be particularly guided by the interpretation of principles of gender equality, non-discrimination and women's empowerment.
>
> —Beijing Declaration and Platform for Action

WE HAVE COME FROM FAR

Up until the late 1980s, it was a different world. The majority of youth lived in rural areas which did not have easy access to electricity or good road networks. Transportation was scarce. Many African nations were in civil turmoil and had unstable governments. Communication in general was quite poor.

Back then, the average African youth's world consisted of what they were taught by parents, relatives, and neighbours. Grandparents played a key role in transferring oral traditions and culture to the children before they were taught at school by teachers. Children had many opportunities for storytelling, unravelling proverbs, singing, and dancing in the evenings around a fire. They learned a lot from their elders. They also listened to the local radio, which started at five o'clock in the morning and closed at midnight in most nations. It was indeed a narrow and limited world view.

Those who had a national television station had the privilege of watching programming that ran from five o'clock in the evening until midnight. Most of the programming was locally produced a few old episodes of shows produced in the UK and USA were available. This meant that interaction with the rest of the country, much less the rest of the continent or the world at large, was minimal.

After that, there was no other media outlet unless one was lucky to own an audio or video cassette player. Do you remember the way those cassettes used to get spoilt? The tapes seemed to entangle and disentangle into really frustrating knots.

Cultures are products of people, place, politics and history, and change over time. Different people have different views about the cultures in which they live, and within any country or community there are many cultures. Culture and tradition can enable or obstruct, and be oppressive or liberating for different people at different times.

— Susie Jolly, IDS

Simple home-made board games like draughts and snakes and ladders, and card games like poker were popular in some areas. Boys and girls from the whole neighbourhood would huddle together, watching others play. Others ran all over the place, playing hide and seek, cat and mouse, catch, hopscotch, and many other games.

In their games, they learned how to make friends and become good losers and winners. They learned how to resolve conflicts and relate to each other in the gender roles society reflected. One favourite game was creating a make-believe family in which girls and boys role-modelled a mum, dad, and children. It was called 'house'.

The 'mums' got bits of food from their mothers' kitchens and pretended to cook in tins, take care of babies, and clean. The 'dads' issued orders which seemed more like military decrees; they meted out instant discipline through the cane. Sometimes when the group did not have any boys, some girls would enjoy the role of 'dad' and really get into it.

All children collectively had fun until the real mums and elder sisters called the girl children to return home and assist with domestic chores. Boys continued with other games outside until they were called in to bathe and eat. That was the basic African world up until the late 1980s.

From the 1990s on, Africa rapidly developed and opened up to the world. This meant opening up to twenty-four hours of FM radio and cable television bringing international content to the audience on a real-time basis. People became more exposed to a world that they had not experienced before. Books, magazines, theatres, and easier transport made the world into a 'global village'. Computer and mobile phone technology, as well as the internet, brought information to our fingertips. The young people of Africa were rapidly connecting with the rest of the world.

Young people around the world were soon wearing the same types of clothes, listening to the same types of music, watching the same movies, and develop similar interests. No one was left behind any more. The information gap narrowed.

Adolescents up to 18 years old are also holders of all the rights enshrined in the CRC. They are entitled to special protection measures and, according to their evolving capacities, can progressively exercise their rights. Investing in adolescent development is imperative to fully realize the rights of all children.

—UN Convention on the Rights of the Child (CRC)

It is a very wide, very inclusive, and vert different world Africans are living in today. It is a crowded world. Given this rapid rush of information, we were forced to adjust in every area of life—including family, relationships, career, governance, and leadership—in order to become relevant in the wider world body.

Africans were not given an opportunity in many cases to step back and examine the new information that was pouring unchecked into every area of our society. All these changes have had significant impact, positive and negative, on all aspects of our lives.

People began to realise that society faced a challenge in the area of gender equality and balance. We recognised that we did not have a gender-equal society. Change in that area has been really slow or elusive. Some aspects have not changed at all.

While there are gender lessons from overseas that we can learn from, the pace at which information is coming to Africa is just incredible. Gender awareness only began to creep into African societies thirty years or so ago. What is relevant in other countries may not be fully relevant for Africa. The challenges and opportunities facing the typical African family are sharply different from those faced by people in other parts of the world. Yet other countries had standards they presented to Africa, measuring whether we understood what gender and its attendant issues were.

The agenda for gender equity and equality which nations in the West are already enacting is relevant to Africa too, but it needs to be improved and adapted to unique African realities. However, Africa has had no time to internalise that agenda and choose what is good in it. That causes some people to reject everything wholesale.

Some African societies have deep concerns about the issue of gender. They fear that the West, for instance, is endeavouring to develop new sexes and gender-neutral societies. In Africa, this is very frightening. We are at the basic level, where we would like to see women, men, boys, and girls develop healthier attitudes towards each other. I am sure that, as we interact in the globalised world, we shall learn new things and become more tolerant of

216

new genders. But currently, we are guided by existing moral systems and fear of the unknown.

We want our daughters to grow into women who celebrate their femininity and who live in an inclusive environment. We want our sons to grow into responsible men who understand, appreciate, and encourage the growth of a society that is strong and balanced in gender terms.

We want a society in which people of different sexes live and work in harmony—a society which has fewer and fewer socially excluded groups. I see this as a very powerful way of actualising our dream of gender justice. The focus on teaching girls and boys at a very early age, creating awareness and recognition of gender discrimination in all its forms, is a powerful proposal.

A male friend of mine who reviewed a draft of this book sent me very incisive questions. I was overjoyed because I knew he had tried to internalise the messages in the book. He already has two daughters, and I am sure they are blessed to have a gender-aware father who is thirsting for more knowledge. He asked questions, like:

1. How do we achieve this within our cultures?
2. Do we have to segment our society and break our cultures into positive and negative?
3. How do we weed out attitudes, norms, and beliefs that fuel gender discrimination without infuriating our communities into a backlash?

My simple and humble answer is, 'Let's focus on awareness building and education.' Education is key because education shapes the mind, and the will to change starts in the mind. I imagine if Wangari Maathai were still around, she would inspire us again with her words, 'If a seed is planted, a forest will grow.'

—Wangari Mathai, Nobel Laurate

Another inspirational giant of our times, Antony Robbins, maybe would also remind us, 'To be successful one needs to start making those small yet giant steps toward change.' I hope every African will reject the choice of inaction. 'A year from now you will wish you had started today!'

—Tony Robbins, motivational speaker

It is true that the issue of gender equality is not going away anytime soon. It's our choice to start our change today. 'If you run you stand a chance of losing, but if you don't run you've already lost.'

—Barrack Obama, US President

Another quotation, which I am currently using on my emails, reminds me about hope. I am naturally a very optimistic person, so this directly appealed to my heart. It says, 'Hope is that stubborn thing inside us that insists, despite all the evidence to the contrary, that something better awaits us so long as we have the courage to keep reaching, to keep working, to keep fighting.'

—Barrack Obama, American President

Changing whole societies on gender is like a very slow gravy train, but it's still moving. We must embrace the little changes. We must be watchful to learn how to change the way we have been thinking about gender roles. We need to rethink how decisions are made in the allocation of tasks and resources: first at the household level, then at the community level, and finally at the national level.

We should ask ourselves:

- Who—men, women, or both—has access to which products and services?
- How do we, as a society, move from vulnerability to resilience?
- How do we ensure equal opportunities, irrespective of one's sex?
- How do we empower women, through knowledge, attitudes, skills, and exposure, to take control of their lives?

And how do we respond to all questions positively, without demolishing some of the incredibly positive aspects of African culture—the very things that make us the authentic African gender brand? Can't we develop that gender brand into a high-quality African product, a brand to be bought rather than a commodity to be sold?

We must be willing to continue learning from other societies, while at the same time preserving our own very rich, very diverse, and very colourful cultural identity that makes us African. We are made up of particular tribes which must define our fascinating sexes in an acceptable and accommodating way.

I am very proud of my African heritage. The DNA that makes me truly African is intangible but deep inside. I am very proud of being a Muganda woman and wouldn't think of swapping it for another identity. I wouldn't hesitate to highlight the many strengths my culture holds. But I am not comfortable with some elements of our gendered relations of power. Those elements need to change.

I am as sure as night follows day that one day, these discomforting elements will fall by the wayside. I know my culture is dynamic. We can make improvements.

My late dad was very progressive in his will when he ensured that all his eighteen children, irrespective of sex, inherited from his property. On the other hand, I know that his polygamy brought many issues to our family.

The purpose of this book is to progressively introduce gender, initially at the most basic level, to create awareness so that you begin to question the status quo.

I encourage you to consider 'gender compensation', a process by which boys and girls are encouraged to cross artificial boundaries and explore activities or roles beyond traditionally ascribed gender roles. This will yield harmonious gender relationships based on mutual love and respect.

As your awareness increases, I hope I will sensitively take you into the realm of very complex gender issues which will challenge you to address women's practical gender needs. You will be challenged to embrace gender transformation from a cost-benefit viewpoint. You will be challenged to proudly embrace your own gender identity roles while you appreciate the value of other people in society and the genders they represent.

I know very many people who are interested in promoting gender justice, but many of them keep asking, 'What are the tools and tactics for me to use to live a gender-balanced life?'

I also know that gender issues are often buried in complex concepts, which discourages people from digging into deeper feelings that they are unable to openly express. I have endeavoured to help the reader understand that a person's gendered roles are as unique to them as their fingerprints.

Gender is developed and not inherent. My hope is, at the end of this book, you will find gender equality is a necessity and not an option in everything you do and say.

CHAPTER 28

Try Being an African Teenager for a Day!

One of the biggest challenges we face today is the risk of losing a whole generation of unguided, unchaperoned, and unaccompanied youth during their teenage years. Boys are literally going crazy with testosterone raging inside their bodies. Girls are mesmerised with oestrogen, wondering what has happened to their bodies. Girls and boys meet, and it's like the crash of the titans—the meeting of Donald Trump and Kim Jong-un to discuss denuclearisation of this world. They drink, they twerk, they have unprotected sex, they get exposed to lifelong threats like drugs, alcohol, HIV, and unwanted pregnancy. These become the most certain realities of their future lives, undisputed and unchallenged!

We are losing our sense of shock. These things happen daily, and we have started taking them for granted. I want to differ. As a parent, I want to believe that today it may be my neighbour's son or daughter, but tomorrow it will be mine. Therefore we need to do something about it.

Our sons have grown up in a world where they were socialised to be male in a hypermasculine way, without parental guidance. Their being and acceptance in society is therefore linked to power. What is the best way to demonstrate your power if not by dominating as many girls as possible?

Masculinity: possession of the qualities traditionally associated with men – 'handsome, muscled, and driven, he's a prime example of masculinity' – It is also synonymous with characteristics such as risk-taking, virility, manliness, maleness, vigour, strength, muscularity, ruggedness, toughness.'

—James Dobson, Evangelical Christian author

So as a hot-blooded 17-year-old, why would one not exercise one's manhood by escaping from school to go to a discotheque at lunchtime? A young man's morale can be boosted by a combination of rowdy friends, alcohol, marijuana, vibrant music, and hectic dance. However, whereas boys can take on high risk activities to impress their friends, better still girlfriends girls on the other hand think hard about resultant danger.

—James Dobson, Evangelical Christian author

Listen to a group of teenagers talking, and you will hear words like these:

'My almighty mobile and Mr Kash are lovely friends.'

'Of course we will become drunk and disorderly and use vulgar language, but who cares?'

'Our pretentious parents will curse us, but what the hell? Have they ever tried being a teenager in 2018? Do they ever feel the rush, crash and banging of mad hormones? Do they appreciate that when our blood races, it's like a race car whose engine has been tampered with and is meant to win?'

'OMG, she is so *penge*! Look at those pawpaw boobs and bums. The pretenders! Let them hashtag their dreams. OMG! She is so *penge*! YOLO!'

Recently I read a hilarious book about developing one's special brand. The writer took us through the experience of a young man at school, trying to score points on a girl. He mentioned some of the attributes that made his peers deem him smart. These included things like 'having confidence the size of Africa!' He accumulated souvenirs, including 'ties, sweaters, and hairbands, to the extent that one girl gave him her skirt!' He gave advice to his peers on 'how to get them girls' and 'how to develop a six-pack through daily exercise'. As I read, I was in stitches—but then it struck me that actually the writer was describing a universal young man's sense of masculinity.

—Mureithi Chris, Kenyan author

On the other hand, girl children are socialised to be feminine. They dedicated with great love and tenderness, They are intelligent, caring an creative

This connotes submissiveness, superficial beauty, and subordination to men. When I searched for its meaning, I got the following description online saying that: 'Femininity This is the quality of being female; womanliness. They gave an example that 'she celebrates her femininity by wearing makeup and high heels' – It is synonymous with womanliness, womanly qualities.

Consider these descriptions also:

'Femininity is knowing how to listen – men love it!'

—Jane Fonda, actress

You must be meticulous in your clothing, make-up, skin — to be clean, fresh, and nice all the time.

—Sandra Dee, actress, Golden Globe, award winner

Notice that, though these descriptions are not from African women, they tend to emphasise a woman's looks and behaviours that are pleasing to the opposite sex. So when our boys and girls behave in ways that articulate the masculine and feminine characteristics we have allowed them to be bombarded with since childhood, we should not be surprised.

Zackny Carson said to the Kenyan electorate prior to the elections in March 2013 that 'choices have consequences'. Similarly, our children's behaviour is the result of our training. Period. The only difference is that from a gendered perspe.ctive, the consequences are more dire for a girl child if she is unlucky enough to fall pregnant.

With that message at the back of your mind, follow me on this journey of adolescence lest you start judging the youth and forget how you used to be yourself.

THEN ENTERS SOCIAL MEDIA, THE TORNADO WITH A BIG, BIG BANG]

Social media is a fantastically powerful tool for communication. We value it for mobilising people for humanitarian causes, like the earthquakes in Haiti and Nepal. One can also easily organise and fundraise on Facebook, Twitter and WhatsApp for a church conference, wedding or birthday party. Social media is also good for reaching people overseas and keeping in touch with relatives, friends, and in-laws.

The benefits notwithstanding, social media has taken over the lives of modern young people. They are developing artificial friendships based on the number of 'likes' they accumulate. But are these genuine friends, or are they simply keeping up appearances? Our children are developing unrealistic expectations about life and are addicted to a contrived reality.

Our children are on their own most of the time, as we parents chase after the almighty Mr Kash, as they call it. They are in all sorts of adult places which our generation dared not visit, lest we suffer huge repercussions from our hawkish parents. Children as young as 14 are now in pubs. They copy whatever they see and share everything about themselves on social media, with classic negative mental health effects. No wonder suicide is no longer the shock it used to be.

Social media can have debilitating effects, especially on young girls. They may suddenly find themselves in a very competitive fashion industry, where looks and clothes are the basis for humiliation. They are called 'cool' once in a while, but are mostly abused and dehumanised with phrases like 'totally needy toenail', 'fat idiotic cow', or 'ugly dumb frigid bitch'. Our children are seeking and waiting for positive affirmation from us, their parents. But as parents, we have reneged on our responsibilities to nurture them and positively affirm them into assertive, curious, and inspired people.

Our children are very lonely. Through the media, (like TV, internet, music, radio and advertisements) the unguided youths pick up the wrong lifestyles and people as their role models.

That's why they have shifted their attention to strangers instead of their parents. And they receive none of their expectations! We parents are not there; we are just an illusion or fantasy. We are like a passing soft wind. We are invisible but felt strongly. We have left no mark but dust. Our children don't know us! Instead they have peers' and strangers' insults, which they deeply internalise in their psyches.

These messages and friends from social media have become our children's undiluted realities. This has a huge impact on girls' sense of self-esteem and self-worth. Everything that they see and hear is based on physical beauty, body size, and sexual submission. Their minds are twisted so much that some believe they can score points through the ability to shock with nude selfies and live sex tapes. Alternatively, they may get access to such images of their supposed 'enemies' and use those images to embarrass, intimidate, and ultimately silence them.

Through social media, girls make comparisons and adopt negative, competitive stereotypes and behaviour. Who has the most likes? Who has the best body? Who has attracted the largest number of sex-hungry boys with errant hormones all over the place, wishing to plant their wild oats? Then they face the challenge of managing strange people's abusive attitudes and behaviours publicly, without parental support. In the process, they are also learning cowardly behaviour, hiding behind anonymity to abuse each other.

In Western countries especially, suicide as result of social media abuse by trolls is becoming a common, frightening reality. I recently listened to a BBC documentary about 'waited adults'—youths who seem to be constantly waiting for something peculiar yet ordinary to happen, delaying adulthood. It sounded so queer and so tantalisingly insane!

As I reflect on the relationships between girls and boys, I recognise that my four sons and one daughter are growing up in a world that is totally different from the one I experienced before the 1980s.

Some time ago in Africa, police arrested more than two hundred young people in the shoddy suburbs of a city, in a series of discotheques, at the lunch hour. That number could form the whole student population in a small private high school. One wonders, how did they manage to mobilise themselves in such large numbers? I am tempted to blame social media. But the real questions are:

- What were our children doing in a discotheque instead of being in school?
- Where were all the caregivers? The teachers at the school?
- What were the parents doing?
- What had the teachers written in the attendance registers?
- Had teachers informed the parents of this mysterious exodus from classes and/or dormitories?
- What about the community? Why had they turned a blind eye? Or do we no longer practise the old tradition in which a child in Africa is reared by the whole community?
- Was this a one-off, crazy-day occurrence? Or is it systemic?
- Who was economically exploiting and benefiting from our children's innocence?

Such incidents are glaring examples that we are no longer looking out for our children. But it's just the tip of the iceberg. We no longer mediate the dangerous world to our children. In my youth, and that of my parents' generation, our mothers and fathers never brought the lantern towards us to burn us, simply because we were crawling towards it. They would stand firmly between the lantern (i.e., the harsh environment) and our innocence to explain the dangers and consequences of our actions.

In those days, when the only destiny for girls was marriage—and a girls was expected to be a virgin until marriage—girl children were an especially protected species. Mobility was heavily constrained. Parents, neighbours, and the community combined to monitor where their children went. They were very caring, to the verge of exhibiting madness and meanness!

Before you judge that teenager, and before you judge that boy for your daughter's pregnancy, calm down. Honestly ask yourself, 'Did I play my parental role effectively? Are there things I could have done differently?' Rather than beating your daughter up, ask, 'As a parent, how do I support my child now, in this condition?' Think about more than your anger at lost school fees, your disappointment, and the snide comments of neighbours, friends, and relatives.

What has happened to my generation of parents? I agree the economy has gone awry. Chasing after jobs and money seems to be the big elephant in the room. It is great and honourable to provide for one's children, but at what cost are we doing this? What is the value of big money when we are losing our children, our future, to alcohol, drugs, cradle-snatchers, AIDS, abortion, and crime?

Our youth, boys and girls alike, are living an illusion. They are confused and literally going crazy. They want to find their destiny. They search for their purpose in life. They want to contribute to the world in a big way, for they have *big* dreams.

PARENTAL RESPONSIBILITY

But they wonder whether they are growing up in fairy-tale land. They miss their parents greatly and have no guidance or role models to emulate. They are trying to be good, but their surroundings and attractions are too powerful for them to resist. So they sway relentlessly from one side to another. They are locked in a maze.

Dear parent, as you host that birthday party, that graduation at home, do you bother to ensure your child does not get exposed to alcohol? Do you pay attention to who talks to them? Do you deliberately stay sober and move around like a matron in a boarding school, monitoring effectively so that you know what is happening to your children?

Do you talk to them and warn them in advance not trust everyone who smiles at them or flatters them about their 'mature' looks? Do you tell them to beware any visitor with a big bottle, smooth flirtation, and flattering language? Do you discourage their naive responses in such situations? Do you warn them against entering empty rooms where they could become entrapped? Do you question their ability to trust at that age?

Remember, teens get defiled or raped on such occasions. Most children who are sexually attacked experience these attacks at home, committed by close relatives and friends of the family—under your very nose. The majority of victims are coerced into silence through threats of violence to them or to you, the parent.

Our children have immense periods of 'nothingness'—blank spaces filled with boredom. They are also under extreme pressure from peers to conform, to be accepted, to be part of the 'gang'. Under the influence of powerful social media, they dare to experiment with sex, alcohol, and drugs.

LOCKED IN A CHILDHOOD MAZE OF ANXIETY AND FEAR

Instead of feeling more mature, young people are thrown into a maze of anxiety, fear, and depression as a result of this premature sex. The boys feel incapable and unfulfilled, not knowing whether they did it 'right'. Girls battle with fear of the possibility of unwanted pregnancy. What a mess! They are bowed down heavily by these diverse social and economic pressures. They believe it's 'cool' to have sex early, but as soon as they try it, it becomes 'so uncool'.

We should wake up as parents and play our role. We must stop behaving like ostriches, burying our heads in the sand and assuming sex, alcohol, and drugs are for adults only—or maybe other people's children and not ours. Wake up! Sex, alcohol, and drugs entered your home long ago. They did not use the front door, so don't check there. When they knocked quietly on the back door or bedroom window, your expectant son and innocent-looking daughter sneaked them inside. Over time, they have gained confidence and are comfortably seated in your sitting room. They choose when to go in and out of your bedroom, using your children as couriers.

Probably as you read this book, your uninvited visitors are looming large in your house. They are like the proverbial elephant in the room, and you have the unenviable task of chucking it out—but how? You love your children as much as you hate their drug habits. But these have become one and the same. Your situation is like the dilemma the Baganda refer to: you have found a huge, poisonous snake coiled in your cooking pot. If you hit it, you will break the pot and can no longer eat. If you spare it, you will be at high risk and you will still have nowhere to cook, so you will not eat. Either way, you will starve. What a task! What a predicament! It's not only disgusting but scary too!

Wow! Wake up and start to frankly and boldly have those hard, open, straight talks with your demure-looking daughter. Don't spare her the gory details and facts. Spare me the decency; this is a life-or-death issue. It's called 'tough love'. For all you know, she may have become sexually active at 11 years old, introduced to illicit sex by your pot-bellied neighbour, your younger brother, your houseboy. Ask the right questions. Challenge and question even further. Know that in this hashtag generation, our children may be more exposed, worldly, and intelligent than we are. Before you give an answer to their questions, they have already visited Google and got an answer, just in case boring Dad or Mum is ignorant—or worse, curious. So be firm and make no apologies for reining in your truant teens.

Housegirls and houseboys may be your surrogate mothers and fathers, but they will never take full responsibility for your children's parenting. I know a case where the watchmen at the gate were the suppliers of drugs to children of a well-respected, decent couple. Do you monitor your child's interactions with the employees in your compound? What about those who take them to school and pick them up?

I am not saying you should lose trust in all your employees, but trust must be earned. As the saying goes, 'Prevention is better than cure.' I remember a popular local drama when HIV and AIDS had just hit Uganda. One of the actors said that as you walked on busy Kampala streets, you could silently count 1, 2, 3, 4 … and assume that every fifth person you met was already infected with HIV and AIDs!

Imagine how scary that situation was. Anyone can exploit and abuse your gullible daughters or tough-looking, yet naïve sons. Be on the lookout. Don't leave anything to chance. It's not a crime to monitor and protect your own!

TAKE THE DRIVER'S SEAT

Of course, local leaders who allow dingy clubs and discotheques to lure minors during the day are also responsible. Nevertheless, parents, remember that the buck stops with us. The rest of society simply supports us. They do not take responsibility to nurture and bring up responsible youths.

Imagine you are on a long journey, and your vehicle breaks down near an isolated African town. You know nobody and cannot communicate in the local language. Aha, the African communal spirit that is so generous suddenly takes centre stage. People gather around you and try to guide you. Maybe it's a mechanical problem; they will guide you to the local mechanic. Or maybe the battery has run down; they will all push until the vehicle starts. Someone else may even sit in the driver's seat temporarily to achieve this urgent communal goal.

Now tell me—what happens when the vehicle starts? Well, you enter the vehicle. You take the driver's seat. You continue with your journey, because when people help you, they do not become responsible for your car and journey.

That is the same as being a parent to a potentially truant teenager.

The community, teachers, neighbours, and government officials (e.g police) are like kind African villagers. They may push your vehicle—the truant son or daughter. Teachers will try to discipline your child using school rules, regulations, and codes of conduct. Neighbours may counsel your child and threaten to report them to you. Government will make deterrent laws and policies that govern the schools.

But when push comes to shove, you take the driver's seat. You drive to your destination. You are the only one responsible for taming your child's truancy and ensure he/she focuses on working towards his/her destiny. Driving on rough terrain would be easier if you started your journey early, before it rains. Another Baganda proverb says, 'When a tree gets bent in infancy, trying to straighten it in maturity is futile. It will simply break.'

For a girl child, ensure you build her self-esteem and feelings of adequacy so that she will be confident when the she becomes a high achiever later on in life. Positively affirm her and let her know that she is beautiful, intelligent, and capable in her own right, both externally and internally. For example, Madonna said that 'I have an iron will but feel that inadequacy-being inadequate and mediocre.' Similarly, Oprah Winfrey said that, 'I discovered I was adequate, have an incredible career, but no life. What we see on TV is often a façade.' So ensure your daughter does not seek confirmation from strangers or from boys in the neighbourhood. Let her know how precious her virginity is, not to be taken by any Tom, Dick, or Harry and at the risk of unplanned pregnancy.

—James Dobson, Evangelical Christian author

We now have many depressed young people. Really? At that age? How can we support our girls to withstand all the pressures in their lives? They have household chores which are repetitive. They have siblings to care for like surrogate mums. They experience taunts and abuse from other girls, coupled with pressure to look beautiful. They endure jibes, humiliating remarks, flirting, and sexual approaches from the boys, teachers, and sugar daddies. They suffer corporal punishment at home and at school. It's tough, very tough!

Let's agree: no matter how much we parent, young people have to go through that phase of exploration, when they do not care what impact they create. If we are frank, we did outrageous things at that age too. We were no angels. Maybe sharing some of our own experience with our children may break that communication barrier.

THE JOY OF CHILDHOOD

Young people have to have fun and enjoy being young before they become adults with all types of responsibilities. Yes, young people can find fun even in very important issues. Imagine that a youth sent the following WhatsApp message to friends after HIV awareness training: 'It's from the deepest pit that one begins to climb the highest mountains. As for those people who keep going for HIV testing every three months, don't worry. One day you will find what you are looking for.'

Or how about the adolescent who decided to prank her mother when she sent her the following message: 'My mum said, "Follow your dreams." So I went back to bed'

How would you respond to that?

Some time back, after elections in Tanzania, a tongue-in-cheek message trended on Whatsapp in the region: 'Tanzanians need to be investigated. Acting all calm and especially so mature during and after the election. Are they even Africans?'

Of course you can imagine where that came from. Uganda? Present, sir! Kenya? Present, sir!

Forgive me if I imagined wrongly that it's only a youth who could dare say that. I assume that an adult would be more conscious and informed. Nevertheless, it was a funny and sharp insinuation.

We love our children dearly when they are young. Why do we ignore them when they become adolescents?

CHAPTER 29

When Compassion is the Most Innovative Solution to the Vagaries of Teenage Pregnancy

When any society stops giving birth, they stop the development of a new generation. It means the potential extinction of that particular group of people. We tend to celebrate the birth of a child as a blessing and a good thing. The birth of a child ensures continuity of life, propagation of one's lineage, and increase of a society's potential for socioeconomic productivity. It is largely the female's role to ensure that this vital cycle of life is assured. Yet the challenges some women face for performing this noble task are almost insurmountable because of the lack of gender equity and equality in our societies.

Can you imagine trying to change such a thing in most African nations? Women still are given a lot of problems when they are pregnant. If they want to take leave, they will not be paid for it. So they suffer to give birth and then must try to return to the office as quickly as possible. Sometimes they return when they have not even healed properly. Naturally, the children suffer also when they are weaned from breastfeeding before they are ready.

It was only in 1993 that the USA allowed women to take employment leave to give birth and still return to work. Before that, the right to return to their jobs was not guaranteed.

In Africa, one of the most frightening and challenging situations for a girl is falling pregnant as a teenager. She will be kicked out of school and, in some societies, even out of her parents' home. She may be moved to her grandparents' home to raise her child. She may become an outcast in her village. Yet the boy who made her pregnant will continue to go to school without any consequences at all.

Do you know that in many African countries, if a woman gets pregnant while in an office job, she is at risk of being fired for being 'lazy' or 'too tired' or 'too weak' to work? Many young ladies are afraid to become pregnant when they have acquired an office job.

Teenage pregnancy is shunned and despised as a bad thing, yet an innocent life is about to be brought forth. What a sad beginning for that life, and what a terrible and vulnerable situation for the young girl to be in. She loses her opportunities, but the boy will never be stopped. Don't you think this ought to be changed? Shouldn't boys be held equally responsible? What about feeling some compassion for the girl?

The most that most males will do is ask the girl to get an abortion. The responsibility still remains on the unfortunate girl to make this terrible choice and suffer the consequences. Some nations make similar assumptions in their policies, making the pregnancy entirely the girl's problem. Governments have said that she can abort whenever she feels like it—thereby risking her health and future prospects of having babies.

Can you imagine how painful it will be to change this situation and make boys and men responsible too when such a scenario comes up? Can't our governments listen attentively to women who have endured this situation? Of course, many women wouldn't volunteer that information because of the stigma attached to teenage pregnancy, especially in Africa.

Unfortunately, issues concerning sexuality, pregnancy, and birth are shrouded in secrecy. In the meantime, the babies of yesterday are teenagers today and will be mothers and fathers by evening! Shouldn't some level of knowledge be imparted to them by their parents before adult responsibilities start?

Children need to develop awareness concerning physical changes, gender roles, and how these affect them and the society at large. That way they will be able to navigate this complex but vital stage of their development. We can educate them or lose them, period! They will make better choices, practise better ways of relating to each other, and change how they think about their relationships.

——— ❧ Chapter 30 ❧ ———

Targeting Adolescents

Culture and tradition are not frozen or stagnant; the individuals and groups partaking of any culture or tradition actively shape and reshape it in their daily endeavours. Culture changes because it is enmeshed in the turbulence of history, and because each act, each signification, each decision risks opening new meanings, vistas and possibilities ... Given accelerated flows and interactions of diverse cultural products as a result of globalisation, does it make sense to still talk of individuals and groups as belonging to given cultures like fettered slaves and zombies, or confined like canned sardines?

—Professor Francis Nyamnjoh,

Until recently, most gender education and awareness programmes targeted adults in the workplace and community, and young adults in institutions of higher learning. There had not been as much effort to make teens aware of gender issues. Few people introduced gender awareness in the areas of creative arts popular among young people. Few deliberately created publications specifically targeted to adolescents.

Nevertheless I know that young people are also suffering from gender discrimination. Young women in colleges struggle to select courses they want, as some are deemed to be only for male students. Since education was liberalised in many parts of Africa, many universities have come up, especially in the cities. Unfortunately, the majority focus on infrastructure for teaching, not accommodation. Consequently many girls have difficulties finding places to live during college. They end up cohabiting with men because they cannot afford rent. Job-seeking women have to pay with sex for the jobs they trained for. There are also huge challenges to youth marriages as societal support systems have collapsed. Couples struggle to pay immense bills, again resorting to dangerous means of survival.

Targeting teens requires a paradigm shift regarding where we embed gender awareness in the culture. It is a departure from business as usual and provides an opportunity for transforming society's thinking. Social media has been able to revolutionise the way we do things mainly because of its uptake by younger generation. We can benchmark on this.

In your teenage years, you are all about growing up and the new experiences of your body changing from a child to an adult. Your life revolves around going to high school, more responsibilities, changing relationships between boys and girls, and basically a lot of self-discovery. Many girls, especially in the rural areas, unfortunately get pregnant along this journey, and they are prematurely thrust into motherhood roles.

Most teens don't pay too much attention to gender roles. Those are things they think they will bother with when they grow older. They do not realise that if they don't become aware of basic gender issues as they grow, they will become very disappointed when the negative factors of gender affect them later. When they are in college, and even more so when they seek employment or enter relationships, the negative factors are likely to affect them.

Did you know that it was only in 2009 that US President Barack Obama signed the Lily Ledbetter Fair Pay Restoration Act? Before that in the US, women were paid less than what their male counterparts were paid in the same job position. The same happens in most African countries: women are paid much less than men. Don't you think that is something you need to know early and begin to think about changing?

You need to learn early about the situation we have now. How does it affect you as a boy? How does it affect you as a girl? What needs to change in order for you to lead a lifestyle which will give you equal opportunities in your daily life?

I have four adolescent sons and one daughter. I want them to be part of a gender-balanced generation. If you learn about gender awareness, then you will have a better understanding of your own family, why mothers and fathers behave the way they do, and why there are some things which are demanded of you to make you a 'good boy' or 'good girl' at home, at school, or in your community at large. You will become socialised in a better way.

The gender awareness campaign did not start in the late twentieth century, as some people imagine. It has been a regular part of society throughout the existence of humanity on earth. Why not start learning and adjusting to proper gender balance as early as possible?

NEVER TOO YOUNG TO BE A GENDER ACTIVIST

> I raise up my voice not so that I can shout, but so that those without a voice can be heard.

> —Malala Yousafzai, Nobel Laureate

You have seen how it has taken an entire century to bring gender equality and balance into the arena of sports through the Olympic Games. Gender awareness campaigns in every other aspect of life—including job opportunities, work balance in the home, leadership, responsibility for pregnancy, and childcare—will take their own length of time to bear fruit. Nevertheless, one thing is for sure: gender awareness is not going away. The earlier and faster we are aware of this, the faster we shall achieve good fruit for our efforts.

MALALA'S STORY

If you are an avid fan of social media, you are likely to be familiar with the name of Malala Yousafzai. In a place called Swat Valley in north-western Pakistan, the Taliban had banned girls from attending school. A local girl, 10 years old, called Malala Yousafzai saw the terrible future that the Taliban was relegating the girls to. Even at that age, she was intelligent enough to know that education is very important in liberating girls from ignorance and helping society to develop.

Malala began to write a blog when she was about 11 years old, under a different name. She wrote it for the British Broadcasting Corporation (BBC), giving details of life under the oppressive Taliban regime. She wrote about her own views on promoting education, especially for girls. Journalists from the BBC decided to make a documentary about what was going on in that part of Pakistan. When the story went viral on international news and social media, many people and organisations around the world began to campaign for equal education opportunities.

241

The local Taliban tried to take revenge on Malala by shooting her in the head as she travelled on a school bus! She suffered critical injuries, but she managed to survive due to expert medical care and security in the United Kingdom. Her work was recognised by many. She recovered, and in 2014, Malala became a recipient of the prestigious Nobel Peace Prize for her fight for girls' education. She is the youngest Nobel Laureate to date.

Malala has received many other accolades, including the Sakhanar Prize, Simone De Beauvoir Prize, and National Youth Peace Prize, among others. She has become an international speaker on issues that surround education and empowerment of young people, especially young girls' equal rights in developing nations. Isn't she inspiring?

Even though so much has been achieved in the past hundred years to bring about gender equality, there is still a very long way to go, especially in the nations of Africa. Like Malala, you are never too young to take this gender awareness campaign seriously. You do not need a degree to become a gender activist. You just need to have humanity, see where there is unfairness and injustice, and express yourself.

Today you are fortunate to have very active social media, where you can express your views and observations on those practices that seem unbalanced and unfair. Ask questions and you will be surprised at the many lessons you will learn. You will be surprised that you too have something important to contribute to this conversations about creating gender awareness. If you learn what gender awareness is and why it is important, you may become part of the growing voice that is asking for positive change in the gender agenda for Africa.

Who knows? One day, like Nelson Mandela and his colleagues, like Malala and her colleagues, you may be remembered as one who brought positive change to society through the gender awareness campaign.

Before you become a gender awareness activist, it is important to understand exactly where we are coming from in Africa on this issue. There is important background to the gender awareness campaign in Africa today.

CONCLUSION

No matter what one's age, one can be inspirational like Malala. One simply needs to be observant about what is happening in society, and then become angry—angry enough to stand up for what one knows is right and fair. The world needs many more Malalas—young people who can fight for other young people on gender discrimination issues.

To make a difference in this world, you do not have to have a big position in society. You simply need to have a big heart and a strong voice. As Malala has said, 'One child, one book, and one teacher can change the world.'

History makes us believe in the power of one:

- in 1645, one vote gave Oliver Cromwell control of England
- in 1776, one vote gave America the English language instead of German
- in 1845, one vote brought Texas into the Union
- in 1875, one vote changed France from a monarchy to a republic
- in 1923, one vote gave Adolf Hitler leadership of the Nazi Party

Therefore, never underestimate the power of one individual deciding to take on fate and change the status quo. Be that individual. Be the person who will rewrite history when it comes to making a difference in the world.

Over time, I have come to realise that it is not only teenagers who succumb to peer pressure. Parents too can be very vulnerable to peer pressure. They allow their children to do things because their peers allow the same. Most teenagers have developed skills to manipulate their parents, and unfortunately parents fall victim to these tricks all the time. As a parent, take a stand. It may not be very popular in your culture, but as long as it is the right stand, that's what matters most.

Countries are also victims of peer pressure, imitating blindly what other nations are doing. Cultures are victims of peer pressure, importing into a locality what may be relevant in other parts of the world but are harmful, even dangerous at home.

It is high time that someone stood up and said no to the insanity in our society. It could be a lonely voice, an isolated concern, but never forget the power of one. It only takes an individual to start a revolution.

As Africans, we have copied many things from the West and tried to paste those copies into our cultural framework. This practice keeps on backfiring with dire consequences, leaving many to live remorseful lives.

For how long are we going to stand unconcerned in the face of social and moral decay among our youth? For how long are we going to be bystanders, using the excuse that we are but one individual? I challenge every man and woman of high morals to stand up and disrupt the status quo. It is possible to reverse the trends. Someone once said, 'Never doubt that a small group of thoughtful committed people can change the world: indeed it's the only thing that ever has.'

Margaret Mead, American conservative anthropologist

CALL TO ACTION

- Take time to walk and talk through your own community. Observe and document areas of gender discrimination that require change. (If you choose to document on video, remember to seek people's consent before taking the picture or video.)
- Imagine that one day, the situation is different. What would your community look like? Dream and dream big! Identify and list ways you can contribute to good change. For each way, identify the people affected. Identify the people with the power to change the situation.
- Approach others with whom you can make the desired change. Explain to them your plans and dreams. Encourage them to dream too. Together, share your plans. Then start to take action. Make small changes every day. Document, share, and celebrate the small changes *every day*.
- Never underestimate yourself. The small steps you take towards social transformation can change the world. The late Wangari

Maathai said, 'It is the little things that citizens do that makes the greatest difference, and my little thing is planting trees.' What is your little thing? I urge every young person who feels concerned about today's social misfits to stand up and start doing their little thing in a little way. I challenge every parent to seize the occasion and lead the campaign. Take it upon yourself to inspire and influence young people.

—Wangari Mathai, Nobel Laurete

CHAPTER 31

Gender Awareness through the Years

It is the woman who controls the whole house … it's her job, that's what she's supposed to do … We have to change this idea that women are not only supposed to work in the house … but she also has the ability to go outside and do business, to be a doctor, to be a teacher, to be an engineer, she should be allowed to have any job she likes. She should be treated equally, as men are.

—Malala Yousafzai, Nobel Laureate

Where did this whole gender awareness campaign start from? The idea of equality between males and females started long ago in history. Until the end of the 1800s, women were treated as the inferior sex. They were excluded from taking part in public life, including politics, education, and certain professions like medicine and engineering.

So there was very little a woman could do except grow up, learn how to help in the kitchen and house, hope to get married to a rich man, have babies (especially boys), and take care of her family. She was not expected to have any education except perhaps learning how to draw, sew, play an instrument, sing, and dance. Hence the majority of women were illiterate.

As early as the second century AD, the very popular Greek philosopher and medical doctor Galen believed that women could not control themselves. Women always had to have someone else make decisions for them. They could not think for themselves or exist without a man controlling their lives.

Philosophers like Galen had great influence on the traditions and beliefs which justified the dominant view that women were, in their minds, spirits, souls, and bodies, weaker and inferior to men. His teachings were followed by many men even up to modern times.

Such beliefs are the reason why some rights-aware people in history began to seek equal rights and opportunities for everyone: in education, ownership of property, justice, politics, sports, and many other areas. The gender awareness campaign is all about challenging and changing those wrong ideas and bringing equality in every area for women, men, boys, and girls.

In the next section, I show a very brief timeline of moments when people took notice of the unfairness in the way females were treated. This publication is written with African adolescents in mind, but you will notice that I give a lot of information about nations in the Western world. This is because many of them got involved in this campaign many years ago. Furthermore, they have well-kept records of their history in this regard. In Africa, our developments were transferred through an oral tradition that was not always preserved, making us miss a lot of our rich history. In many ways, we are only beginning to build our records. I hope that in coming years, when we learn more about gender awareness, history will become full of positive African examples of gender awareness progress.

SOCIAL EQUALITY

> I don't really understand why a woman wouldn't feel like she deserves equality, equal pay, and equal rights. We need to just not only maintain the status quo but push forward and really continue the good fight for equality for people everywhere.

—Reese Witherspoon, Hollywood actress

The earliest account of gender equality is found in the Bible. In the beginning, when God created males and females, he gave them equal opportunity to rule over all things. This is written in Genesis chapter 1, verses 28 to 31. One sex was not made superior than the other. They were given the instruction together.

1600 BC: One of the earliest gender equality petitions is again in the Bible, recorded in Numbers 27:1–9 probably more than four thousand years ago. It is the story of the daughters of Zelophehad. Their father died and left only five daughters, no sons. Therefore there was no boy to inherit his land. The daughters went before their leader, Moses, and made a petition to receive their inheritance from the father. It was discussed among the elders, and they figured that the girls too could own land. So they adjusted their laws to make room for females to inherit when their fathers had no sons.

Do you know that in many communities in Africa today, girls still do not inherit property from their fathers? Don't you think you ought to know what it is like in your own community? 'In the nineteenth century, the central moral challenge was slavery. In the twentieth century, it was the battle against totalitarianism. We believe that in this century the paramount moral challenge will be the struggle for gender equality around the world.'

—Nicholas D Kristof, American journalist and political commentator

1792: British author Mary Wollstonecraft wrote a book called *A Vindication of the Rights of Women*. She wanted to prove that women and men could enjoy equal rights. In those days, girls were good for taking care of the house chores, getting married, giving birth, raising their children, and caring for their husbands. They were not allowed to have any formal education, get jobs, or own property. If they managed to do any of these things, they were despised by society.

1848: An attempt was made in France to create equal opportunities for women and men. It faced a lot of opposition.

1851: Sojourner Truth, a black abolitionist, women's rights activist, and former slave, delivered the famous 'Ain't I a Woman' speech at the Ohio Women's Rights Convention.

1859: Isaac Reeve published 'The Intellect of Woman not naturally Inferior to that of Man'. He was pointing out that males and females were similar except for a few biological differences. Moreover, given the same opportunities, both men and women could excel because their intellectual capacity was equal.

1868: Frances Power Cobbe published 'Criminals, Idiots, Women and Minors: Is the Classification sound?' In those days, people believed that women, children, idiots, and criminals had the same kind of mind. They were not different. Only men had superior minds. Can you imagine how some people might have hated to see such a book that challenged the status quo and this very wrong way of thinking about women and girls?

Do you know that today in Africa, some tribes still think that adult women and little children have the same mindset and intellect? It is okay to beat up women to 'teach them a lesson' and 'keep them in their place'. What do you think of such a custom?

1946: The United Nations established a Commission on the Status for Women in 1946. Its mission was 'to raise the status of women, irrespective of nationality, race, language or religion, to equality with men in all fields of human enterprise, and to eliminate all discrimination against women in the provisions of statutory law, in legal maxims or rules, or in interpretation of customary law'.

1947: Equal rights for all people was declared in Japan. This meant that women could vote, get education, own property, have a say in their marriage, and so on.

LEADERSHIP AND VOTING

We need to move beyond the idea that girls can be leaders
and create the expectation that they should be leaders.

—Condoleezza Rice, former US Secretary of State

1806 BC: The Egyptian pharaoh Sobekneferu was the first female head
of state.

1848: Five women, including young housewife and mother Elizabeth Cady
Stanton, were having tea when the conversation turned to the situation of
women in America. Within a week, they organised a two-day convention
in Seneca Falls, New York, to discuss women's rights. The participants
signed the Declaration of Sentiments, which called for equal treatment
of women and men under the law and voting rights for women. The
American women's rights movement had begun.

If there were no women voting, obviously there were no women standing
for political office. So there was no representation of women and girls
in the government. All decisions were made by men only. Why would
they make laws that were convenient for women too? Imagine how many
women had talent to lead. They lost the opportunity because they were
suppressed. So what happened?

In most African censuses, women are in the majority. However, in those
nations, men are the majority in parliament, so they can easily refuse to
change unfair or unequal laws. For example, it is very difficult to pass a
law that, when a girl gets pregnant, the father of her child should take full
responsibility for her and the child until the child is of independent age.
There is no penalty for interrupting a girl's education.

Why? Because there are very few voices of responsible women who have a
proper understanding of gender in these parliaments. This situation can
only begin to change when girls learn from an early age just how important
and necessary gender awareness is.

1893: New Zealand becomes the first country to allow women to vote. This happened because of a gender campaign that had been going on for many years. Women (and some men) decided to campaign for equal rights for men and women in choosing who would lead their country, form governments, and write the laws.

1919: The right to vote and stand for office was given to European women in Kenya in 1919; in 1956, those rights were extended to African men and women under certain conditions related to educational level and property ownership. In 1963, all Kenyans, regardless of colour and other previously restricting factors, were given the right to vote and stand for election.

1920: The USA allowed women to vote after many years of people campaigning for equal rights to vote in elections.

1930: South African white women were allowed to vote. Black women had no similar right to vote until 1994, after apartheid was banned.

1992: More women run for and are elected to public office than in any other year in United States history to that point.

2006: Ellen Johnson Sirleaf becomes the first elected African female president, in Liberia. Joyce Hilda Banda of Malawi became the second African female president in 2011. In 2014, Catherine Samba Panza of Central Africa Republic became the third African female president.

2011: King Abdullah of Saudi Arabia granted women the right to vote. However, that right did not go into effect until 2015. Prior to this decree, Saudi Arabia was the last remaining country in the world that did not allow its women to vote.

2015: Lieutenant Commander Zimasa Mabela, a South African woman, became the first woman in Africa to command a navy vessel.

2016: Hillary Rodham Clinton became the first woman to be nominated by a major party (the Democratic Party) to stand as a candidate for president in the USA. She stood against property billionaire Donald Trump. She won the popular vote by more than three million votes. But she lost the election due to the structure of the American electoral college. What an initial breakthrough! What courage! What a shame! What a loss! What a shock!

EDUCATION

> The future must not belong to those who bully women. It must be shaped by girls who go to school and those who stand for a world where our daughters can live their dreams just like our sons.
>
> —Barack Obama, American President

1715: Britain's Elizabeth Elstob published *The Rudiments of Grammar for the English-Saxon Tongue*, the first Anglo-Saxon grammar. She did this at a time when women were not supposed to learn to read and write. If they were caught reading, they were punished severely.

1792: American Sarah Pierce opens a school in her home with one student. By 1816 she had taught 157 girls.

1826: The first public high schools for girls are opened in New York and Boston. Very few girls were accepted in the public schools. Only boys could go to public high school before this time.

1837: Mount Holyoke College becomes the first college for women. It was founded by Mary Lyon in South Hadley, Massachusetts, in the USA.

1945: The first class of women is admitted to Harvard Medical School. Before this, they would not accept women to study medicine formally— yet the first doctor and nurse in the home is usually the mother. She instinctively knows when any member of her family is unwell and usually knows just what to do. She gives first aid even before going to a hospital. What a sad contradiction!

1947: Cambridge University admits women to membership and degrees. The statute limited the numbers of women to one for every ten men. This was not good enough, because there were many well-educated girls with potential to join the university.

1947: All UK medical schools become coeducational. Before that, they did not allow women and men to go to medical school together. Only a few colleges admitted women for medical studies.

1948: Education was proclaimed a human right in Article 26 of Universal Declaration of Human Rights. This meant that every nation that was part of the United Nations had to ensure that everyone received an education.

Even today, there is a very high percentage of females who have never been to school and do not enjoy this basic equal opportunity with males. For example, in Somalia 95 per cent of girls aged 7–16 are illiterate and have never been to school. In Niger it is 78 per cent; in Liberia 77 per cent; in Mali 75 per cent; and in Burkina Faso 71 per cent. These are very high numbers of uneducated females who may never get to know what potential they have.

Most of the time these girls are married off as soon as they reach puberty so their families can get a dowry. This means girls get married as young as 9 years old to men who are much older than they are. They have no experience in being a housewife or a mother. They literally lose their childhoods to become child brides and child mothers.

Many times girls develop a condition called *fistula* as a result of giving birth to babies when their bodies are still developing reproductively. This is a terrible condition which makes them become very smelly because of leaking urine and faeces. So they end up being rejected again by the men who have brought this condition upon them.

These girls may never have the opportunity to learn about gender equality. They may never know that they have as much right as men do to education, meaningful representation in politics, choice in how they live their lives, and exploration of their great potential. If you cannot read or write, you have to depend on other people to do it for you. How dangerously vulnerable can you become if someone gives you wrong information and you don't know?

──•❀ CHAPTER 32 ❀•──

The African Gender
Awareness Journey

In Africa, the woman's 'place' was not only with her family; she often ruled nations with unquestionable authority. Many African women were great militarists, and on occasion led their armies in battle. The Africans had produced a civilization where men were secure enough to let women advance as far as their talent, royal lineage and prerogatives would take them.

—Zack Hendrick Clarke, author, *African Warrior Queens*

In the previous chapter, you read about the changing world from the early 1980s. However our gender awareness journey in Africa is affected by even earlier history. It means we have to look deeper and further back in order to understand why we are as we are today with regard to the gender agenda.

In most ancient African societies, the roles were very clearly defined. There were roles which every member of community played, and these occupied their days. The roles were based mainly on one's sex and age. People were simply classified as children, unmarried young people, married couples, and the elderly. Everyone knew what society expected and what the norms were. This formed the basis for understanding intercommunal difference. The communities also had clear boundaries based on clan and physical location.

There were roles for men: e.g., hunting, the bulk of farming, fishing. Their role was to bring home the spoils (meat) and protect the community from warriors. They rightly earned their title as head of household.

Younger boys tended the cattle. Once they came of age, they were initiated into adulthood and became hunters and warriors in the community. They lived in a dangerous world which was constantly under threat of attack from neighbouring communities and from wild animals. There was always much to do to protect their own and extend the territory of their communities or kingdoms. The younger heroes/vigilantes therefore earned respect. They had to be nurtured by the women to stay alert and grow strong—ready to take over the mantle of their fathers or 'carry the heavy family grinding stone'.

Elderly men formed the council of elders. They were the celebrated 'retired generals' of their time. They were weak physically but strong intellectually, based on long experiences through their travels and knowledge exchange with far-off communities, traders, and warriors. They held secrets about their communities and had enduring contacts outside the community. When they seemed to be lounging under the oldest or biggest trees, where community meetings were held, they exuded wisdom passed down in oral traditions. They used local proverbs to discuss, unravel, and judge complex cases like marriage and land disputes.

Within these councils of elders, a few of the older women were also allowed to participate in various but subtle capacities, guiding the community and shaping its direction. They mentored the younger people through retelling folklore, purposely naming the babies, and handing down knowledge during marriage and funeral practices. They used song, dance, drama, and other means of passing on oral education and always ensured there was a succession plan in every area of life. They ensured there were men who could become leaders when the older men were too weak to lead, or if they died.

The older men quietly, supported by older women, were the gatekeepers of culture in all its manifestations, including expected gender roles for girls.

Women did all the domestic work around the homestead. They ensured that the household was intact. They ensured continuity of the family by birthing and raising children. They received the spoils from their warrior husbands and produced food, clothing, and shelter for the family. In some communities, the women built the homesteads. In others, they did the repair work and inner decoration of the huts and created a clean and comfortable living environment. The kitchen was their space, which they organised and ruled with vigour—it sustained life.

The women taught the little ones the basic duties of family and community welfare and their roles in them. Daily chores like grinding millet, collecting water and firewood, cooking, and washing dishes were not simply chores, but spaces for socialising, sharing, learning, and enjoying each other's company. Women had decided to have fun as they worked.

There were some communities in Africa where the roles of women extended beyond the home. For example, in a number of ancient West African kingdoms, women ruled as warrior queens who had female warriors and horsewomen. They did a fine job of protecting the kingdom and conquering other territories. Many white explorers were surprised to encounter and even fight with these 'Amazon' women of great strength and military expertise. They ably fought alongside their male counterparts.

Among the Maasai in Kenya, the women are the builders of the *manyatta* homesteads. Indeed these women's work was never done!

Younger women helped around the home. They learned from their mothers and aunts how to become good wives, mothers, and aunties to their nieces. They learned how to cook, clean, fetch water and firewood, and raise little ones. They were real surrogate mothers. They were trained in personal hygiene and love in marriage. They had to especially learn patience and the spirit of giving.

In most of those communities, the daylight hours were spent in family- and community-building events, while the evenings were spent relaxing and socialising around firelight, recounting the day's activities, listening to self-made music, and recounting their history. It was in those evening hours that the lazy were chastised, for in the ancient African societies no one was found with empty hands. Everyone was engaged in some type of work.

In a number of African cultural groups, women took serious leadership positions. They were not only mothers and wives, but wise and influential political leaders. Women chiefs arose in numerous African tribes.

A friend of mine recently sent me an interesting WhatsApp message. I felt that we, the current generation of parents, used to be mesmerised when we heard about these ancient women. But these days, we are just nostalgic, because we have no such strong women to emulate today and show to our exceedingly stubborn children. In her message, my friend said, 'We the People born between 1950-1975 ... We stayed near our parents, we had no cell phones ... We used to visit our friends ... We are a unique and the most understanding generation because we are the last of a generation who listened to their parents.'

CHAPTER 33

Modern Restless Days Arise

Enter modern days through colonialism, global trade, HIV and AIDS, climate change, and international conflict. With these came the dramatic and restless invasion of the powerful digital age of internet, mobile technology, and social media. Community organisation changed and is still changing. Roles and community routines also began to change—their definitions based on sex and age were no longer current.

'Community' no longer referred to the fixed geographical location of a village. Apart from communities recognised by tribe, race, blood relations, and territorial boundaries, we now have virtual communities made up of people with a 'common interest' in terms of needs, functions, aspirations, and shared same infrastructure, like schools, workplaces, and water sources. Communities do not necessarily live in a confined geographical location. Some are local and others are international.

For example people living with HIV and AIDS may form a community because they have similar health challenges, needs, and interests. The Harley Davidson motorbike riders' community is found in many nations. Think also about the supporters of football clubs like Manchester United, Arsenal, Real Madrid, and Liverpool. They have never met physically, but when they win, they rejoice together, and when they fail, gloom encompasses them wherever they are. These communities are temporal, mixed, and ethnically and culturally diverse.

Modernity brought a great shift of roles between men and women as more girls went to school and more women sought employment. The consequences included delayed marriage, later childbirth, and fewer children, and hence a smaller family unit. Soon the work ethic and attitudes of both women and men changed significantly. People, especially men, disappeared into towns, cities, mines, and overseas destinations, leaving their villages to the old, the wives, and the little children.

With modernity, some roles in community became completely redundant. We developed what we perceived as safer communities, with modern weaponry and police, and an organised military at a distance. Inter-tribe war and strife became rare. Men who had hitherto been warriors lost that role of protecting the village.

We developed modern ways of farming, and more people became redundant in this area too—replaced by machines. We confronted the vagaries of climate change and used modern farming methods. Transport and trade replaced common neighbourhood interdependence and self-sustenance, which used to happen through weekly market days.

Today, for the average family especially in urban areas, food is 'produced' in the supermarket and corner shops. Food is obtained for the household by going to the office or factory. In the rural areas, farming continues but there is no more hunting to survive. In some nations, men and boys were sent en masse to become soldiers, fighting people for causes they did not understand. Others were sent to the mines, or had to go great distances away from their homes to find income and education.

What happened to the roles of males? I imagine they were initially missed. But human beings cannot exist in a vacuum. When an important thing is removed, somehow it will be replaced by something else. But can men really be replaced? Of course *no*.

'We've begun to raise daughters more like sons … but few have the courage to raise our sons more like our daughters.' The perceived balance in traditional society was systematically broken. So when male roles were challenged and began to disappear rapidly, they had to be occupied by something else.

—Gloria Steinem, American feminist, journalist and socio-political activist

New inter-ethnic communities began to form in urban areas. Intermarriage and polygamy reigned. With it, a clash or harmonization of cultures began. There were huge manifestations of intercommunal difference.

The terminology used in most African languages still suggests that 'my wife is sitting at home' while the man goes to the city to find work. In other words, the new roles signified that men went to work and earned money. Therefore when you earned money, that meant you had worked. Anything that did not earn money could not be 'work'. Therefore women who did subsistence farming, household chores, and childrearing were considered to be 'sitting' at home and 'eating' the meagre remittances they received from their husbands in the cities.

This highlighted the gender issue of valuing women's and men's work. The roles of men are deemed more powerful and productive than those played by women at home. Society finds it very easy to undermine the reproductive, productive, and communal roles women play to secure the family's socioeconomic well-being, simply because women's work doesn't result in a salary at the end of the month.

Who should pay a woman for all her work? Who is the beneficiary of a woman's labour?

What about the older folk? Their so-called 'wisdom' was challenged and eroded as people acquired new interactions, knowledge, and skills. People respected and adopted alternative value systems that often clashed with traditional sources of knowledge. People got their knowledge from books, schools, libraries, and international conferences. As the years went by, knowledge also came from TV, radio, and now the internet.

The youth could no longer relate to older men's wisdom and guidance. Their modern spouses (sometimes from a different ethnic group) could no longer tolerate the old people's 'laziness and interference'. Their young, educated, and beautiful spouses would say that they had 'not married the whole clan'. Some unlucky old people were abandoned in the villages. A few lucky ones were integrated in their sons' modern households. Others were put in religiously based old people's homes. Overall, these traditional community leaders had to submit to a central government, which greatly diminished the role of old people as advisors and counsellors. This role was taken over by political administrative structures.

What about female roles? Female roles remained intact and even increased. Women still get pregnant for nine months. They still give birth and are still the principle caregivers within the home. As many became de facto single parents, they took on a disproportionate burden of familial and caregiving duties compared to their male counterparts.

Beyond that, the modern female is encouraged to become an income-earning breadwinner, slowly encroaching on the male role as the family's main provider.

The saying is 'a woman's work is never done'. Women's days became longer as they pretended to balance multiple roles as wives, mothers, and income-earning employees or businesspeople. They continued to be the unpaid and unappreciated managers of homes and carers of children. Sometimes women have the help of other women, such as household employees or adolescent daughters or grown daughters-in-law.

Many women have become what is referred to as 'social widows'. They have living husbands who are absent for long periods of time. Women have to play the roles of both father and mother, and are a dominant role model to both daughters and sons.

Husbands are more often out of the picture of parenting. Stressful, antisocial working hours combined with unhelpful social habits keep men away from home and absent from their parental responsibilities. They are increasingly linked to material support rather than caring and emotional involvement. They are never at school meetings. When the children are sick, fathers send money for treatment but hardly hold the child's hand in hospital. As adolescence sets in, with all its confusing realities, the fathers are not a viable recourse for advice and support. Think about it: what type of children would emanate from this new but necessary care system?

What about the boys and girls? They are still greatly loved by their parents, who have become too busy to parent them effectively. Modernity has filled the vacuum. It has introduced a new mentor in their lives. Children are now mentored by the media, which pumps them with uncensored images, stories, and experiences. This has influenced children with cultures and traditions they have never known and whose meaning they do not fully understand.

Nannies and house-help have become the new mothers. They are also, in some cases, part-time wives. They are teachers for both females and males. They are the real role models, similar to matrons in boarding schools, which have been turned into safe havens for 'socially orphaned' girls and boys whose parents are too busy to care for them as they grow up. These children are the victims of the diminishing voice of their male family heads, loving mothers, cultural background, and national ethos. But what kind of adult will emerge from this modern parenting system?

THE IMPACT OF CHANGES TO GENDER ROLES

There has been a major change in the way gender roles are played within our society. There are also changing ideas about what used to be the family unit and homogeneous community. Many do not consider how gender roles have changed greatly over the past one hundred and fifty years. Those changes have brought a great imbalance in the way people operate in society. This imbalance has created people whom we refer to as 'socially excluded groups'.

This is where the discussion of gender has started to find voice. To many people, the whole issue of gender is a terrifying and often greatly misunderstood concept. We still uphold the traditions that strictly defined our gendered roles within very narrow confines of a homogeneous community, with each family having a male breadwinner and head of household. Unfortunate are those families and communities who are still unaware about gender. They never realised that a woman adds great value and love to her family.

If your eyes are positive you will love the world but if your tongue is positive the world will love you. A womans's love is in action. She looks with her heart and feels with her eyes. A woman is the bank where her family deposits all anger, worries and hurt. A woman is the cement that keeps her family together and her love lasts a lifetime.

—Mother Theresa, Great Monday quotes

CONCLUSION

The African gender awareness journey has seen a shift in the roles of males and females.

- A gender role includes specific rights and obligations. It has a certain social status and power associated with it.
- A person's role can change from time to time. Roles can change drastically depending on social, economic, and cultural changes in the community.
- The roles males and females play are influenced by the cultural norms of that society, their social status in that society, other people's expectations, and the image an individual wishes to develop for him- or herself.

Now you have a better idea of the background of the African gender agenda. The next lessons are a journey that will explain complex and often controversial issues related to gender awareness through practical day-to day experiences and realities of both males and females in Africa homes, schools and workplaces.

CHAPTER 34

Do You Have an Authentic Brand?

Before you can become an effective and self-actualised defender, fighter, and disrupter for gender justice, you have to do something about yourself first. Find out about yourself. Who are you—the real you? Can you attract people to respond to your cause?

Hear this. Every man has a history, and we know a lot about this. What we hardly know is that every woman has 'her-story' too. We can hardly access that story because we have told her that she does not have one. Rather than confront the gatekeepers of patriarchy, she has used a very strong needle to sew up her stories because they are hardly documented and shared.

Briefly, here is my story—the Grace Mukasa Story.

I grew up surrounded by love, both at home and in school. Call it luck, attitude, temperament, or character, but I have always been a very lucky and likeable girl among siblings, fellow students, and older women. My siblings will attest to this.

My mum mainly had boy children. As a middle girl child in a family of ten children, I came to appreciate my mother. She was like a powder keg of energy: dormant at times, yet volatile when need be. My father adored me. He was the good cop! My mother pressured me—she was the bad cop. She kept me on a very short leash. I was her treasured sidekick, like an all-important handbag, to be picked up and moved with everywhere. This made me privy to huge amounts of adult conversations. I learned early that a child is to be seen and not heard. I attended funerals, weddings, clan meetings, and friend meetings.

I had the best and worst of gender experiences while growing up. Having a privileged position with both parents brought consequences from my male siblings. I did not help my case because I could never keep my mouth shut, even if my life depended on it. As soon as my parents came back, I would eagerly snuggle next to them and narrate everything my brothers had done during their absence. This earned me some slaps and punches from the culprits, but I never seemed to learn.

The woman I call my mother was an enigma. She was very welcoming and generous to her relatives. She was, however, an exacting taskmaster. Discipline was a key driver in her life. She constantly pushed us to our limits during her short time with us. Luckily to me she was a 'possibility legend' who taught me to thrive on a positivity and possibility mindset, even after her early demise. She pushed me to excel in school through her nonstop words of love, challenge, and advice. I learned to anticipate disciplinary actions. They were her brand of parenting. Apparently she knew she had terminal cancer long before we children found out. So she decided to talk to me constantly about life's challenges.

When I personally learned about making my brand, I felt overwhelmed and out of my depth. However, I had already read Mandela's book and knew how to hold difficult conversations with myself. From that moment onwards, I started to question myself. I reflected on my achievements and I confronted my failures. I deliberately assembled what I frankly believed to be the true worth of my life as Grace Alice Mukasa (GAM)—or was it my brand equity? I went into deep introspection and a heart-searching journey of self-discovery.

I put my life in five-year clusters. For each cluster, I tried to remember the most dramatic events plus the most significant people who had affected my life, whether positively or negatively. I listed who, what, how, why, how much, and when, thereby capturing my treasured achievements, my great failures, and the major lessons learned. As I meditated on my journey, I began to rediscover and confirm my dearest passions, my most inspiring dreams, my desires, and ultimately my real purpose in life.

I analysed my self-worth at the time and challenged myself to determine whether I had invested in myself optimally to acquire real value. I literally went on the road to rediscover myself, learn what I really wanted in life, and believe in myself. It was a tedious and long-winded journey which took me through two years of very deep personal conversations with myself.

I met Pepe Minambo, a great motivator. He reminded me of my worth when he gave me an inspiring book whose title was, *'You're Born an Original: Don't Die a Copy'*That book, that book! It just made me realise and believe that I was born an original. The rest is history!

— John Mason

One of my greatest motivators was Tony Robbins; I started to 'awaken the 'giant within me' At that moment, I questioned why I had all along been employed and not become self-employed. Why was I helping other people to execute their dreams and visions rather than my own? Why was I living far away from my family and missing out on my children's growing years? I started to dream very big dreams as prompted.

—Anthony Robbins, *Awaken the Giant Within.*

I decided to plan for that time when I would turn the tables, become an employer, and fulfil my own passion for advocating and facilitating women's empowerment. But first I had to deal with myself. I started my long climb. I started to conquer my personal inhibitions. I documented as I made progress up my personal Everest.

However, change is not linear, nor is it easy. In September 2016, I suffered a massive stroke that affected my left side. I am lucky; I am right-handed. In December 2016, I asked myself, 'What next?' If my mother were around, what would she say to me? Would she allow me to sit, mucking around? Mopping in self-pity when I never saw her shedding tears as she fought her greatest personal battle with Cancer?

I resolved to fight and not allow the stroke to define my destiny. I resolved to document my experience with stroke. I resolved to walk every day to exercise my legs. I resolved to continue researching and writing books on gender. Hence *Gender Is a Choice* is in your hands now.

This publication has been written with lots of love, hope, confidence, and a sense of fulfilment that it will transform millions of women and girls' lives and livelihoods. It hope it will also touch the hearts of men and boys and all people who are vulnerable and suffering silently from gender injustice coupled with other forms of vulnerabilities—people with disabilities, people living with HIV and AIDs, orphaned children, people living in fragile contexts due to conflict and climate change, widows, and single mothers. It is my hope that before you think of saving others, you will start with yourself.

Robin Sharma, in his inspirational book *The Leader who Had No Title*, says that every leader has their personal self-raised barriers to their own successes, which he refers to as a personal Everest. I thank God that as I was struggling to find myself, literally at the crossroads of my career, I crossed paths with Pepe Minambo, a motivational speaker and serial writer of incredibly inspirational books. Like the Baganda say, 'It was as easy as pushing someone who is already squatting, for me to be convinced to register for his Saturday lessons on how to become a motivational speaker, together with one of my sons, Ronald. I had already presented at many conferences as part of my international NGO roles, and I was already aware of my personal strengths and weaknesses (personal Everest) to conquer. I was eager to get feedback. I was very ready to challenge myself to excellence.

Pepe Minambo was a very humble and patient mentor to all of us in his academy. He attended to our needs as a whole class, yet treated and professionally responded to everyone as an individual.

I once saw and got intrigued by a book titled '*Every Woman Has a Story: Many voices, many lessons, many lives*' but until then, my own journey had never resonated with me as an important story that could be told. Pepe a motivational speaker and author, listened to my personal journey, and his conclusion was 'amazing'. He challenged me by asking why I had never written my story and shared it to inspire other African women. He even helped me to secure the services of a ghost writer to support me in this new venture.

—Daryl Ott Underhill

Suddenly I found myself planning and multitasking seriously. I was an employee in a strategic and demanding job as Regional Director for Practical Action in Eastern Africa. I gave it my total commitment Monday through Friday. Every Saturday morning, I was a highly motivated student with a motivational speaker, Pepe Minambo. On Saturday afternoons, I worked with my ghost writer on my personal story (which I will publish soon). On Sundays and during many evenings, I was in my own world, living my dream and enjoying my passion by writing this gender book or literally burning the candle for my PhD.

The more books I read, the more writing I did, and the more knowledge I acquired, the more it became clear to me that I was not yet maximising my leadership potential. I hardly had time to pursue my passion to empower women and the less powerful. I was not realising my dream. As an employee, I was too busy fulfilling someone else's vision, while mine lay dormant.

I also had an issue with pursuing my career in Nairobi, Kenya, miles away from my growing children and lonely husband, who were based in London. This made me have very deep conversations with myself. I knew I had to use my agency effectively. I had to make my priorities clear. I had to make critical decisions about my future. By the time I completed the Motivational Academy training, I was very clear about what I needed to do to fulfil my purpose and live a happy and meaningful life.

I resigned from my job as Regional Director for East Africa. Not that it was the first time I had done this. I had done the same five years earlier as the CEO of AMREF UK, when I realised that I needed to bring my young daughter back to Africa to appreciate her heritage. Prioritising her future stability was more important to me than holding on as a CEO. But many of my friends didn't agree with my choice. At that time, I established a real estate company with one of my sons in Uganda, called Grace Impact Africa (GIA). The company is meant to serve university students (especially female students) and middle-income families by finding them affordable, decent, and safe hostels and homes. However its launch was postponed indefinitely when I suffered a massive stroke soon after registration.

This time, I relocated back to the UK and joined my family. I envisioned establishing a Grace Mukasa Leadership & Business Centre for Women in Africa to serve my purpose on earth—to transform the lives and livelihoods of African women by developing their leadership and business skills.

In preparation for this gigantic journey, I went on a major trip to the US to sit at the feet of an international giant, Tony Robbins. I was seeking inspiration and knowledge from this world-acclaimed motivational speaker at his oversubscribed annual conference, 'Date with Destiny.' Again, the rest is history.

—Tony Robbins, motivational speaker,

My reason for sharing my journey is to inform you that finding your voice and creating a personal brand is never an easy process. I also want to reiterate Pepe's message that 'Great people climb on the shoulders of giants in their journey towards greatness. Find your own giants. It is a tortuous journey, but it's doable once you have confidence in yourself and dedicate your energy consistently until you become a master at what you do.

—Pepe Minambo, African author and motivational speaker

My aim is to let you know in simple terms how to demystify gender discrimination in all its forms. I want to share with you the underlying causes of this inequality. I want you to understand why it is very challenging and one of the greatest limitations on your inherent God-given potential as a human being, as a woman.

This is a campaign of love and passion for women and girls. I want them to become empowered and to work collectively and effectively with men and boys to defeat gender injustice. It is a long term campaign. We are in it for the long haul. It will be like a tiring journey, with two steps forward and one step back. The reality is, gender discrimination is not going away anytime soon. It is part of every society today. It is resilient and elusive. Even societies which have in the past suppressed such campaigns are being forced again today, to make changes to balance the scales of gender roles, resources, opportunities, and decision-making power. And you are a very important partner in this campaign.

The most important message in this book is that every woman and girl has a unique, valuable, and intimate story. That story is 'her-story' which explains why she is the way she is, and which no one can take away. She possesses an arsenal of knowledge, skills, talents, character traits, values, and unique passions that are valuable to her and to the rest of society. Every woman has experienced vulnerable events and adverse experiences which, when uncovered, refined and developed, can form the basis of a very strong character. She just needs to give it a voice and begin to change her life by asking, 'Who am I not to become great?'

I call upon every woman and girl to wake up every day with a very powerful goal in life. Every woman must wake up with big dreams in her mind plus lots of plans to execute towards their goal every day. Every woman must be ready to take action and actually do what they planned to do. When you wake up, talk to yourself, affirm yourself positively, and say the following loudly to the world.

I recognise my greatness because:
- it's a new day
- it's nice and beautiful
- I am a great person
- I do great work
- I am authentic and credible
- I am unique

273

- I am special because God created me for a good purpose
- it was not a mistake, because God does not make mistakes
- I have something of value to offer to the world
- I am a solution maker
- the important thing is *not* that I fall sometimes
- the most important thing *is* that every time I fall, I stand up again, dust myself off, and move forward
- I am a conqueror and a survivor
- I am a winner
- above all, I am grateful

Repeat it again before you sleep because what the mind dreams, the body will execute.

We must all positively affirm the girl child and encourage her to believe herself, in her enormous capacity, in her intelligence, and in her greatness. If that happens, she will confront the world with confidence. She will be assertive. When people challenge her, she will ask why. When they say a thing is impossible, she will ask why not. She will exercise her agency to make meaningful choices for herself and to act as an agent of change for her peers.

But before you start to play your role, this book is meant to sensitise you, to build your awareness about the true but sombre realities about our gendered lives. The book challenges your conscience and makes you examine your moral fabric. It will spur you to do something about gender discrimination because it the right thing to do. It will remind you that, just as Mandela realised in the prime of his life, we are all born equal. We hold rights by virtue of being human. No one—I repeat, *no one*— should take away that dignity from you based on your sex, age, IQ, or social background. You are a great human being and an individual with inalienable human rights. For all the women and girls in Africa, this book is a clarion call to *you*. Acknowledge your humanrights.

A friend of mine one day sent me an inspirational quotation: 'Life is the most difficult exam. Many people fail because they want to copy others not realizing that everyone has a different question paper.' Isn't that an amazing insight to use to change yourself based on your personal attributes?

Realise that you are an amazingly fantastic and unique human being whom God created without limits. Be creative and 'draw outside the lines' You can even create a better picture. By understanding gender, you can break the chains that hold you back, that block you from being competitive, and that stop you from creating your own authentic brand.

—Pepe Minambo, African autor and motivational speaker

One of the most celebrated psychologists of the twentieth century, created what is popularly referred to as the Maslow hierarchy of needs. This theory is based on the hypothesis that at various stages of life and growth, we have different priorities and motivational factors.

—Abraham Harold Maslow, Psychologist

This theory is also relevant for gender justice. As one leadership writer, mentioned, a person, cannot give what he/she has not owned first. Gender justice promotion requires effort from men and women who have acquired a lot of self-confidence, self-esteem, and self-worth. The fight for gender justice can be significantly successful if it is led by people who are already empowered and confident in themselves and are ready to share their personal worth with others. They are ready to give because they have reached a level of self-sufficiency. They have autonomy. And by this, I mean their sense of self-worth is credible and legitimate in the eyes of the people, not an exaggerated, narcissistic view of themselves based on an overinflated ego. [Hence the meaning behind the title of this book.]

—Steven R Covey, leade hip authority, Teacher

---**❧ CHAPTER 35 ❧**---

The Process of Achieving Self-Actualisation

People who are at the lowest level of Maslow's hierarchy of needs are motivated to fulfil basic needs like food, water, sleep, and sex. Once people have achieved basic needs, they aspire to safety needs, including security, order, and stability. Upon achieving basic and safety needs, human beings prioritise the need for love and belonging. It is at this stage that people start to share themselves with others, as with family and friends.

Through the achievement of these three stages, a person starts to feel comfortable with what they have achieved. The person then develops a need for esteem, or recognition by others. They prioritise the aspiration to be competent and be recognised as such through higher status and other measures of success. Now the person is at the cognitive level and can be creative in stimulating themselves intellectually. They can be innovative and begin to explore new things.

Next, they reach the aesthetic level, at which stage they need, prioritise, and aspire for harmony, order, and beauty. Finally, they reach the highest level of the hierarchy. At this level, they have grown and achieved so much that their needs, priorities, and aspirations are for *self-actualisation*, a term Maslow coined to refer to a state of harmony and understanding.

The self-actualised person is fulfilling their full potential. At this stage, the person is aware of their purpose in life. They are very concerned with maintaining their authentic brand so they focus on themselves and try to build their own image. They may look at this in terms of feelings, such as self-confidence, or in terms of accomplishing a set goal. They emphasise the positive qualities in themselves. A person at this stage of growth becomes more purposeful. They want to contribute to society and leave a positive legacy.

Of course you do not only have to build your authentic brand. You also have to be consistent and live according to your brand. There are many people and corporations with great brands who have lost authority and authenticity when they acted in a way that was in contradiction of their initially known brands.

BRANDS THAT HAVE STRUGGLED WITH THEIR AUTHENTICITY RECENTLY

- Toyota, the giant manufacturer of vehicles capable of overcoming the rough terrain in sub-Saharan Africa, for lack of safety of their vehicles
- Volkswagen, the world's largest automaker in 2015, for emissions cheating, rigging, and deceit in their diesel vehicles
- Tiger Woods, the renowned golfer, for infidelity in marriage
- Samsung, the major manufacturer of mobile phones, for Galaxy 7 phone batteries that burst into flames
- Lance Armstrong, the record-breaking cyclist, for doping and lack of integrity
- Oscar Pistorius, the great South African Paralympic athlete, for the murder of his beautiful girlfriend
- OXFAM GB, the international charity, for failure to deal decisively with staff who exploited vulnerable women during humanitarian responses

Remember also that you cannot brand yourself in a crowd. You are yourself, an individual with unique emotional intelligence, experiences, mistakes, life achievements, character, and values. Look around you. You will realise that great companies have a brand and make a promise in their vision statement and then deliver on it.

ENDURING, AUTHENTIC, AND AMAZING BRANDS WITH EQUITY

- Apple, the computing innovator, delivers on new technologies
- BMW, the luxury car maker, builds the ultimate driving machine
- FedEx, the delivery service that promises when your parcel has to be there overnight, it will be
- Google, the internet giant, organises and universalises information usefully
- Coca-Cola, the soft drink company, inclusively cures thirst everywhere in the world
- M-Pesa in Kenya, the money transfer innovator, allows you to transfer and receive funds wherever you are, Immediately

Similarly, great men and women, the ones we all admire and respect, have established unique, enviable brands for themselves. They have won coveted prizes and left amazing legacies behind.

a. Nelson Mandela, human rights campaigner, fought for freedom and had an amazing power to forgive his enemies
b. Wangari Maathai, gender and environmental activist, lover of trees
c. Princess Diana, member of the UK royal family, combined female beauty, charm, and power with a compassionate human heart
d. Mother Theresa, saint of Calcutta, fought for the rights of the poorest of the poor and provided loving care to themAbraham Lincoln, president of the United States, abolished slavery
e. Barrack Obama surmounted all obstacles to become the first black US president
f. Hillary Clinton, former US secretary of state overcame gender-based adversity. She was the first woman nominated by a major party, so she was the first woman who had a meaningful chance

to win. And while she did achieve the popular vote, the Electoral College went to Trump.

g. Martin Luther King Jr, civil rights leader, demonstrated incredible power to dream and courage to prophesy during turbulent times— 'I have a dream that my four little children will one day live in a nation where they will not be judged by the colour of their skin but by the content of their'

—Simon Sebag Montefiore, British wrier and actor

All these heroes underwent amazing pain to achieve their dreams. Painful changes must continue to take place until gender equity and equality is created. You can make some changes as an individual, but you will make more significant change through collective action. Fighting for gender equality is a very complex, controversial, sensitive, and elusive agenda. You need to acquire knowledge, build capacity, and leverage the capabilities and talents of other people to form a critical mass for change.

Despite the challenges of fighting for gender equity and equality, success brings an extremely rewarding sense of achievement. Think of the millions of people whose lives can be changed as a result of your intervention. Mother Teresa said, 'If you cannot save a thousand people, save at least one.' Because that is a human life you will have saved!

—Mother Theresa

As Pepe Minambo, one of the best motivational speakers in East Africa, asked:

Is it enough or be good when you can be great?
Is it enough to settle for a c when you can get a B? ...
Is it enough to be ok with B when you can get a straight A?
—Pepe Minambo, African author and motivational speaker

It is in recognition of the above challenges that I wrote this book. I am very passionate to inspire you, to enable you to believe in your greatness as a woman, to recognise that you are greater, smarter and have the X-factor that you have never exploited.

I have been blessed with great knowledge, skills, and exposure. This book is part of my contribution to humanity. I know I am the rough-cut diamond whose tremendous intrinsic value and potential has not been tapped fully yet. I never limit myself and I am versatile. Positive thinking is my mantra and I encourage all women and girls to adopt the same attitude because I know and believe that 'Positive thinking will let you do everything better than negative thinking will.'

—Zig Ziglar, American author and motivational speaker

I read somewhere that positive and negative thoughts become self-fulfilling prophecies by leading to positive or negative outcomes. Once you know this, why would you waste your time thinking you are unable or incapable?

Rather than standing in that negative space that pulls you down, jump into the positive space that enables you to be opportunistic, happier, and successful. It is the transformative space of *possibility thinking*.

Take it from me. If you are both positive and optimistic, and then decide to invest in your growth every day, you will grow every day! It does not matter whether you are a woman or man. It does not matter what circumstances you were born in. You will be able to identify the triggers for your negative thinking and take control of your emotions to deliberately steer yourself back into the positive space. Dr Seligman, one of the world's leading psychologists, studied our thought patterns and concluded that we think and explain events in three basic dimensions: permanence, pervasiveness, and personalisation. If you are on the negative end, then whatever happens is the end of the world. It is final and cannot change. And it is all about you. On the other hand, optimistic people tend to believe that events are just events and will pass. They see opportunities even when

faced by challenges. A specific event does not crowd the whole world. It's not about me, me, me.

—Martin Seligman, American psychologist

KNOW YOUR POTENTIAL

You have the inherent potential to do great things in this world. But first things first! You need to believe in yourself. You need to be self-aware. Discover your strengths and areas for improvement (note that I have not said 'weaknesses'). Take deliberate action to grow yourself into that great woman you dream of, desire, want, and believe you can be, no matter what.

Dr Feuerstein, a great psychiatrist from Israel, emphasised this in his acclaimed approach to mediated learning experience (MLE), through which parents can improve their interactions with children. His assessments revealed that every child has the propensity to learn. My organisation, Redd Barna (Save the Children, Norway) trained us as trainers to train school teachers and other carers to treat children with greater love and care. However, I used MLE as an important tool to use at home as a young working parent. I was in highly demanding leadership roles and used to travel a lot for field work. I used MLE to keep my children grounded in our family values through the way, I communicated with them. I don't have any regrets looking at the way they have turned out as young men. It is up to the parents to mediate the world's harsh environment and support the child so the child achieves their potential. I would recommend it to every parent.

—Reuven Feuerstein, Israel Psychologist

I recently learned something that was said by Dr Myles Munroe, who is one of the greatest motivational speakers of our generation. He aptly summarised the meaning of any person's potential in four sentences:

1. Potential is who you are that you haven't yet been
2. Potential is how far you can go that you haven't yet gone
3. Potential is how much you can achieve that you haven't yet achieved
4. Potential is what you can become that you haven't yet become
— Myles Munroe, Bahamian evangelist, author and motivational speaker

That is potential. It is universal. It is futuristic. It is gender neutral. So it is never too late to realise your own potential and take massive action to achieve it.

NEVER UNDERESTIMATE YOURSELF

The greatest undoing of most women is the fact that they have been systematically and relentlessly told they are inferior, until they have come to believe it. They undervalue themselves. The greatest obstacle to women's empowerment most of the time is not men alone, but fellow women who have inadvertently become gatekeepers of patriarchy. Such women are most often the women we love, respect, look up to, and believe in.

These are the women who pull others down inadvertently because they have grown up in a patriarchal society. That is the only one they know and perceive as natural. They have been socialised to accept that men have God-given rights over women, and it's a societal norm which must be maintained for the society's good.

Usually these women are the elderly, respectable members of our communities—cultural leaders, grandparents, aunties, family friends, mothers. They feel responsible and duty-bound to pass on our cultural attributes to the younger generation. Let us be inquisitive, challenging and smart. They counsel and prepare our youth, especially during rituals like birth, initiation into adulthood, marriage, last rites, and burial.

Then there is a second group of women who are close to us as friends, neighbours, and colleagues at work. We normally refer to them as women, who practise PHD ('pull her down'). They may have envy and go to a great extent to beat back any woman who dares to aspire.

Do not get me wrong. I am not condemning our cultures wholesale. I am also not pretending to be an expert on culture. I know there is a lot of deep, indigenous knowledge and valuable lessons acquired over generations that are captured in our myths, beliefs, and taboos. Our culture should be understood and fiercely protected as our society's national treasure. I am simply saying that as we live this culture and pass it down to the next generation, let us inquisitive, challenging, and smart.

We should not take in everything without questioning those aspects of our revered culture that disadvantage, disenfranchise, and disempower half of our communities—women and girls. We need to objectively analyse our culture and weed out those aspects that are not tenable for achieving gender equality.

FIND YOUR VOICE

Never undermine or underestimate yourself. I once read that faith is the emperor of dreams. A great emperor is born from one tiny sperm. A large eagle grows from one small egg. A giant tree grows from one tiny seedling. Everything begins small. It is faith that builds the staircase to your dreams.

Always have faith in yourself and the universe. One will not get you anywhere without the other. Both must be equally strong to reach your desires. Not a single bird makes its first leap from a tree without faith. Not a single animal in the jungle starts the day without faith. Faith is the flame that eliminates fear, and faith is the true emperor of dreams.

At a Youth Takeover of the UN event, dubbed Malala Day, on 12 July 2013, she said that.

Dear brothers and sisters, do remember one thing; Malala day is not my day. Today is the day of every woman, every boy and every girl who has raised her voice for their rights. There are hundreds of human rights activists and social workers who are not only speaking for human rights, but who are struggling to achieve their goals of education, peace and equality.

—Malala Yousafzai, Nobel Laureate

Thousands of people have been killed by the terrorists and millions have been injured. I am just one of them. So here I stand, one girl among many.

283

Grace Alice Mukasa

I speak- not for myself, but for all girls and boys. I raise up my voice- not so that I can shout, but so that those without a voice can be heard. Those who have fought for their rights: their right to live in peace, their right to be treated with dignity, their right to equality of opportunity, their right to be educated.

Malala is today one of the most powerful voices in the twenty-first century when it comes to gender equality and human rights. The only reason she is making a big difference in the world is because she found her voice. Now she is using it for every person in need of equality and empowerment.

Find your voice and change your world.

TWO GREAT DAYS IN A PERSON'S LIFE

Someone once said that, there are only two great days in a person's life: the day they were born, and the day they discovered why they were born. Period!

—Mark Twain, writer, humorist, entrepreneur and lecturer

Just imagine—someone may live for 75 years, which comes to about 27,375 days. But out of all these many days, only two are critical! The first, the day you were born, is obvious. Everyone goes through it naturally and passively, without assistance. However, you are capable of being active on the second most important day of your life. It's the most critical, because this is the day you can utilise your creative juices and find your voice in this overcrowded, noisy world. This is the day you discover your true worth and the legacy you will leave in the world. It is when you discover the *real you*, separate from the crowd!

Without this second great day, your life will be meaningless. It will be empty. It will be blown away by the wind like chaff. Even if you live a hundred years, your life will not be different from the life of a still-born babe, because you served no purpose in the world.

I am grateful to God because, after a long career journey, I have finally found my voice. God put me in one place, and I was forced to have the time to deliberately commit it and use it to fight for gender equality and justice.

Have you found your voice? Have you discovered what makes you cry, sing, and dream? Is there anything for which you can sacrifice your life? for it was concluded that, 'If a man has not discovered something that he will die for, he isn't fit to live,' What will you die for? What is that one thing that will define your legacy here on earth?

—Martin Luther King Jr., civil rights leader.

Finding your voice as a woman in a patriarchal society, where everything is organised in a way that benefits men and boys, is not an easy task. But once you find that voice, it is not easily silenced! 'The most common way people give up their power is by thinking they don't have any.'

—Alice Walker, 1983 Pulitzer prize for fiction winner

You have the power to overcome negativity and live a nice, beautiful, happy life!

CALL TO ACTION

- I challenge every African woman and every African girl to go on a journey of self-awareness.
- Discover and write down who you are (you can sk your friends, colleagues at work)
- Define your personal brand. In so doing, you will be able to identify your purpose in life and hence in fulfilling it, you can become self-actualised and make the world a better place for both men and women.

CHAPTER 36

Gender and Development of a Personal Brand

I learned a fundamental life lesson: self-growth and self-development are key pillars to success. I learned it long ago, as a young, untrained, and struggling manager with Save the Children–Norway. I learned then that my organisation did not own me; it owned the job I held at the time. However, I owned my personal growth, development, and career.

My mentor at the time told me that I should never surrender my opportunity to learn and grow to my employer. Every time I got a new job, I should use it as an opportunity to learn new things and offer distinguished service. I should also ensure that the knowledge and growth uplifts me to a new level. That's why I have worked very hard to build and nurture my brand—an authentic brand—because I knew Warren Buffet's 4-word secret where by commodities are bought and brands are sold.'

—Warren Buffet, American Invester

In 2004, I was promoted from within, as a regional coordinator, to lead a team of twenty-six and very sharp young professionals dispersed in twelve districts of Uganda. I was really out of my depth. I now realise one of the greatest challenges of leadership is to be promoted from within to manage your former peers and 'partners in crime'. It's tough managing people who, until recently, were your colleagues. One day, you are lambasting

286

management with them at every opportunity; next day, you are suddenly on the other side of the fence.

I think my managers then had identified my leadership potential, but I did not believe in myself at all. I was simply a *position leader* who depended on my job description and title to make others do what I wanted them to do. You can imagine the anarchy I unleashed on my colleagues. I was not yet a leader. I didn't know how to influence, build trust, and gain the respect of my team. I lacked practical experience and had no patience. I was a toxic manager.

I had very little confidence, low self-esteem, and great insecurity. I did not believe in myself. I felt that everyone who gave me honest feedback was an enemy working in the spirit of a Pull Her Dn down (PHD) syndrome because I was young and a woman.

Those were my weak excuses. As the saying goes, 'Experience is the name everyone gives to their mistakes.' When I look back today, I chuckle, because I realise that I shamelessly broke all of the twenty-one irrefutable laws of leadership which are ably explored by the leadership guru Zack C. Maxwell.

Then one day a colleague kindly introduced me to Stephen Covey's ground-breaking books: *The 7 'Habits of Highly Effective People'* and, later on, *'Principle-Centered Leadership.'* These two books became my 'bibles.' I studied them from cover to cover, again and again. The more I read them, the more I became self–aware. The more I read them, the more I became exposed to leadership tactics. The more I read them, the more I realised my great potential and the more I challenged myself to 'sharpen my saw'. I wanted to become not only a leader, but *great African leader.* I wanted to coach and mentor young leaders, especially women

—Stephen R. Covey, leadership authority, teacher

I still remember the many nights I sat with my feet under a table, bum on a chair, sometimes without electricity, in a rural district town called Soroti in Uganda. I literally burned the midnight oil. Then a miracle happened. I started to dream, *very big dreams*! I vowed to become a great woman leader across Africa.

287

And it happened. I have been a leader in several national and international NGOs. I have led in Africa, Asia, and the UK. As I was preparing to apply for a visa recently, I reviewed my passports and realised that to date, I have travelled in more than fifty countries on this leadership journey. 'What a great achievement!' I congratulated myself. That's when an inner voice reminded me, 'The great are humble!'

I am a fascinated and avid reader of new inspirational books on leadership and women's empowerment. Every airport I pass through, I go to the duty-free bookshops. I normally walk in with the intention of buying one book and walk out thirty minutes later with four or five new books. That is my weakness. I just can't help myself. I cannot walk away from a good book title.

Some of my close friends say that they envy me and find me very inspiring. I smile back while at the same time I humble myself with the reminder not take my success for granted. I know I am still on my journey of seeking new knowledge. I am forever looking out for people to help me grow, not only in my leadership but holistically.

Before I learned about the impact of socialisation, I thought all my passion to learn depended on reading books as an adult. However, now I know better. I was a beneficiary of a socialisation process which was progressive in nature. I grew up in a big family which valued the extended family system, surrounded mainly by boys (my brothers and cousins), plus many relatives who came in and out of our home.

Consequently, I quickly realised that if I was to survive, I needed to learn and devise strategies to fight for my space and defend myself. I learned to do my part in a very good way to survive my mother's wrath. I also knew that if I did a good job, there would be a reward. My mother was a natural coach. She never tired of explaining the what and why and how of any daily issues I faced. She did this up to the very end.

I remember one special day when I visited her in hospital, where she was literally on her death bed. She was heavily medicated, and everybody was just waiting to hear the news that she had breathed her last. I was coming from school with my friends. As we surrounded her bed, she gestured to me to come near. I knelt down, and in a surprisingly clear voice, she whispered, 'I know I am dying, but don't despair. They have tried all they could do. There is nothing more they can do. I know your brothers will always love you, so don't fear; you are not alone. However, as soon as you bury me, go back to school. Your brothers will love you best if you are educated, have a job, and become somebody in this world. So read hard and never drop out until you have collected my degree for me.'

Oho, what a will and legacy she left me! The following day, after her burial, I escaped from the mourners and went back to school. And instead of one degree, I collected two!

I was taught a lot about being a woman by my no-nonsense mother, but she was also a very empathetic person in her parenting style. I was grounded in the values of my culture, but the way she mediated her parenting to me made me develop a curious mind. I always asked why I did things and how I did them. I realised early that I could ask. First of all, my parents believed that, despite being a girl among many brothers, I needed very good education. They found it imperative to put me in an exclusive girls' boarding school. I had no distractions and was well cared for and instructed by great nuns in a convent school.

My mother, especially, never tired of telling me frankly about the virtues of hard work, courage, persistence, resilience, and integrity. She not only told me about them, she role-modelled those values and behaviours. For example, by the time she died, I was 17 years old. She had already inculcated in me the routine of waking up at 5 a.m., as soon as the Muslim call to prayer sounded across the mystical twenty-one hills that make up the core of Kampala city.

I was pleasantly surprised later on to learn about the foundational practice of successful people: they break down the first hour of the day into 'four fifteen-minute segments'

—Lolly Daskal, writer and Executive Leadership Coach

1. fifteen minutes of prayer
2. fifteen minutes of exercise
3. fifteen minutes of reading
4. fifteen minutes of planning

I am also a proud beneficiary of the holistic training and role-modelling of nuns in a Catholic boarding school: St Theresa's Girls Primary School, Bwanda. Again routine, hard work, and consistency were unquestioned values to succeed in such a school. You had to simultaneously practise education, religion, and garden work at specific times of the day, every day—as they say, *religiously.*

Lastly, I believe I was able to build the brand that I am today because I looked deep in myself and discovered the real Grace in me. I am very passionate—once I believe in something, I go for it. That is the innate skill I have utilised very well in my leadership. I love and believe in people. Empathetic skill enables me to reach out and connect very deeply with the people I lead. I inspire the potential buried deep inside them, and I develop it.

I am confident because my parents constantly affirmed me and rewarded me. I believe I have something unique in me and I can always add value. I can therefore speak out and share my ideas without fear and question why or why not. I am a strategic thinker with excellent ideas, planning, and prioritisation skills. These skills make me an excellent creative contributor, even as I recognise that I am not the best at detail. In fact, I hate it.

I normally bubble with creative ideas and innovative solutions to challenges I face, especially as I wake up early in the morning. I was advised recently to keep a notebook next to my bed because by eleven o'clock, my great ideas tend to mysteriously disappear inside where they came from.

I am fascinated at the way my unwavering integrity makes people trust me and show incredible loyalty to me, even when I am away.

These form some of the strengths I have. Some seem innate. Others I have struggled to harness and grow all my life. I see myself first as a compassionate human being and a woman. Thereafter I juggle my ever-changing identities as a loyal wife, ever-loving mother, and inspirational leader. I started to speak positively to myself as a restored person. That's has been my focus throughout this formidable fight with Stroke. I live everyday in the magnificent spirit of recovery. I can positively use Zig Ziglar's quote that this stroke is just a detour and not a dead end street. Rather than moan in sorrow full loneliness, I decided to mix in a church netwok of Ugandan born-again Christians living in London. I also decided to document and share my experience of defying stroke with other people (patients, families carers and the diverse range of medical professionals), in the hope that they will get greater awareness unlike me who was literary ambushed on September 4th 2016.

I made a choice, at a very young age, when I got the opportunity to lead, 'To stop swimming at the shallow end where everyone seeks shelter.'—that is, in their comfort zones. Mediocrity became my antithesis. I challenged myself to become not just any leader, but a credible leader. I wanted to be an African woman pacesetter, leaving behind me a trail of inspired and successful young women and men. I don't begrudge them their success; I am incredibly proud of them. In some instances, especially now, we have reversed roles, and they have become my mentors.

—Chris Mureithi, Kenyan Writer

This required me to set the bar very high, surf the waves, and swim at the deep end. I always remember that 'success is not for the chosen few, but success is for the few who have chosen'.

—Robin Sharma, Canadian writer and premier speaker on Leadership

Robin Sharma also said, in his very inspirational book *The Leader who Had No Title*, that to be a leader, one has to learn very early to define one's personal brand and decided to build strong and deeper relationships with all the people one meets in life.

I suffered a stroke in September 2016. It was very tragic and confusing at first. Then one day I started talking to my stroke. I assured it, 'You may think you are my partner in pain, but that is it. I will not allow you to steal my destiny.' From that time forward, I embraced my new social status as a person with disability.

I decided to protect myself against self-stigma. I confronted all my personal pains, fears, and losses to be on the razor's edge.

Most people hide in their shells when the going gets rough. They retreat into their bunkers. They push away anything that pushes them the least bit out of their comfort zone. And sadly in so doing, they also push away their chances for growth, masterly and lasting achievement. 'Never forget that Dude. The brave eat their fear before fear eats them.

—Robin Sharma, Canadian writer and premier speaker on leadership

So I ate my fear every day. I wrote something every day. I achieved at least one success every day, and thanked God for it every day before I slept. I vowed never to sleep during the day but to stay awake, seated and alert, to strengthen my core and my beleaguered brain every day. I walked twice every day. I vowed never to be a negative statistic in the UK books. Consider this: 'I learned that courage was not the absence of fear, but the triumph over it.' I am grateful I learnt that important lesson.

—Nelson Mandela, freedom fighter, South African president

Take courage, fellow women and men. One day you will be the real issue. When they say many women stop school at primary level, you will say, 'Not me!' When they say most girls drop out of school when they fall pregnant during teen age, you will insolently say, 'Iam not dumb!' When they affirm that all women lack the self- confidence to be leaders, raise your voice and answer, 'Not me!' When they assert that, due to reproductive roles, most women cannot pursue higher educational degrees, shout, 'Not me!' When they pronounce that women cannot balance leadership power and marriage, reply, 'Surely, I gave it my all. It takes two to tango!'

Defy failure. Deny it space at your table. Your mantra should be to become the standard!

> **Be the standard**
> - When the rest sit, I stand
> - When the rest stand, I stand up
> - When the rest stand up, I become outstanding
> - When the rest become outstanding, I become the standard
>
> —Chris Mureithi, Kenyan author

Therefore open your mind, assess what your brand is today, and define what your authentic brand should be. Your authentic brand must be real, credible and aligned to your consciously developed reputation (Not a fake charade.) It's like you are paying for the name and image that you will have created over the years. People will know you and they share your values. Create the real you in your brand. People will be telling themselves that they trust and like you. They will be wondering how to get somebody with the qualities you represent, in their lives

Have a very deep conversation with yourself like Nelson Mandela. If possible acquire his book, *'Conversations With Myself.'* Read it, reflect and learn from your personal experiences, because every one of us has a unique story. Your personal story gives you unique perspectives, reveals your strengths, and abilities (X factors). Normally when we remember our negative experiences, we tend to focus on the pain they caused us. We don't bother about the coping mechanisms we used to overcome the challenges.

For example, when I lost my mother as a teenager. I used to focus on the deep, sharp, and unimaginable pain, loneliness at the time. I was very angry and in my heart I kept asking, 'Why me; Mum why did you leave me so early; whom have you left me with?' In my grieving state, I could not imagine coping without her. But I did cope! Of course it was not easy. There were so many problems but I overcame all of them. I even became pregnant while still at school, however unlike the fate of most orphans and girls who get unplanned pregnancies, I remained focussed and never dropped out of school till I got my degree!

However today I clearly see the resolve, creativity, resilience, persistence and integrity I developed. As you know necessity is the best source of all creativity. I learnt to focus on my education like the eagle. I had a polygamous father, who disappeared soon after our mother's burial. He used to send people to bring us food and that was it. He had conveniently forgotten we were still at school and needed fees, transport and scholastic materials. Most importantly he forgot we needed love and left us to pick up our emotional pieces, on our own! Nevertheless, I stepped in the gap and became the surrogate mother and leader to my nine siblings. I made sure we continued going to school, cooked, and maintained our home just like my mum used to do.

Just on the day after her burial, I went back to school and made a vow to continue until I got a degree. I had promised my terminally ill mum to do this. I knew it was hard but the right thing to do. I knew I was my father's favourite daughter, so I exploited that special position. I made enquiries and followed up my father at his new home and literary demanded for school fees - for my self and my siblings. To get rid of me, I think, he made arrangements for me to collect rent from his tenants and pay for school fees. (The rest is a story for another book).

That major life experience shaped my character and values (Y factors). If you reflect on your own life experiences you will discover your own too. You build your brand based on solid values, and that gives you credibility, leadership, and authority in a particular area (Z factors). Through your experiences, good and bad, you learn and grow your character. In responding to the vow to my mother, I built on my integrity, leadership caring skills. I became a problem solver, and compassionate for my siblings to receive school fees too. No wonder I ended up as a leader in the NGO sector, which uses a lot of similar values and skills. So, in answering challenges, you make decisions about what you will do to cope and make a difference in life.

Today I challenge you to start on your task to deliberately develop your authentic brand which has equity. This is like expressing your legacy, reputation, and intellectual property. The potential value of your brand is a combination of your X, Y, and Z factors. Personally, reflect on the key questions. Start to dream and *dream big dreams*. The journey has started, and we have agreed you shall build this boat while sailing. Jump on and let's go!

CALL TO ACTION

- Complete the following worksheet to begin developing your sense of your personal brand.

Key question/process	Answer	Action(s) you will take to enact what you have discovered

Write down the story of your life (ten attributes for each generation starting at five years)
 	
• Highlight the good and the bad (at home, at school, at work, in marriage).
• Reflect on how major events affected you: strengths developed, fears developed and conquered, and values you exhibit today.
• What did you learn?
  o How did the lessons strengthen your character?
  o What emotions did you experience?
  o Which emotions have you kept up to today, and which have you dropped?
  o What values did you use and develop?		

What makes you unique and authentic?		

What attracts you to other people, especially as a woman or man? (Forget the socialised aspects of femininity and masculinity, because we are trying to fight gender discrimination and inequality)		
What makes people like you, resent you, or hate you? (Some of these characteristics represent your strengths and values that you should retain and build on, and others reflect areas to drop or improve on)		
Why should anybody care to know you? What is uniquely important about you and can add value to others?		
What are your X factors (most dominant natural strengths and abilities)?		
What are your Y factors (most dominant character traits and values)?		
What are your Z factors (your dominant skills and passions)?		
What are ten unique life experiences that have enabled you to grow your character—the one we see today?		
What is your purpose in life, your service to society, and the legacy you will leave behind?		
What is your vision in life?		
What type of brand and legacy do you want to leave behind in this world? When you die, what will people genuinely miss about you?		
Who are you? What is your unique identity? What makes you different from all other people in this world?		

Who have been the most important people at various stages of your life? Why? • List them • What did you learn from each of them (negative or positive)? • What will you do or not do to put that learning to good use?		
What are your unique dreams and passions? What are the things you plan to achieve before you die? List them. Dream big.		

CHAPTER 37

The Six Gendered Spaces in Practice

In chapter 10, we examined the six socialising agents in general. These socialising agents are found within certain contexts. Those contexts are what I refer to as 'gendered spaces'. The agents of socialisation impact people within spaces which have the same names.

In this section of the book, we shall examine the six gendered spaces. I will use the illustration of one family, the Ketanuga family, to show socialising agents at work within the gendered spaces.

It is important for women to appreciate each other and celebrate the goodness of being soft and feminine, while we also appreciate men for being firm and masculine. What has been happening since these gender wars began is that everyone has been struggling for their survival. If we can understand why gender is so important and why it has been the way it is, then we will be able to learn where we went wrong, walk it back, and get a fresh start.

We will develop scenarios that will help you to see how some of these six socialising spaces play a key role in shaping gender roles. The six are the family, the school, the workplace, the community, the media and religious centres, and the government.

SPACE 1: THE FAMILY

Mr and Mrs Ketanuga have six children. Jack, 15, is the firstborn. Imora, 13, is the second born, Peter, 11; Mary, 8; Junior, 6; and Oscar, 3, are the younger four in the family. Mr Ketanuga is a consultant with a non-governmental organisation that assists rural livelihood development through sustainable agricultural and animal husbandry. Mrs Ketanuga works as a nurse in the community hospital.

They are a typical middle-income African family who live in one of the estates in the capital city, in a three-bedroom house. Both parents are educated and working. The younger children are surrounded by love and positive affirmation—sometimes tough love that is firm when they have to be disciplined. They enjoy both Mum and Dad.

They have one maid who helps to take care of the children at home. She is a day maid; she does not live in with the family. She has her own family of three children and her husband.

Mr Ketanuga works until 5 p.m., and on a daily basis he stops at the local bar to unwind with his colleagues and other people with whom he is does business. He arrives home between 9 and 10 p.m. He does not like cold or reheated food, especially maize meal or rice. So Mrs Ketanuga has her kitchen organised so that when he comes home, they will warm the vegetables and stew and cook fresh maize meal or rice for him. Sometimes he wants steamed bananas, and they have to make that dish fresh.

Since the maid must leave as soon as the children have returned from school at 6 p.m., the food must be cooked by someone else. Mrs Ketanuga taught Imora and Mary how to cook, so they usually run back from school to help her. Mrs. Ketanuga normally comes in from work at around 7 p.m., as the hospital is usually very busy in the evenings. She is always very tired because nursing requires that she is on her feet most of the day.

When he comes to eat his supper, Mr Ketanuga does not like to sit alone at table. Usually Mrs Ketanuga waits up and sits with him while he eats. If she is absent, then Imora and Mary wait up to serve him. Jack and Peter sit and converse with him while he eats. They talk about the day and then go to bed. The girls quietly wait up in the kitchen. After Dad is done eating, they clear away the dishes and pack any leftover food.

According to their culture, men and boys are not supposed to enter the kitchen. It is girls' work. Men and boys who stay in the kitchen with their mothers and sisters are teased and called names. They feel very sad and ashamed.

Even though Jack is a sensitive boy who loves his mother dearly and would like to be more helpful to her, he does not do household chores because that is girls' work. He fears being bullied and called names at school.

In their culture, boys and men used to do outdoor work like tending cattle, hunting, being warriors, and farming. Since they live in the city, these jobs do not exist. The boys socialise by staying out and playing football or pool. When they come home, they just sit around and read or watch TV while the girls are busy helping their mom or the maid with various household chores

THE KETANUGAS' FAMILY VALUE

Ketanuga normally goes on night duty every other week. Whenever she leaves the house, she tells Imora and Mary, 'I have left the house in your hands. Let me not find it in a mess; otherwise you will be in trouble with me. Make sure everyone is fine. If there is a problem, call me. Make sure you check on Oscar at night if he wakes up or starts to cry. Be quick to comfort him because he might wake your daddy up with crying. You know your dad has to go to work in the morning and does not want to be disturbed!'

Even though their father is in the house with them, the girls have to be in charge when their mom goes on night duty. Sometimes this is very difficult for Imora, because she is tired and has to go to school the next day. She wakes up many times to take care of her little brother. In the morning she is still sleepy. This affects her studies, so she is not as active in school as her brother Jack.

During the weeks when Mrs Ketanuga does night duty, it is very difficult for her. She has to stay much longer hours, and she worries a lot about her children at home. There is a shortage of staff in the hospital, but they get paid more for working overtime. When she gets home, she has to ensure that she is awake by the time the children come home so that she can spend some time with them, help them with homework, and catch up with anything that she was not able to do before.

301

Then she has to wait for her husband to come home, hopefully by 9 p.m. She prepares a warm bath for him. She warms and cooks his food and serves him. She ensures that he is settled in before she goes to work. Many times Mr Ketanuga delays and comes home late. So Mrs Ketanuga is late to reach the hospital and has to cheat to explain her frequent tardiness.

She had tried to explain this situation to Mr Ketanuga, but it seems like every time she mentions it, he comes home even later the next day. She now prefers to tell lies at work. She remembers that, during her first years of marriage, she got in trouble with Mr Ketanuga's clan, relatives, and friends. He complained in a clan meeting that she was neglecting her duties as a wife because of night duty. He said that he never saw her during those weeks, and she was always complaining of tiredness from working at night.

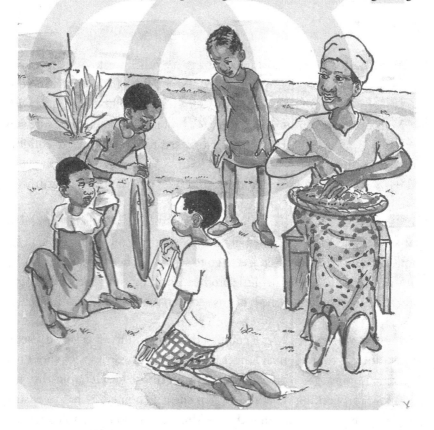

It was not possible for her to answer back and explain that she could not leave the job. She couldn't explain that her income was also helping to pay for the family's day-to-day household needs, including food, toilet paper, water, electricity, and books for the children. Mr Ketanuga's money was paying mortgage on the house they wee living in (at least for him he had a tangible asset he could show for his expenses).

She remembers that clan meeting with a shudder. She felt really humiliated, lonely, and frightened. The clan elders reprimanded and warned her to put more effort into being a good wife and mother, even though she had a job. A job was not more important than her husband and family. Her mother-in-law and Mr Ketanuga's two divorced elder sisters were especially tough on her. They threatened to get Mr Ketanuga another wife if she did not change and give him 'peace'.

Mr Ketanuga looked down throughout the meeting and never tried to defend his wife, even though he knew the true situation. That was their culture.

So Mrs Ketanuga had learned from long practice to balance all the work as a wife, mother, and nurse, in that order. She became a wife who was present for her husband no matter what happened at work. But she had to pay a heavy price for her obedience. She is constantly tired and stressed. She has regular headaches. Sometimes she feels nauseated due to failure to eat well.

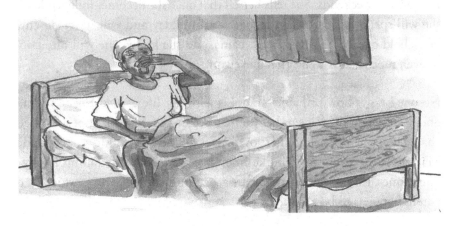

She is lucky now because her daughters are growing up fast. They can help her with the repetitive work around the house. Their small arms, legs, and backs are becoming important indeed. The money Mrs Ketanuga earns also helps her to pay for the maid.

It suddenly hits her. For her to be successful in all three roles, she has to heavily depend on other women—her young daughters and the maid! Her older daughter, Imora, has become the surrogate mother to Oscar and Junior. The maid does all the work at home that a wife would do—washes clothes, irons clothes, cooks the food, scrubs the house. She goes to the shops and markets and bathes the children.

By the time the maid goes home, she is also very tired. Yet she has to do more work for her own family. Like Mrs Ketanuga, she has to make sure she is a good wife, good mother, and good maid!

On the weekend, it is always spring cleaning. All the dirty clothes are removed for washing, and the house is thoroughly cleaned from top to bottom. Mrs Ketanuga, the maid, and the girls wake up early to do these chores. If Mrs Ketanuga is not home, then the girls and the maid get a head start. They have learned that it is their role, and there are consequences if they do not play their roles well.

Imora hates weekends. She tells herself that once she becomes independent, she will spend her Saturdays in bed until midday and will never do any household chores. She has nice dreams, and she knows she will hire two or even more maids to do the housework.

No one knows how unhappy Imora is with her life as a surrogate mum. She is a quiet girl who keeps her thoughts to herself. She does not share her challenges. She does share her joys. After all, no one would understand. Mary feels the same way. Unlike Imora, she vents her frustrations loudly. Sometimes this rebelliousness earns her punishment from whichever parent happens to be around.

However, Jack loves the weekend. He gets to sleep in with his brothers and his dad, because waking up means that they will be in the way of the ladies cleaning the house. He only dislikes that they have to eat their breakfast later than usual. He thinks this is because the women talk too much instead of doing their work.

After breakfast, the boys watch TV programmes. By that time, Imora and Mary are already too tired to enjoy anything on TV. Also, they have to wash up dishes used for the sumptuous Saturday breakfast. Imora often joins Oscar in his afternoon nap while their dad goes off to socialise with his friends and catch up on business deals.

If Mrs Ketanuga is at home, they do their hair and release the maid early. Saturday evenings are usually the most fun part of the day for the Ketanuga household. The work is done. Sometimes Mr Ketanuga comes home early with takeaway food. The whole family gets to eat together and catch up on the various issues that have arisen. Since they don't have to cook supper or wash up, the girls get to rest a little. That is usually a time of real joy. This does not happen very often, about once a month.

Because of the extremely heavy schedule that Mrs Ketanuga has had for a long time, she has developed a heart condition and a back condition. These were caused by the stress that comes from closely spaced pregnancies, prolonged overwork, standing for long hours both at home and at work, and little rest and recuperation for her body.

However, these conditions have not stopped her work schedule. She has worked tirelessly through her bouts of illness and exhaustion. She normally has to force herself to get out of bed after very little sleep. The doctors have informed her that her workload must become lighter. But when she looks at her family, their lifestyle, and their needs, she does not quite see how it is possible to work less, unless she hires more help. Still, that would not lighten her duties as a mother or as a wife.

After getting the doctor's advice, Mrs Ketanuga tried to confide in her best friend, Maude. They were childhood friends, having attended primary school, secondary school, and university together. They shared a room at university and shared intimate experiences as they got their first boyfriends. Maude had a very difficult marriage and had since separated from her husband, John.

Mrs Ketanuga:	My health is not so good. My pressure is very high. The doctor has recommended that I stop working. That I slow down.
Maude:	And …
Mrs Ketanuga:	Of course you know I can't. Not with the children's education and Ketanuga no longer reliable.
Maude:	What do you mean? Is he having affairs? Does he beat you? Put down your tools! That foolish man, you must divorce him!
Mrs Ketanuga:	But … but …
Maude:	Do not even think about it. He cannot harass you like that. Wake up, girl. Start a new life before it is too late, just like me.

Since that time, Mrs Ketanuga has cut off the links with her dear friend. She was taken aback by the judgmental way her friend reacted to her dilemma. She in fact feels very angry with Maude for trying to take over her life. She deeply loves her husband of twenty years and has never thought of divorce. She is simply frustrated by the way he is preoccupied and doesn't pay much attention to family. He is rarely around to support her with parenting nowadays, as he used to in earlier years. It seems something from work has been bothering him.

Imora has become increasingly withdrawn and is losing weight, Mary is angry at everybody. She snaps and behaving like a volcano wanting to erupt. Jack is always watching English Premier League with his friends. Mr Ketanuga, in the meantime, is home less and less. He stays out on flimsy excuses and broods and paces whenever he is home. At weekends he travels to the village on his own.

All this worries Mrs Ketanuga. She swears to continue working for her children until she drops dead!

When Mrs Ketanuga thinks about her family, she wonders how Jack and the boys would take care of themselves if anything ever happens to her. At least Imora and Mary have been trained in the various chores in the house. In the worst-case scenario, they can work as housemaids. They know how to think on their feet with regard to any challenge in the house. She is happy they have mastered the art of multitasking, using their brains, hands, and feet to deliver service in an efficient and effective way.

Her inner self, however, revolts violently whenever she thinks about their fates as wives in the future. Will they always toil away for others, even when they are sick and tired? Will they ever lead happy lives? Will they ever have a break? Who will speak for them now that their childhood has made them deaf and dumb in the face of unfair gender treatment at home? Is it their fate to lead the same life she has led herself?

What about her husband? He could easily marry another woman and she would take care of him, maybe even better than Mrs Ketanuga has done. Mrs Ketanuga feels she has miserably failed him as a wife. She cannot help but blame herself for his current strange behaviour.

What about her boys, Jack and Peter? Her dear, darling Jack gave her a lot of joy and brought respect from her husband's clan when he was born. She smiles widely whenever she remembers that time. Mr Ketanuga treated her like a queen. He was very proud of her. But how would the boys survive with a stepmother? Why are they so uncaring and unsupportive of the girls at home?

Has she inadvertently created uncaring monsters by allowing the boys to selfishly look on while the girls toil away at household work? Has she failed to impart social and survival skills to them as a parent—skills to care for others, skills to look after themselves? These boys are her greatest challenge and fear. They have lived all their lives totally dependent on a female taking care of them. Has she spoilt them?

Mrs Ketanuga feels trapped because it is not her fault and it seems too late. The culture she has been born in, socialised in, and married in has not allowed her to train and treat her boys the same way as her girls. She wonders whether she has been foolish to adhere to those unhelpful cultural norms when she has spent most of her time in the city.

Her children will not necessarily get married to people from her cultural background. What if they marry into cultures in which men are expected to contribute to half the household tasks, like Mr and Mrs Agunatanza? He was from Mrs Ketanuga's culture, but his wife is European. He had to learn how to cook, take care of their twin girls, do the laundry, and many other chores.

Mrs Ketanuga wonders why she has been so narrow-minded about her sons. If they knew how to do things like the girls, she would not even need to think about a second maid. The load in the house would be lightened. She is aware of most of their home activities and shortcomings, but what about their activities in school, where they spend a big chunk of their daylight hours?

With such thoughts churning around in her mind, all she can do is pray for another chance to raise her children better.

SPACE 2: THE SCHOOL

The Ketanuga siblings go to the same school. Like most public schools in Africa, their school does not hire staff who will clean the classrooms, sweep the compound, slash the grass in the field, or wash the school toilets. The only workers apart from the teaching staff and the administration are the tea girl, a messenger who runs errands for the office, and two security guards. The school depends on its pupils to clean the school.

The students are expected to clean the classrooms and around the school compound, cut the grass, and wash the toilets. Therefore, part of the supplies each student is supposed to bring to school is a broom made of reeds.

Again, because of the culture of the community, it is the duty of the girls to ensure that they bring brooms to school. In each class, the girls have a roster for sweeping, washing the toilets, and collecting the garbage. The boys in the upper school have the duty of burning the rubbish in the school incinerator.

Only at the beginning of the term, when the grass is long, are boys required to bring slashers so they can slash the grass. Otherwise, as in their homes, daily hygiene at school is left to the girls. Should they default in it, they face consequences. The boys have more time to play and socialise while the girls do the cleaning.

Sanitation and hygiene are very important aspects of the school that the Ketanuga siblings attend. When the morning chores are completed, during assembly time, the teacher inspects the hygiene of each student. Students must have a clean uniform, clean hands, and neat hair. Their personal hygiene gives them merits, but it is tough for the girls to maintain after morning cleaning. The general complaint in the school is that the girls are not as hygienic as the boys. They therefore get consequences for this default on a daily basis.

This creates a certain dislike for school and demoralisation among the girls. The teachers often separate the girls for talks, encouraging them to work as hard as the boys and to improve their concentration in class.

In fact, the Ketanuga siblings are really lucky. They go to a school in the city. Had they attended a rural school, Imora and Mary would have missed the early morning mathematics lessons every week on Tuesday and Thursday. Mrs Ketanuga remembers very well her school days in a rural area. They had to collect water and firewood for cooking the school lunch—together with their female teachers! No one seemed to care that mathematics was a key lesson for both girls and boys. No one seemed to question why, at the end of the term, the girls did very badly in the final mathematics examinations. No one seemed to notice that many girls slept during class hours.

WOE, BELOVED GIRLS, WHEN PUBERTY HITS!

Then a new challenge develops for the girls in Imora's class—the mother of all challenges! Their bodies start to misbehave and bulge out of their clothes. Their breasts grow rounded and large, with prominent nipples. One morning as the girls prepare for school, Imora exclaims to her mum, 'I hate that blouse. The boys keep staring at my chest.' Of course her hips compete in size too.

Skirts suddenly became too tight and too light.

One day, while seated in class, Imora feels sharp cramping in her lower tummy, extreme pain, and pulsating headache. She feels something leaking onto her panties. It is not urine—her bladder is empty. She stands and furtively checks her skirt behind. She is horrified to see her skirt has a *big red dark spot*! She quickly removes her school sweater and ties it around her waist. She feels really sick and starts sweating profusely. She fears putting up her hand to ask the teacher for permission to go out.

The pupils in her class have developed a habit of making bad comments about her body whenever she stands up to answer the teacher's questions. She has therefore decided to protect herself by making herself invisible. She avoids busy spots in the school. She avoids asking teachers questions. She always enters class early and comes out last. She has slowly become a very silent and lonely girl.

In that season, no one ever questions why girls' performance seems to deteriorate as they enter adolescence. No one realises that many girls quietly suffer from headaches, backaches, and painful cramps at particular times of the month. Sometimes they even faint. No one seems to notice that when girls go to the stinking toilets, they take a long time, although sometimes the teacher punishes them for delaying.

The toilets have no water, yet the girls must change their sanitary towels. When they finally come out, with dirty hands and sweaters tied around their waists, the boys are patiently waiting nearby, watching like hawks, ready to make negative comments and laugh at them. One day Imora says to her sister, 'The boys are so mean. I feel like running away!'

No one notices the shame girls feel when asking for money from their dads every month to buy sanitary towels. Few pay attention to girls who perform badly and tend to miss certain classes on certain days. Many girls simply begin to lose interest in studies because they feel they are not intelligent enough to pursue the subjects. The girls and those around them don't realise that this is just a symptom of their change in puberty. Some girls eventually drop out of school completely.

Imora has so many questions but very few answers. She wishes her mum was available during the day. She wishes her mum would not come home looking tired and miserable. Imora would then have asked her, 'Why have the boys in class started staring at my chest? Why has no one taught me about menstrual hygiene? Why must I suffer those terrible headaches and stomach pains every month? Why is it a taboo to talk about it anyway?'

She might also have asked why the government or school had not put any water in the toilets, restored toilet doors that had come off the hinges, or included sanitary towels in the school requirements. Why were the sanitary towels so expensive? Why couldn't they develop ones that could be reusable? Why did no one seem to care? Why did the teachers pretend not to know? Why? Why? Why?

Imora feels that her mum is the most frustrating. Why did she find it so hard to explain to her daughters the body changes of puberty? She seemed to suddenly talk in proverbs and indirectly, as if becoming a woman were a shameful process.

THE LONG WALK OF SHAME

Imora would remember that day forever—the day she made the long 'walk of shame' from the back to the front of the *whole* class. The English teacher, Mr Omadi, forced her to remove her sweater from around her waist and walk to the front of the classroom. He angrily shouted at her, 'Why are you always so shabby? Remove it!'

She became transfixed in one place and started sweating again, but refused to respond to the teacher. No … she just couldn't do it! She would die of shame! She started to explain, but the words wouldn't come out. She stammered and shook. The teacher forcefully removed the sweater, and suddenly everyone, including the teacher, was laughing and shouting at her. Her green skirt was stained with the *big red dark spot*!

The head teacher heard the commotion. He came round. He was a helpful and supportive man. He comforted Imora. He explained to the rest of the class that what had happened to Imora was normal for any girl as she matured into a woman. He told the class, 'You must all be happy and celebrate womanhood. Imora's body is preparing her to become a great mother and wife when she completes her education. Let us all clap and wish her well. In the meantime, let us help her to change and become more comfortable.'

He took her to the office. He wiped away her tears. He gave her some water to drink. Handing her a tablet of bathing soap, a five-litre jerrycan of water, and a new skirt and sanitary pad, he sent Imora to the school bathrooms. When she came back, he once again reassured her she would be OK. He allowed her to go home and rest, with a note for her mum explaining further. He invited Mr Omadi for some straight talk over lunch.

In most public schools in Africa, few really sit back to think about the day-to-day experiences that most of these girls go through. They have started the day earlier than the boys. They have been working at home from the time they woke up. The older girls assist in collecting water, making breakfast, and looking after their siblings. They do not start the day with the same mental capacity as their brothers, due to tiredness.

As they develop into women, they find it hard to cope with the changes in their bodies, coupled with bullying from their peers and seemingly uncontrollable hormones. They start attracting lots of attention from teachers, their brothers' friends, and older men on the road, especially when their parents are away. Their gender-specific needs—for menstrual hygiene management, privacy, guidance, support, and protection from defilement and rape—are hardly responded to. When there are consequences for making mistakes at home or at school, girls are unable to start class in the same frame of mind as boys. They are confused and lonely, and so much more is expected from them!

After school, Jack and his younger brother stay behind for extracurricular activities. They play physical activities, including football, volleyball, rugby, tennis, hockey, and basketball. They socialise and learn to be leaders.

Imora and Mary, on the other hand, have to rush home and look after their siblings. The maid has to leave, so the girls have to do the evening house chores and hopefully have a little time left to do their homework. Many are the days Imora and Mary receive corporal punishment at school because of failure to complete their homework. Sometimes sheer exhaustion causes them to make silly mistakes.

Imora wonders how long she has to undergo this. She wonders when she will ever get the wherewithal to move out of her parents' home and just be in her own space. Having such frustration with her mom, she wonders whether she can try to speak to her father, Mr Ketanuga.

Imora smiles to herself. She cannot even imagine starting a conversation with him about her challenges in school. In the past few months, her father has been returning from his workplace looking like he is about to explode! She wonders what is going on in that office he had once been so proud of.

SPACE 3: THE WORKPLACE

Mr Ketanuga's work requires him to travel from time to time in the rural areas. He has a number of work colleagues with whom he shares the office. For the longest time, all the team leaders were male. Management said that whenever they advertise they got mainly male applicants. And the few women who applied could not be shortlisted due to very poor applications.

The women applicants lacked consistent experience in leadership positions. Most of them had had breaks in their careers to go on maternity leave or care for sick relatives, so they missed out on promotions. Many had not had very good tertiary education because they had been pulled out of school to help their mothers with household work and with their siblings. Also, some had dropped out of school because tertiary education where technical skills were developed was considered 'too much to spend on a girl'. The parents had made what they believed was a rational choice to keep the boys in school and remove the girls. After all, it was the boys who would inherit the father's property and propagate the family lineage. Mr Ketanuga was proud his wife has upgraded her education and even graduated after marriage.

Some of the women who already worked in the office were very well qualified, but they seemed intimidated by the 'big positions'. They felt that those positions were reserved for their male counterparts. Also, when they did the same category of work as the men, they got less salary despite producing equal output. So these women did not see the point of pursuing a busier, more prominent position when the pay was not very attractive.

The work was quite intensive. It involved working late in the evenings and over some weekends, as well as field travel. In some instances, the good jobs meant working far away from home. Few women could manage to be away for long trips. They seemed to always have new babies. Their husbands interfered and refused them permission to travel. Without understanding these circumstances, most of the male employees and managers presumed that the female staff were not as committed as the male staff. Mr Ketanuga agreed with this view completely. He really would have preferred that their organisation was all male. It would have been more efficient.

No wonder most female staff preferred to stay in non-managerial positions. These jobs were very good for women because the jobs were flexible and allowed them to balance their household roles as wives and mother with those at work, as employees caring for the needs and interests of their bosses. The only challenge was that these jobs could be very measure. They paid less, and one hardly played any role in decision making. Staff couldn't develop their careers or leadership capacity. They retired with very little pension.

Their boss was retiring. He had worked with the organisation for twenty-five years and was going to become an advisory consultant. It meant that a new boss was required. Mr Ketanuga has been working with the organisation for twenty-one years. He hoped to be considered for promotion. Surely he had more than enough experience to run the organisation?

During the days when the board of directors met to discuss how they would fill the position, Mr Ketanuga was quite anxious. He hoped that they would nominate him for the position.

Finally the chairman of the board of directors called for a meeting for the team. The former team leader gave a small speech to thank the organisation for supporting him, then gave the chairman an opportunity to speak. Mr Chairman made a few introductory remarks, then told the team that the board had been in discussions with the foreign trustees of the organisation. The major issue that had been brought up was that now the organisation needed to become more gender-balanced.

Mr Ketanuga did not quite understand what that term 'gender-balanced' meant, but it gave him a bad feeling. It sounded to him like that 'women stuff' that was being peddled around by some advocacy groups he knew. He didn't care much for that term. The team had twelve competent men and one lady who was the secretary to the CEO. What exactly did they mean by 'become more gender-balanced'? The kind of work they were involved in was labour intensive—did they need more secretaries?

While he was thinking, the bombshell dropped. Mr Chairman called upon a lady who had been sitting quietly in the corner. He introduced her as the new team leader!

What! A woman? OMG!

Mr Chairman went on to share information about her high education qualifications, strong capabilities in the areas of consultancy and programme development, expertise in food security, and agricultural know-how. She was going to lead this team into a new era.

Mr Ketanuga looked her. He thought she had a big, roving eyes and very curvy body. She was wearing a well-fitted skirt suit. She looked extremely confident, but Mr Ketanuga felt there was no way this woman could be educated, experienced, and up to the level of a team leader. He was unimpressed, but he kept his expression cool and controlled. A woman? The world was going the wrong direction!

Everyone clapped and smiled. There was an animated buzz for about two minutes. Mr Ketanuga did not understand what everyone was excited about. A lady to be his boss? It was a very difficult pill to swallow—a very sad day in his career.

He now remembered a very funny story from one of the neighbouring countries. The country had accidentally got a female vice president, and every time the president would go abroad, she had to chair the army council. At first the generals thought it was a bad joke. A woman to preside over important military meetings? She turned out to be very competent ... but that was not where his thoughts were right now! A woman was *not* a team leader.

Mr Ketanuga thought of resigning. At least if it had been a man who was going to lead him, it would have made his disappointment less palatable. But a woman?

Then he thought of his now-ailing wife, and he became agitated. His dear wife could no longer work long, demanding hours. She had taken a long sick leave. She required expensive medicines and rest, coupled with physiotherapy The family income had been reduced. He also had to pay the mortgage; otherwise he would lose his precious house. School fees, uniforms, food ... The maid had not been paid for the last five months, and she was looking at him in a funny way ... How had his wife managed to juggle all those costs before?

320

'Oh, let me not even think about it,' he concluded. He realised he had to swallow humble pie and give the new woman team leader a test run.

In her maiden speech, the new team leader said she was passionate about gender in the workplace. She talked of improving the organisational culture and making the office a safe place for both male and female workers. ('Seriously?' the men whispered. 'No staff has ever died in office!') She talked of improving work habits to lessen the need for overtime and antisocial working hours. ('Really? She must be mad.')

She said the job descriptions would be reviewed to incorporate gender issues. She said she would review the performance systems to ensure equality. ('Yeah right! She's raving mad.') All staff would be sent for training to become more gender sensitive. She went on and on and on … and Mr Ketanuga thought she had gone out of her pretty head. She needed a manicure and not a leadership position!

During the next few months, she began to introduce the idea of gender awareness in the workplace to Mr Ketanuga and his team. Those months were depressing for him. Every fibre of his being resisted the thought of a female team leader. He took to drinking more alcohol and being a real sourpuss to his family. They had withdrawn from him.

Mr Ketanuga wondered why his new boss was so passionate about gender awareness, what it meant, and how it affected society. He had imagined that she might be a single woman, but was surprised that she was a full-time wife and mother to a rather lovely family who seemed to be into all of that gender stuff. When the senior staff were invited to her home for a get-together, her husband and sons were busy helping with chores and doing things he had only witnessed his friend Mr Agunatanza doing. Yet these were fully African males. It was strange, but they seemed happy working together—washing dishes, serving guests, yet having intelligent conversation with them. The conversations he held with her husband fascinated him and gave him respect for this whole gender thing. It seemed she was practising what she preached. And her family were an accepting congregation!

Incidentally, the woman was not a bad manager. She was compassionate and focused, and the company made a profit. Everyone seemed well cared for. Mr Ketanuga began to grudgingly have respect for her. He looked forward to their regular meetings. He even toyed with the idea of surprising his wife with a fully cooked breakfast. The moment he thought of that, though, he freaked out. He needed more time to acclimate to this gender agenda.

It was in this state of mind that he went for a one-week gender workshop and retreat. He had promised himself that nothing could change him at 45 years old, and with twenty years of marriage behind him. But if this was what he had to do to keep his job, the he would pretend to be interested in gender. Little did he know that this workshop would shake the core of his fundamental attitudes, beliefs, and behaviours towards the opposite sex.

The workshop illuminated key gaps in the relationships he had with his wife, daughters, and sons. He began to realise that he had to take personal responsibility for gender awareness. There were a lot of changes he needed to start making, starting in his home, immediately. He left the workshop and travelled home with a spring in his step. He was a man with a mission. Things were going to begin to change in his home and in his community!

Thinking of his rural home, the community which had shaped his culture to be so gender unbalanced, he wondered—where could one start with such people?

SPACE 4: THE COMMUNITY

Mr and Mrs Ketanuga and their children normally travelled twice a year to his ancestral village home, which was about two hundred miles from the capital city. He went alone more often, because of work and to see his relatives. On those random weekends, he enjoyed individual time away from everyone to take in the sights and sounds of the countryside. Mr Ketanuga loved the compact country house he had started to build when he got his first job and finished when he was newly married.

Building such a home was one of his community's customs. When a man married, he was required to 'bring light to the homestead'. Every male child in the house inherited a piece of land from his father. If he was to keep that land, he had to build on it. Mr Ketanuga looked back and thanked God that he had been wise enough to do this very early. If he were to try to build that same house today, it would have been impossible because of the many responsibilities he held.

His four sisters had been unlucky in marriage. The eldest, Loyce, who was also his closest confidante, had lost a loving husband of thirty years to AIDS-related complications. The youngest sister was still trying to hang on to a very abusive marriage. The middle two sisters were now divorced. In his opinion, both of them were very quarrelsome and difficult to handle. None of his sisters inherited any land from the family, because girls were meant to go away to their husbands' homes. It was funny because in those homes, they did not inherit any property either. It was feared that if they left for any reason, that inheritance would leave with them.

This put women in a difficult position. Only if they bought property with cash could they really own it. Even then, if they were married, they had to register property in their husbands' names or their children's names. If they did not do this, they would be seen as rebellious wives, and it could make their husbands and clans retaliate in negative ways. Women who could do so bought property secretly, through women's cooperative groups, to have a future nest egg should their spouses divorce them or die.

This tactic became more common when the HIV pandemic arose and wiped out many men and, later on, their wives, leaving orphans who could be easily exploited.

Mr Ketanuga reflected on how not owning land formally was a major issue that facilitated unequal access to economic activities for women. They could have access to the land. They could till the land. But they did not own or control that land. They could never present that land to a bank as collateral in order to access a loan. Statistics showed that women contributed up to 60 per cent of the agricultural labour force, yet men controlled 95 per cent of the land!

His sisters were part of these abominable statistics, and he was among the men who had allowed such a situation to persist. Mr Ketanuga felt a twinge of discomfort at that thought.

His sisters had devoted all their lives to tilling the land. They had had access to it as long as their husbands loved them or were still alive. His sisters who divorced had come back to their parents' home empty-handed. The case of his eldest sister, Loyce, was most painful. When her husband died, his younger brother had chased Loyce off the land, citing the fact that she had not produced male children. He married a second wife and confidently installed her on Loyce's husband land without shame. Nobody questioned that unfair action.

It got worse. The eldest sister of Loyce's late husband did not have children. This woman grabbed Loyce's adolescent daughters and said that from now on, she *did* have children—through her late brother's loins. Some community members whispered among themselves that the sister was in fact not interested in the welfare of her late brother's children. She was looking for labourers for her farm.

Loyce cried helplessly as two men she did not know tried to forcefully put her children on a bicycle and take them away. The children fought back, crying and calling out to their mother for help. She could do nothing about it. The council of elders were all male, and this was how it had always been done in the past.

Mr Ketanuga felt a huge sense of unfairness on behalf of Loyce. Yet he too was powerless to help her. When he tried to speak to the elders, they looked at him strangely and reminded him that this was how things happened in their clan.

Worse still, they suggested that Loyce must have had a hand in her husband's death. They asked how it was possible that she had escaped getting 'that thing', yet it was said HIV was infectious? It was all very ominous and complex.

Mr Ketanuga asked Loyce to return home with him and look after his farm and village house as a paid farm manager. She would not continue being a squatter at home and where she had married. Mr Ketanuga vowed that his daughters would never become squatters like Loyce and other unfortunate women in his community.

Those cultural practices had never really bothered Mr Ketanuga before the gender awareness retreat. Now they really disturbed him. His new female team leader was the one who had really begun to open his eyes to the importance of gender and how there was a lack of balance. It made him wonder why were women and girls always given a raw deal. Who benefitted from such discrimination? Was there any instance in which women were positioned to benefit more than men? What about Imora and Mary? Would they get no inheritance from him? Mr Ketanuga loved his children equally and did not think it fair to leave only the boys an inheritance. How would Imora and Mary feel? How would they be supported?

That evening, he discussed the issue with Mrs Ketanuga. They both agreed to do something about Loyce. They decided that from the land that Mr Ketanuga had inherited from his father, they would cut off pieces and give it to his sisters for ttheir livelihoods.

The following day, Mr Ketanuga called a clan elders' meeting. He dropped his own bombshell! He informed the council of elders that he would sell off a piece of land in the village and use the proceeds to buy other land, far from his clansmen, and register it in his two daughters' names. He concluded by telling them, 'That will be my legacy to my two girl children, whom I love dearly. And no one, repeat, *no one* can stop me!'

The clansmen heard the determination in his voice and saw it in his body demeanour. What new thing was this young man smoking? Who had ever heard of such a thing as giving girls land to inherit? There was little they could do to turn around the claim. They all knew no one could stop him. They concluded that he was slowly going mad. He had lived too long in the city with 'that woman'.

That was Mr Ketanuga's recognition that women contributed the largest labour force for agriculture, mainly as small-scale farmers making substantial contribution to national wealth creation. However their work was labour-intensive and they lacked access to capital, consequently narrowing their range of activities and the growth of their enterprises. The day he made that vow, he slept soundly and was at peace with himself.

Visiting his upcountry home and being in the village really brought into focus some of the gender awareness issues that his boss had highlighted. These made him quite uncomfortable about what kind of person they showed him to be. To make himself feel better, Mr Ketanuga concluded that he was merely a product and a slave of his culture. With that thought, he proceeded to relax on his front porch and enjoy the rural sights and sounds. It was Saturday afternoon.

It had been a long time since Mr Ketanuga enjoyed himself with pals at the bar. He could no longer afford to buy beer for himself and was more conscious of his family needs. He would not waste more money on his pals. He missed the banter though. He now spent more time at home, reading or conversing with his wife and children. The girls had matured and looked after him very well. The eldest girl, Imora, had been pulled out of school after high school to look after her mother. If her mom's health improved and funds allowed, she would later be allowed to go for a certificate or diploma course.

He remembered when Imora used to bring back the best school reports, though. 'That girl was a real gem: hardworking, really intelligent, and never scoring less than 85 per cent on all her exams!' he reminisced. 'Whoever marries her will be a blessed man. She will bear him intelligent children—and she is so responsible. I wish—'

Then his thoughts were interrupted when he heard the village announcer reminding everyone to go for the village meeting. Government officials were coming to lend money, specifically targeted to women who ran small businesses. Mr Ketanuga used not to attend those lousy meetings. His wife did. He used to joke with his cronies at work, 'Women? They use every opportunity to meet and gossip.' He now knew better.

After mapping out his wife's daily routine, as instructed in the gender retreat, and comparing it with his, he realised that those times when women got to bond with others were times to unwind and get things off their chests, because their day was never really done. He wondered how Mrs Ketanuga even found time to talk to him. If time could be related to poverty, then women had time poverty.

On hearing the announcement again, he figured, well, today he was bored. He decided to attend the meeting, to check out what went on there.

HIJACK OF THE WOMEN'S PROGRAMME!

The meeting was held under the big tree next to the community hall. This was the tree where men usually sat and talked about important issues of the village. So women approached the tree cautiously. It was a dedicated, special place for men.

Many men came with their wives carrying them on bicycles. The older men sat on wooden forms in front. The older women sat on mats behind them. The younger men stood aggressively and restlessly at the sides. The children and younger women sat really far away. Many of the younger women, though still unmarried, had both babies and toddlers. Many of them were also pregnant. They did not talk at the meeting. They were too busy looking after the noisy children. They had also come with jerrycans, for they had to go for water soon after the meeting.

There were visitors: four men and one woman. They taught the community, especially women, about good business. The woman facilitator was a great orator. She spoke in very fluent English. She reminded Mr Ketanuga of his eldest daughter, Imora—intelligent, beautiful, and responsible. Had Imora been a boy, he would have done everything to educate her and later on make her his heir. Unfortunately, she was merely a girl!

After their long speeches, the visitors asked for questions. The men responded very well. Most women kept quiet. One woman said, 'Whatever my husband has said is also what I say.' Eventually, after a lot of encouragement and cajoling from the female facilitator, the women opened up to talk about their businesses. They mentioned that, due to several constraints, they had missed out on higher education, consequently blocking their opportunity to enter formal employment. They therefore concentrated on agriculture and small enterprises, which paid less.

Then one woman picked up the courage to speak out for everyone. She spoke with a commanding voice and a lot of passion. She said, 'The majority of us run very small businesses. This is mainly because we lack capital. The formal banks do not lend to us. We rely on family and friends for loans. These are often small and unreliable, sometimes with exorbitant interest rates. We lack access to capital, but not because we are bad at paying back. It is due to our low education levels. Blame our parents! The bankers have very formal and complex processes for applying for loans, and we cannot interpret their policies. Blame the bankers! We lack of ownership of assets required by most lenders as collateral—land titles and car logbooks. Blame our husbands! We women have never been free to use our heads.'

When she sat down, there was spontaneous applause from everyone. In those few words, she had ably articulated the dependency of women. Women depend almost totally on other people for their success.

Afterwards, the visitors registered the women and gave them loans in khaki brown envelopes. Mr Ketanuga was not surprised to observe that the first thing most of the women did was to hand over the envelope to their husbands before they climbed on the bicycles to be taken home. 'By our culture, those are the really good wives,' he mused. 'But hold on. Why are they doing that?'

It was because of the mindset that women could not handle money. They had to depend on men to do it for them. Why were the men taking the money from their wives? That was the surest way to hijack the women's empowerment programme. Why were the women happily handing over their money, knowing well that the husbands would disappear and use it to drink and to marry new wives? Who would pay the loans back? What would it take to genuinely remove the shackles from women?

At work, Mr Ketanuga had been trained. He appreciated now the importance of women becoming economically independent. But still, culture was culture, and gender relationships were complex. It would take more than a meeting to change systemic gender inequality, mediated over many years through the socialisation processes.

But despite this off-putting hijack he had observed at the end of the meeting, Mr Ketanuga was very pleased with his own small efforts to begin changes and gender balancing within his own home. He hoped that the example he would set among his peers and in his community would be enough to trigger changes among his neighbours. He had taken a first step. The next step would be to take this new revival back to the city. There were things that needed to change. The change was going to be painful, but that change was going to start *now*!

CHAPTER 38

A Full Circle to Positive Gender Roles

Mr Ketanuga had gone through different gendered places. He had seen and experienced just how negative stereotypes had moulded and eventually affected him and his family so adversely. He had even had some conversations with his female team leader. She had given him tips and assured him that it was never too late to start making positive changes. She narrated some of her own challenges when she had met her husband, dealing with their community and other peers. Now she was a good example to all who were around her.

Mr Ketanuga had his own lessons at home, in the school where he took his sons and daughters. He had gone through the challenges at work by eventually accepting and even enjoying working with a female boss. He had witnessed how programmes targeted for women's empowerment in the community were hijacked by men. He had learned about socialisation and being gendered, and had seen its impact on communities.

He took all those lessons home. He had frequent family talks with his wife and children, narrating what he had learned. It was humbling to them all how he openly shared the new things he had learned and confessed where he had been wrong.

He had given the children and his wife opportunity to speak out and give their views on the new things. The girls were at first shy, thinking that these were tricky questions and suggestions to show them out to be lazy. But they soon realised he was serious.

They watched his woeful attempts at learning how to cook. It made the kitchen messy, but they had so much fun with their father. The boys thought that it all cramped their style, but they also found hilarious moments to make fun of each other and banter while they helped with chores they had not been accustomed to doing.

Mr Ketanuga realised that his wife and daughters became more productive if more hands were put in to lighten the load on them. He realised how the role of home caregiving was heavy yet unpaid for, and realised how hurtful it was to the females that those roles were not recognised as 'work'. He realised that for the longest time, he had not considered household chores as work because they were unpaid activity.

His new interaction with his family gave Mr Ketanuga more respect and love for his wife and daughters. He had watched his young wife age faster than him. He clearly saw how the health of his wife deteriorated as she played three seemingly impossible roles—as dear wife, active mother, and committed employee—with little support from her husband and male children.

She was overworked, overtaxed and unappreciated. She was under pressure constantly. No wonder she was ill. She worked long hours both at work and at home. Mr Ketanuga felt a profound sense of sadness and loss for the years he had wasted in negative gender stereotypes, leading to the imbalance in his home.

Mr Ketanuga wondered how Imora could have turned out if she had continued with higher education. To him, she was a tragic symbol of the consequences of unfair gender differences. Was it too late for her to go back? Maybe he could bring a female relative from the village to look after his ailing wife.

Then he remembered the horrid advice his relatives had given him when they heard that his wife was ailing and had to resign her job. They suggested that he marry a second wife. Seriously? Were they out of their minds? He shuddered at that thought. To him, that would be the ultimate betrayal of his wife for so many years of unconditional love and support. There had to be another way to make things better for Imora.

Mr Ketanuga decided that evening that charity begins at home. He decided to lead by example. He did not need a relative to make his life easier. He could do that work himself. He remembered that he had vowed to cherish his wife in sickness and in health. What better way to show his love and care than to nurse her himself? He would blunder, but he knew it would be a powerful gesture to her in so many ways.

That night he started by assisting his wife to bathe. He talked to all his children and asked them to work out a roster of how they would share the home workload. The boys were still struggling with various chores and learning how to multitask. It meant missing out on some English Premier League games for Jack and gaining some weekends of doing nothing but girly things for Imora and Mary.

Even Mary stopped snapping at everyone. Suddenly she had a sense of the comical and showed signs of being the family comedian. She imitated her brothers and father and caused everyone to roll with laughter. Imora was gaining confidence too. She could have whole conversations with her dad now. All of these changes really helped to boost their mother's health.

Since more hands made lighter work, Imora was able to join a college for a diploma course. She was happy to start there and imagined how she would work her way up to a postgraduate degree. She intended to surprise everyone and pay her way all by herself—unless she got a scholarship.

It seemed that suddenly Imora was blooming. She radiated happiness. Both sisters improved and began to love education. Mary had just joined high school and enjoyed listening to Imora's college experiences. They became inseparable, sharing their work, issues, and challenges. They worked together to fight off the bullies. They now found it easy to talk to their father. He supported them by talking to their teachers.

The boys were no longer frightened by the kitchen. In fact, Jack started a boys' club in their neighbourhood. With his father's help and experience in community development work, he mobilised boys to teach them the value of gender balance. They began to take these lessons to the schools, teaching very basic lessons about gender.

As a matter of fact, they used *this* book as their reference in giving lessons. Don't you think you should be thankful that you do not need to attend those clubs? You received everything first-hand, right from the source!

CONCLUDING REMARKS

You now have a foundational understanding of what the gender agenda is all about. We have gone on an interesting journey from ancient Africa to the modern day. We have explored the Importance of Gender and four of the six gendered spaces.

As you mull over what you have read, it is my hope that you will join like-minded gender activists like Malala Yousafzai to begin change. You are the change you want to see. If there are areas of this publication that have really spoken to you, and you feel you must begin to do something, then begin to be the change. As you change, just like Imora's brothers and Mr. Ketanuga did, you will realise the sweetness of a balanced-gender existence.

Take these examples to your home. Begin to help your loved ones in areas where they are not gender balanced. Share the illustrations in this book and the story of Flora or the Ketanuga family to those who will listen. This is only the beginning. What has been written in this book is to stir up your mind and give you ideas which you can develop to help others in our society.

The gender agenda is not going to go away anytime soon. It is here to stay, and we must embrace it. The earlier you do that, the better for yourself and those who live around you.

I would like to help you. There are many excellent professionals working in many areas of the gender agenda, and I am one of them. You may have some questions or suggestions. Contact the author here:

Address
Grace Alice Mukasa
Flat 11 Biddulph House
Rideout Street
Woolwich, London
SE18 5EU
United Kingdom

Email
Gracemukasasfm@gmail.com

Together with other like-minded individuals, I facilitate participatory organisation gender audits and train and inspire high schools students, teachers, and other leaders in various aspects of gender, leadership, and development.

In the developing world, the gender agenda is still quite new—about forty years old. New things are always coming up. I encourage you to be inquisitive, ask questions, and explore the furthest horizons of this interesting and vital area of life.

I hope this has whetted your appetite to learn more. You will find more exciting topics in forthcoming volumes in the Gender series.

APPENDIX

Please enjoy an excerpt from book 2:

I Told You Already, She Doesn't Work!

A very important aspect of culture is the definition of work. Your community has its own way of defining work. There are things which people do, and they will be told, 'That is not work.' Therefore what is work, and who works?

The discussion below took place during a census interview. A census enumerator has to interview the head of the household and fill in the census questionnaire based on the answers given. The questionnaire is used by the National Bureau of Statistics to compile data that the government uses to plan and to allocate resources to different sectors of the economy.

Census Enumerator:	How many people live in this household?
Husband:	Me and my wife plus our six children.
Enumerator:	Can you please give me the names and ages of each member of this household?
Husband:	Sure. My name is Tom Senior. I am 44 years old. My wife Frida is approaching 26 years old. We got married when she was 17 years old.
Enumerator:	And the children?
Husband:	Our oldest son, Tom Junior, is 10 years old. My wife got pregnant as soon as we married. I was really happy to get my heir so soon.
	Two years later, we got the twins-two girls, Pat and Pam. They are fine although I wish God had given me boys. She is a very fertile woman, my wife. She was a real great catch for me! The twins are now 8 years old.
	Then we got Lillian. Lillian is a real problem. She has a disability in her legs and eyes. She is always complaining of one sickness or other. I don't like the way she walks in a crooked way. She is lucky her mother never tires of carrying her to hospital. She is four and half years old.
	We then had Emily. She resembles my late mother so much. I even named her after my late mother. She brings a lot of joy to me. Emily is 2 years old, and the baby Rosa is now 4 months old.
Enumerator:	So you have six children, aged 10, 8x2, 4, 2, and 4 months?

Husband:	Sure, and we are going strong. We only need three more boys and then I will count my blessings.
Enumerator:	Now tell me about work and income for the family.
Husband:	I work. My wife does not work. She is a housewife. She sits at home every day. She has a lot of time to relax and gossip with her friends. But me …
Enumerator:	How do you get your food?
Husband:	Most of the time, my wife harvests it from the garden. She grows maize, cassava, tomatoes, beans, nuts, and greens. We use these for our food. Once in a while, I bring back some fish from the market; otherwise it would go bad.
Enumerator:	What do you do?
Husband:	I am a trader. I buy and sell fish in the evening market. I normally start at 4 p.m. and I am not through until 7 p.m. Oh, it is really tough work.
Enumerator:	What do you do before you go to work?
Husband:	I normally wake up at around 9 a.m. By then my wife has finished with her children, and my bath water and breakfast are ready.
Enumerator:	What do you do next?
Husband:	I go to the trading centre to find out what is happening in the world. By the time I come back, lunch is ready. I eat and go back to plan with my friends. We normally sit under the big tree mango tre at the trading centre, The one where we hold the community meetings. While there I discuss

important things about what is happening in the village. for the village. Then I go to buy and sell my fish.

Enumerator: Do you come back home immediately after the market?

Husband: Yes. I come back to bathe off the smell of the fish. My wife knows my routine, so I find the water already warm. I bathe, take some tea, and go to our pub for one or two ... you know. I am a man. If I stay home, my wife may send me to the kitchen or bundle her noisy children on me. She started to do that to Tom Junior—turning him into a woman! I gave her a few slaps and warned her off my heir. So I come back at 10 p.m. or 11 p.m., when they are all asleep and there is peace in the house!

Enumerator: What about your wife? Does she work?

Husband: I told you, she does not work!

Enumerator: How does she normally spend her time?

Husband: She wakes up at around 5 a.m. to prepare breakfast and prepare those who go to school. Then she escorts the twins to school. When she comes back, she clears up their mess and cleans the house. She goes for water next. By the time she comes back, my mum and the baby are both awake. She bathes them and serves them their breakfast. She then serves me mine before she goes off to the garden.

Enumerator: And then?

Husband:	She normally comes back around midday, carrying some food, greens, a bunch of firewood on her head, and a jerrycan of water. Problem she takes long because she meets her friends on the way and stops tobgossip.She prepares lunch and picks up the twins from school. Then she serves everybody with lunch.
Enumerator:	Does she do anything after that?
Husband:	Of course. She has to wash up the plates and put her children to bed to rest. She has to iron all our clothes. She leaves the children under the care of the twins and goes back to her garden for weeding.
	She comes back in the evening at around 4 p.m. to prepare dinner. But before that, she must fetch firewood and water again with her sidekicks, Pat or Pam. Thereafter she bathes the children, feeds them, and puts the younger ones to bed before she monitors and helps the older children do their homework.
	After that she happily listens to the radio as she waits for me to come back. You see, I need to bathe with hot water, and I need my food warm. I also need company as I eat. She is my wife, after all! It's a happy calm life my wife lives, and I love her so much.
Enumerator:	Who helps your wife with all that work?
Husband:	What's wrong with you? I told you alrcady, she does not work!

About the Author

Grace Alice Mukasa, was born in Kampala, Uganda. She is holding dual citizenship for Uganda and UK and currently living in London. She a proud mother of four sons and one daughter.

Grace is an accomplished international development director with a credible reputation as a transformative leader, who is passionate about gender justice and women's rights. She has a Masters in Gender and Development from the Institute of Development Studies (IDS), University of Sussex, UK. She has also acquired an immense arsenal of knowledge, skills and expertise from field practice in different contexts and several on-the-job trainings over the years.

Social change that transforms the lives of the poorest and most vulnerable people is what drives Grace. She has a unique leadership profile as an African woman leader who has directed international development initiatives and infrastructure projects. She is a proficient trainer and advocacy and authority on advocacy and policy influencing agendas. She has worked with five international NGOs leading and directing their wok in Africa (18 country programs in Eastern, Western and Southern Africa); South Asia (6 ountry programmes); and in UK (where she was the CEO for AMREF UK). She has represented the organisations and presented papers on their behalf, usually as a key speaker and discussant on panels in international conferences and national consultations with government.

Grace is a survivor, having suffered a massive stroke in September 2016. Not one to be defined a by her circumstances, Grace now spends her time reflecting, retrieving and writing about her career experiences. Its her hope to share with young people other upcoming women lead and __ practitioners about how to learn, grow and develop into transformative leaders who can inspire, engage and develop high performing teams. She is also plans to share her experience of how becoming a born again Christian enabled her to overcome fear and restore her trust in God's love and healing power.

BIBLIOGRAPHY

Bell, H. (2009): Cutting Edge Pack, <u>Gender and care work: An overview</u>, IDS, UK

Gaventa, J. (2006): *Finding Spaces for Change*, IDS, UK

Chambers, R., 1995 (a). <u>Paradigm shifts of participatory research and development</u> in Nelson, N., and Wright, S., <u>Power and Participatory Development: Theory and Practice</u>, Pg. 30-42, Southampton, IT publications.

Chambers R. (1995): *Poverty and Livelihoods: Whose reality counts?* IDS

Covey S.R. (1989): *The 7 Habits of Highly Effective People*, Free Press

Covey, S.R. (20049): *The 8th Habit, from effectiveness to greatness.* Free Press

Christine de Pisan (1405) *The Book of the City of Ladies*, Penguin classics.

Daskal, L. (2016): *How to succeed as a new leader*, Harvard Business Review (HBR).

Deere CD & Doss CR(2006): *The gender asset gap: What do we know and why does it matter?*, Feminist EconomicsDobson, J. (2014): *Bringing up boys*, Tyndale House

Dobson J. 2014 'Bringing up boy's, Tyndale House (separate from that of Deere CD & Doss CR. (2006)

Feuerstein, R. (2014): *Mediated Learning Experience (MLE): Instrumental enrichment,* Feuerstein Institute

Frits W. 2001): *Empowerment and Evaluation: A Framework for analysis and application,* INTRAC

Hugo de Vuyst et al (2013):*The burden of human papillomavirus infection and related diseases in Sub-Saharan Africa,* PMC.

ICC (2011): *Rome statute of the intrnational criminal court,* International criminal court.

INTRAC, (1999). *The Monitoring and Evaluation of Empowerment; Resource Document,* Oxford, INTRAC.

Jimmy and Karen Evans (2007): *Marriage on the rock: Gods Design for Your Dream Marriage,* Regal.

Kandiyoti D. (1988): *Bargaining with Patriarchy,* Sage

Levtov, R. (2016): *Men, Gender and Inequality: A background Paper for the UN Secretary General's High, Level Panel on Women's Economic Empowerment,* UN

Mandela, N. (2010): *Conversations With Myself,* Macmillan.

Martin E.T Seligman, Ph.D (2006): *Learned Optimism: The cup half full.* Vintage Books

Minambo, P (2015): *Inspiring people one book at a time: Beyond limits,* Evewoman magazine

Mowafi, A. (): *The trials and tribulations of being a good Egyptian girl,* Fe mail

Munroe, M. (2006): *The power of Vision,* Whitaker House

Mureithi, C. (2014): *What makes you special,* Lavinda Ltd.

Munroe, M. (2008): *Understanding your potential: Discovering the hidden you*, Destiny Image

Mureithi, C. (2014): *The shallow end*, Premier Group

Norah, V., (2008): *Self-Made Man: One woman's year disguised as a man*, Penguin Highbridge (audio)

Noland et al., (2016): *Is gender diversity profitable? Evidence from a global survey*, Peterson Institute for International Economi

Pepe, M. (2009): *Be inspired before you expire*, Flame Keepers Publishers.

Robert, L., S.,(1886): *Strange case of Dr. Jenkll and Mr. Hyde*, Longmans, Green & Co.

Simon S.M. (2010): *Speeches that changed the world*, Various Various

Sharma, R. (2010): *The leader who had no title: A modern fable on real success in business and in life*, SUCCESS magazine

Underhill, D., O. (1999): *Every Woman Has a Story: Many voices, many lessons, many lives*, Grand Central Pub

UNHCR, *Uganda Annual Report* (2014)

UNHCR, *Kenya Annual Report* (2014)

UNHCR, *Chad Annual Report* (2014)

UNHCR, *Sudan Annual Report* (2014)

VanKlasen L. and Miller V. (2002): *Power and Empowerment*, IIED

Walter I. (2011): *Steve Jobs*, Simon & Schuster

Wangari M. (2008): *Unbowed: My autobiography*, Willliam Hainemann Ltd.

Wendy S., (2007): *Young women reclaim self respect and find its not bad to be good*, Random House

Williams, S.(1994): *The OXFAM Gender Training Manual*, OXFAM GB

World Bank (2012): *World Development Report: Gender equality and development*, World Bank Group.

Walker, A. (1982): *The color purple*, Harcourt Brace Jovanovich

Printed in the United States
By Bookmasters